WARRIOR PRINCESSES STRIKE BACK

WARRIOR PRINCESSES STRIKE BACK

HOW LAKOTA TWINS FIGHT OPPRESSION AND HEAL THROUGH CONNECTEDNESS

SARAH EAGLE HEART
EMMA EAGLE HEART—WHITE

THE FEMINIST PRESS
AT THE CITY UNIVERSITY OF NEW YORK
NEW YORK CITY

Published in 2023 by the Feminist Press
at the City University of New York
The Graduate Center
365 Fifth Avenue, Suite 5406
New York, NY 10016

feministpress.org

First Feminist Press edition 2023

The stories in this book reflect the authors' recollection of events. Some names, locations, and identifying characteristics have been changed to protect the privacy of those depicted. Dialogue has been re-created from memory.

 This book was made possible thanks to a grant from the New York State Council on the Arts with the support of the Governor and the New York State Legislature.

First printing January 2023

Cover design by Sharanya Durvasula
Cover photograph by Jay Valle
Text design by Drew Stevens

Library of Congress Cataloging-in-Publication Data

Names: Eagle Heart, Sarah, author. | Eagle Heart-White, Emma, author.
Title: Warrior princesses strike back : how Lakota twins fight oppression and heal through connectedness / Sarah Eagle Heart, Emma Eagle Heart-White.
Other titles: How Lakota twins fight oppression and heal through connectedness
Description: First Feminist Press edition. | New York City : Feminist Press, 2023.
Identifiers: LCCN 2022034729 (print) | LCCN 2022034730 (ebook) | ISBN 9781558612938 (paperback) | ISBN 9781558612945 (ebook)
Subjects: LCSH: Lakota women—Biography. | Indian women healers—United States—Biography. | Lakota Indians—Religious life. | Spiritual healing. | Spiritual journals—Authorship. | Psychic trauma—Social aspects—United States. | Decolonization—Psychological aspects. | Lakota Indians—Social conditions. | Women psychotherapists—United States—Biography. | Twins—United States—Biography.
Classification: LCC E99.T34 E245 2022 (print) | LCC E99.T34 (ebook) | DDC 305.897/52440922 [B]—dc23/eng/20220902
LC record available at https://lccn.loc.gov/2022034729
LC ebook record available at https://lccn.loc.gov/2022034730

PRINTED IN THE UNITED STATES OF AMERICA

This book is dedicated to our beautiful uŋčí (grandmother),
Mary Rose Crazy Thunder,
our beautiful iná (mother), Emmaline Eagle Heart,
and our handsome misúŋ (little brother), Troy Weber,
and our children: Aarron, Gavin, Brenden, Elise, and Josalyn,
who are our inspirations for healing and everything we do.

Love,
Re Re and Ra Ra

Contents

Introduction

THERE ARE SO many conflicted feelings that arise when we think about what it means to be a warrior princess. Part of us—the part that grew up watching princess movies—says yes! The other part remembers the liberty taken by our white counterparts to appropriate our culture. But what if the warrior princesses struck back? What if the women lulled into imagining themselves as long-forgotten princesses reawakened? What if we came together to fight for all of the injustices committed upon women and the oppressed? What if we remembered and acknowledged the truth about Native American history in the United States of America? The one where the white cowboy isn't the hero?

Striking back reminds us that the wakíŋyaŋs (lightning or thunder beings) can change our trajectories rapidly, like a storm coming in to sweep us off our feet ... We are all stepping into that storm together. This is the beginning of that day.

About five years ago, we were visiting Minneapolis and both found that we felt individually called to write books about healing. We knew at that moment we *would* write a book together. We didn't know it would be a four-year journey or that we would write this book during the COVID-19 pandemic, but we knew Indigenous wisdom was needed now more than ever. Indigenous wisdom takes many forms; our particular perspective comes from being raised on a reservation, moving on to an urban adulthood, then returning to the reservation again—"a return to the heart" is what we call it.

1

Even though we are identical twins, we both have unique experiences, some heartbreaking and some joyful, that originated from our lens of growing up on Pine Ridge Indian Reservation in southwestern South Dakota—a place where we know we were privileged enough to grow up, despite being essentially poor orphans. Even though mainstream society perceived us as poor and our tribal community always made the top twenty poorest counties in the United States, we did not feel poor. We were very privileged to be rich in Lakȟóta culture.

When we were young, we thought we were going down two separate paths. From thirteen years old, Emma knew she wanted to help heal others so they would not feel alone in their pain, and she eventually landed in psychology, psychotherapy, and energy work. She began in advocacy, working with Native American youth in the public school system and with domestic abuse and sexual violence survivors in the court system. Sarah's path was a bit more scenic: at sixteen, she wrote articles for *Indian Country Today*, then fell in love with marketing and advertising at an Indian casino outside San Diego, and then Tȟuŋkášila called her to work as an advocate at the Episcopal Church, which would take her around the world, and then she landed in philanthropy. Sarah discovered she was meant to help heal too. Through Sarah's journey of advocacy and cultural education, she healed through narrative as a macro-visionary. Emma healed on a micro level, assisting tribal members in grassroots communities.

We discovered that leadership is not a one-size-fits-all approach and that the old tenets of a single-vision job approach were not working for our people. In fact, this Western approach is stifling our people and our ability to flourish. It did not connect all of the issues or the solutions, and it definitely did not take into account our holistic worldview. The age-old approach of defining a person by a single job for their entire lives thrives in systems that benefit by keeping the status quo.

Through working with many tribal communities, we know there are many perspectives. There are always at least two sides to a story and we invite you to see these stories through our eyes. We can only claim and share our own perspectives, which are grounded in the Lakȟóta worldview we learned from our grandmothers, aunties, and uncles who raised us. We have been fortunate to have many spiritual leaders and extended family in our lives who taught us to understand how the Creator works with and through us. We have also read many self-help books and have gratitude for those who have come before us. We believe it's time to write a self-help book from an Indigenous feminine perspective.

We understand there is a paradox of suffering and enlightenment. We decided to share our stories because we know we are not alone in these experiences. These are not the stories of perfect Lakȟóta wíŋyaŋ (women) as we've been stereotypically portrayed or raised to emulate. Some may not approve that we are telling our stories of heartbreak, shame, triumph, and everything in between. In fact, some of these stories are even considered taboo to talk about in tribal communities. We will share them anyway because we want those who are struggling to know they are not alone. We will lay bare our own individual and family pains, we will share our experiences of lateral violence, but we will also share our vision for the future, which is entrenched in collectivism. We don't tell these uncomfortable stories to shame anyone but to shed a healing light on humanity from a contemporary Indigenous feminine lens. Everything happens for a reason. Everyone is on a journey of learning and healing in their lifetime. Everyone has a role to play in not only their individual understanding but also that of others. You must only take a step backward and attempt to see another's perspective from your heart.

We know our lived experiences are almost never heard in the mainstream discourse of issues that affect so many women:

violence, lack of knowledge of reproductive rights, racism, sexism, alcoholism, drug abuse, identity struggles, spirituality crises, suicide, trauma, leadership struggles, lack of storytelling opportunities, and climate change. We knew we had to ensure that the firsthand perspectives of Indigenous women brought up in these underprivileged circumstances would be heard.

Also, we use "we" a lot in this book. It is not the royal "we" but the collective "we." We use it to refer to ourselves as twins, to our tribal collective perspective as Oglála Lakȟóta, and to all of us in this world. In fact, it's very difficult for us to even use "I" because we are taught that collectivism is a higher value than individualism. We did our best to share our story in a way that you could receive it.

We very vulnerably and humbly offer our stories and knowledge for you to learn, grow, and transform your understanding of Native American and Indigenous peoples from the eyes of two Oglála Lakȟóta čekpás (twins) who feel called to help shift the world into a paradigm of healing now and in the seven generations to come.

Wóphila Tȟuŋkášila for this opportunity.

Wóphila Tȟuŋkášila for guiding us.

Wóphila Tȟuŋkášila for the helpers in our lives.

Wóphila Tȟuŋkášila for always loving us.

Mitákuye Oyás'iŋ.

When I look back at difficult moments in my life,
I now know it is my ancestors who gave us strength and guidance.
I know this because despite all the vitriol and hatred directed our way,
I felt protected and I felt strong . . .
I didn't feel alone.
I know that protection and strength didn't come from just ourselves.
—EMMA EAGLE HEART–WHITE

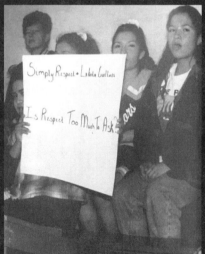

CHAPTER 1

The Original Warrior Princesses

BY EMMA AND SARAH

"YOU KNOW, PEOPLE are saying the reason you're protesting is because you're mad you're not going to be warrior princesses," our high school principal said after calling us to his office on the first day of our senior year. We looked at each other in disbelief, carefully holding back laughter. There were so many things wrong with that statement that our poor, sweet principal just didn't understand.

We were seventeen, protesting our high school's then-fifty-seven-year-old Warrior homecoming "ceremony" in rural Martin, South Dakota. We should have been celebrating our senior year, but there we were making the town of one thousand one hundred uncomfortable and angry by protesting the mascot and this "ceremony." Would he listen if we told him about the sacredness of Lakȟóta women in traditional Lakȟóta culture? Or how a pretend "medicine man" dancing around women to choose one for the "big chief" was extremely offensive to our spiritual leaders? Aside from the cultural appropriation, could he not at least see how utterly sexist the whole "ceremony" was? The female students taking part in the school's annual Warrior homecoming ceremony dressed in what they thought was authentic Lakȟóta regalia: big 1980s-type hair with fringed midcalf leather dresses, barefooted and singing a forlorn "Indian Love Song"—all of which made us want to puke. Nothing about this "ceremony" was authentic. So NO, we did not want to be a sexualized

7

Pocahontas-type "warrior princess" chosen for a man like a piece of meat.

In 1994, we were two young women part of the Oglála Lakȟóta Nation, growing up in the LaCreek District of Pine Ridge Indian Reservation, one mile outside of the white farming community of Martin. Martin, like so many small towns in rural America, consists of a single main street with a grocery store, video rental, and a handful of small shops. The town is sandwiched between two Indian reservations; in fact, Martin used to be part of the reservation until Bennett County was ceded to the federal government in 1912. While its majority of white inhabitants had ample opportunity to get to know the culture of their neighboring reservations, this unfortunately never happened. Even today, many of the people living in Martin are completely removed from rez life, as is the case for most Americans.

"Wíŋyaŋ" means *woman*. The root words are "wí," meaning *sun*, or literally *luminary*. "Íŋyaŋ" means *stone* or *rock*. The stone is the first ancestor and therefore the wisest; it is used in ceremonies and is indestructible. Together "wíŋyaŋ" combines two of our most sacred aspects in Lakȟóta life.

Our great-grandmother Emma and our grandma Mary Rose were both alive during our childhood. Uŋčí (Grandma) Mary Rose is still with us, but Great-Grandma Emma, whom we lovingly called Old Grandma, has since passed on. Old Grandma was a force of nature. A traditional Lakȟóta woman of humility and integrity, who grew up working hard on the homestead and had taught her lineage to do the same. Our extended family of aunts and uncles also played a large role in our upbringing, especially Tȟuŋwíŋ (Auntie) Mabel. In fact, our extended family is our nuclear family and that's pretty common for Lakȟóta families. They were there for us when our parents weren't able to care for us. Our father was not involved in our lives, and our mother was struck by a drunk driver, resulting in permanent brain damage. The woman she was before the accident versus the woman she was after are two completely different people. We were only seven years old when it happened, so our grandmother raised us in our mom's stead. It is not uncommon to find grandparents in parental roles on our reservation, due to our traditional kinship bonds. As čekpás, we have spent our lives intertwined, observing and reflecting with each other. We shared what we saw and learned. We were raised by a very spiritual family, traditionally Lakȟóta and Episcopalian. We grew up with our female relatives watching over us very closely, who made sure to teach us the original stories and traditional knowledge of our Lakȟóta people.

"Čekpá" means *navel, belly button, umbilical cord*, or *twins*.

Old Grandma used to laugh and point by pursing her mouth in our direction (she didn't point with her fingers because that was considered rude), saying she was scared of us when we whispered in our baby language. That made us laugh because we never took ourselves too seriously; besides, the Lakȟóta people value humility, so it was probably better we didn't let such thoughts go to our heads. Native Americans who were connected to the traditional ways in our community would still treat us a little differently, often calling us uŋčís (like we were reincarnated grandmas) because we were twins. No matter what, we knew that there was something bigger in the world than just us. We knew that Tȟuŋkášila was, and is, guiding humanity.

"Tȟuŋkášila" means *Creator, God,* or *Great Spirit*. From the time Lakȟóta children are born, their families share knowledge of a larger spiritual presence in life through prayer.

LIFE ON OUR reservation is a struggle for many. There is much hardship from growing up in a tribal community where, according to the US Census Bureau, 38.5 percent of the inhabitants live below the poverty line[1] (although many outside reports place the rate much higher, at 80 percent and above).* Pine Ridge Reservation is the poorest county in the United States, with a per capita income of only $7,773, versus the national average of $27,599.[2] This wealth divide is driven by an unemployment rate of 89 percent—well beyond South Dakota's 4 percent rate.[3] Our grandma only makes $10,000 a year, and she's supported us and so many in our family and still manages to lend others money when they need it.

Poverty and joblessness are a recipe for high rates of drug and alcohol abuse, and on our reservation, more than 80 percent of residents suffer from alcoholism. The life expectancy for men is 48 years and for women, 52 years—second only to Haiti for the worst life expectancies in the Western hemisphere.[4] We also have the highest infant mortality rate on this continent—beating the US national average by 300 percent. On top of this, we faced the multitude of harsh statistics that Native American youth face. Teenage suicide rates are 150 percent above the national average, and an above 70 percent high school dropout rate is the norm.[5] All of this paints a very bleak picture of where we grew up.

Coupled with these sobering statistics, we had literally zero positive role models or images of contemporary Native American women to look up to in the media at large. It seemed like the common phrase on the reservation, "We are a forgotten people," was turning out to be a harsh and accurate truth. Imagine us, not only facing discrimination from the rural white community, but also seeing no contemporary representation of our people in the media. On top of that, the school

---

*The Lakȟóta people were traditionally a nomadic people, and we still see that with many of us today. Our nomadic ways make it difficult to get a clear picture of everyone living on the reservation and to obtain accurate statistics. Exacerbating this is a lack of funding and interest from the government and outside organizations in taking accurate census data of reservation populations. We have found that Re-Member.org presents statistics in a fair manner with explanation, and we use them as our go-to, unless we find more recent statistics from other organizations.

one mile from our homes held an extremely stereotypical fifty-seven-year-old skit where a "medicine man" gifts a "warrior princess" to the "big chief." That is the perfect recipe for triggering trauma.

Bennett County High School is located at the end of Martin's Main Street, and this is the school we attended our whole adolescence. Every year the school put on a homecoming coronation, where each person in the ceremony would enter the gymnasium in a stoic and slow fashion, with a spotlight illuminating their walk to the stage. The student's high school accomplishments were read to a tom-tom drumbeat. The "warrior princesses" (the homecoming-queen candidates) would sing an "Indian love song" around a fake fire complete with fake logs and a flickering light. Next, the "medicine man" (the runner-up homecoming king) would dance around the "princesses" to a drumbeat, stopping to assess the princesses' appearance—touching their hair, looking in their mouths, caressing their jewelry and clothing—and to weigh them by lifting them from under the arms. Finally, the "medicine man" selected one of the "warrior princesses" by lifting the chosen one completely to standing position, indicating she is the "warrior princess" (the homecoming queen) chosen for the "big chief" (the homecoming king). Making matters worse, the whole school football team, all thirty members, also dressed up as Native Americans for the ceremony, wearing face paint, breechcloths, and feather regalia all provided by the school.

Every year, we had to sit through this gross display of cultural appropriation, surrounded by all these white kids playing Indian. Throughout high school, we tried to understand the significance of this "ceremony," along with a handful of other Native American high school students. We wondered: Why are these "warrior princesses" wearing Native American women's traditional dancers' regalia, complete with leather buckskin dresses? Why is there a "big chief" standing stoically with his

11

arms crossed in front of a tipi wearing a headdress, leather vest, pants, and breechcloth? Why is there a "medicine man" wearing Native men's traditional dancers' regalia, complete with a porcupine-quill head roach and eagle-feather bustle? The media and the scientific community had yet to acknowledge how harmful these stereotypical representations were. We tried to understand how this could be honoring our people, but we could never shake the feeling that this ceremony was wrong and that we needed to do something.

During our junior year of high school, we should have been thinking about attending the homecoming game, wondering who our dates to the homecoming dance would be, marching with the band in the homecoming parade (we were quite the clarinet band nerds!), and focusing on our studies. Instead, we had a telepathically intuitive moment as we sat and watched the homecoming ceremony with quiet disgust. One of us sighed heavily and the other twin said, "I know."

And that was it. We had just agreed to protest.

At the time, we didn't understand how much courage it would take to stand against this fifty-seven-year-old school tradition. Nor did we understand what the consequences would be. We just knew that we had to stand together and speak up against what we saw as a violation of the sacred traditions of our tribe. Our school mascot was also a racist depiction of a Native American warrior head wearing a traditional headdress. It wasn't

Indian princess pageants are still happening all over the United States, but they also occurred at Indian boarding schools. These pageants grew as a parallel to high school beauty contests beginning in the late 1890s, and by the 1920s, the stereotypical Indian princess outfit, buckskin and fringe, matched the stereotype on the silver screen. The popularity of Westerns meant non-Natives also believed they could honor Native people with distorted ceremonies by pretending to be us. But given the reality of who we are—our culture, language, and values— these dramas perpetuate untruths about our people that will never be okay.

uncommon for us to see white people dressed up as Native Americans at the homecoming parade and the school football games, and we felt that this logo and the name of the team, the Warriors, cultivated a culture that made this dressing up seem acceptable. We decided to protest to stop the ceremony and remove the school mascot.

FIRST YEAR

The homecoming coronation ceremony takes place in late September, and students have one day to vote for their chosen "warrior princess" and "big chief." We wanted to drum up as much support for our protest as possible well before it began, so the summer before our senior year, we started telling anyone who would listen that we planned to protest that year's ceremony. Sarah was interning again as a reporter, so we reached out to her contacts in the media. We told the local Native newspaper, *Indian Country Today*, about the protest, and spoke to the local radio station KILI, as well as our friends, elders, and community.

Much of our decision to protest was because we had received traditional Lakȟóta teachings since childhood from our tribal community. We spent summers attending the dozens of powwows and sundances. We were selected by a four-year Lakȟóta mentorship program called Center for Substance Abuse Prevention (CSAP) to become peer mentors in all of our respective schools and throughout the reservation. We learned Lakȟóta values from Lakȟóta leaders who were both counselors and social workers. These Lakȟóta leaders mentored us and taught us leadership skills, and in turn, we also became peer mentors to younger Lakȟóta children at a summer camp for two summers. This mentorship played an essential role in our ability to critique our high school's homecoming practices at a young age.

We felt the delicate racial balance in Martin every time we went to the grocery store or a school event. Growing up, we played along with all of their rules. We loved our school, and we were popular despite racial tensions being the norm. We were cheerleaders; we played in the band; we sang in choir. We ran track and played basketball with these kids at a time when very few Native youth chose to attend the mostly white high school. Most elected to be bussed forty-five minutes away to the nearest reservation high school. Some of the young kids in the tribal community called us "apples"—a derogatory term meant to signify that we were red on the outside and white on the inside—because of our participation in school activities and our friendships with white kids. But these white kids had been our friends since kindergarten. Granted, there were never any sleepovers with us in our tribal community, but still, we considered them our friends. Given this, protesting was a hard decision and one we did not enter into lightly.

Sarah felt apprehensive. She knew the mascot and homecoming ceremony were wrong, but she had also spent her entire high school career as a cheerleader. Since this was our senior year, it was Sarah's turn to be cheerleading captain for the boys' basketball team, an opportunity she was incredibly excited about. We had played basketball as freshmen, but we quit to work in the local café because our grandmother couldn't afford the basketball shoes or traveling money, so cheerleading became Sarah's sports outlet when she could purchase her own necessities.

The first couple weeks of our senior year started rough. Sarah began to hear whispers about our cheerleading coach wanting to kick us off the squad because of our planned protest. When the coach went to elicit support from the school principal, the principal told her, "No, don't do that. If you do, you're going to make it much worse." Instead, we were told there would be no cheerleading captain that year because, apparently, they didn't need one. Sarah says, "I knew this was retaliation because they didn't want me to be captain. After this humiliation I wanted to quit. I didn't want to stand in front of a glaring audience for a school that hated that we were standing up against their tradition, but I didn't have a choice. Fighting racism and sexism was not the type of school spirit they wanted. But I had committed to being a cheerleader, I loved cheerleading, and this was my final year." Even though we both desperately wanted to quit, we decided to honor our commitment. We wouldn't allow them to chase us off.

This wasn't the only consequence we faced. All of our white friends stopped talking to us and would stare at us as we walked down the school hallways. We were shunned, called names, and even intimidated by our peers. People threatened to throw rocks or eggs at us if we attended school events. We were afraid. Even our band teacher no longer spoke to us, after playing clarinet for six years—we were second and third chair, to boot. Our math teacher, who was also the football coach, openly glared at us. We sucked at math and he was no help, so the feeling was mutual.

Even worse, other Lakȟóta people began taking sides as well, because they felt like they had to. Our very own LaCreek tribal community was split. They seemed to ask, *Who are you two to rock the delicate racial balance in this small town?* They were afraid of retaliation against our tribal community, since the Native Americans in the area were already accustomed to facing discrimination and didn't want to make it worse. A few of the tribal members didn't even see a problem with the ceremony. Not everyone living on the reservation was as connected to the sacredness of our traditional ways at that time, so for them, the ceremony wasn't a big deal. Even for us, no one ever told us this ceremony was racist and should stop. We just knew, intuitively in our hearts, that it was wrong and that we had to end it—even if we had to stand alone.

Many townsfolk accused us of wanting to be "warrior princesses" and said we were causing a scene for attention. Years later, we would come to understand how this is a common tactic employed against marginalized groups to devalue our opinions and make it seem as if our motives are disingenuous. Heck, one local wrote an editorial saying we were "two young, dumb girls who didn't know anything." This was an adult openly attacking two teenage girls' credibility to devalue our perspective and fuel a fire of racism. It was sickening. It was scary. Thank God for Uŋčí, our grandma.

Our grandma grew up in the country, and her parents farmed and kept horses. Our great-grandparents had one of the first Native nursing homes on their lands constructed from tents. They were devoted Episcopalians and served as delegates to the Inestimable Gift Church, a nondenominational church in Allen, South Dakota. Grandma raised her children in LaCreek for several decades. Our mother and her siblings attended Bennett County High School—so she, too, had witnessed the same homecoming ceremony. Our family worried as they listened to us share our experiences, and our grandma supported us with words of wisdom and encouragement. They even tried to confront the teachers at our school about the hostility we'd been facing.

Grandma knew there were some good people outside of the tribe who tried to understand Lakȟóta ways. These people would donate food for memorial dinners and come to the local powwows. When it was time for our protest, she saw the backlash we were facing for standing up against this small town, and she prayed for the white folks because they didn't understand. Grandma told us, "People I considered childhood friends started distancing themselves from me." There were many wašíču, *white people*, that she didn't talk to for a long time because of our protest. Grandma said, "I felt so much anger at these people that were supposed to be my friends. Their children were so mean to my grandchildren. A Lakȟóta friend said to me, 'I often think, "Why did the white man treat the Native Americans like that? We all have a soul and a mind. The white man thought we are animals."' Just think about that and someday you'll understand how I feel about certain people in this town."

One day leading up to the protest, Emma went to her biology class, where all ten students usually sat at the same table in the center of the classroom. When she sat down to join them, all the students—her childhood "friends"—got up and sat on the other side of the classroom. Emma says, "I just sat there for a few moments looking down at my books with tears in my eyes. I fought back those tears, but I was filled with overwhelming sadness. I was trying to be strong to face them, but it was hard feeling the coldness in their gazes. I had a difficult time comprehending why they couldn't understand what we were doing. Didn't they understand the deep pain this 'ceremony' and mascot causes our people?"

Emma left the class and headed to the main office to call her CSAP counselor, Chris Eagle Hawk, to get her mind off of what was going on. As they spoke, he could sense something was seriously wrong. Emma sat down on the floor and quietly explained the situation to him because she knew the office staff was listening. She wept silently.

Chris Eagle Hawk replied, "Be strong. You are doing the right thing. You are like the brave leaders and warriors who come before us, Crazy Horse and Sitting Bull. Be strong, my girl." Tears streamed down Emma's face at hearing the kindness and strength of these words. Crazy Horse and Chief Sitting Bull were such strong, brave leaders and warriors. In this moment, she felt the opposite. But she thought, *I need to be strong.* Emma quickly wiped away her tears before the staff could see.

After the call, Emma says, "I knew I needed to be bulletproof to face the pure anger and hatred from the staff, students, and the community, but I also needed a moment to cry, so I went to the bathroom. Somehow Sarah intuitively knew I was there. I shared with her what Chris Eagle Hawk had said and she began to cry too."

We stood there, in our pain and rejection, facing each other in silence. As twins, we often could intuit what the other wanted to say without saying anything. At seventeen years old, acceptance by our peers meant everything to us—particularly to Sarah, who had tried to do everything right. She always got good grades, was popular even among the white students, and participated in many extracurriculars. Nothing could have prepared us for the pain of rejection we would feel from the school faculty, our community, and our childhood friends. In this moment, we let all the grief come through us while we cried and held space for each other.

After some time, we brushed our tears away, gathered our courage, and walked out of the bathroom ready to face them again. Emma says, "When I look back at difficult moments in my life, I now know it is my ancestors who gave us strength and guidance. I know this because, despite all the vitriol and hatred directed our way, I felt protected and I felt strong— strong beyond my own capacities. I know that protection and strength didn't come from just ourselves."

As the days grew closer to the protest, so did the verbal attacks, taunting, and threats of violence. The white students yelled, "Prairie niggers!" and made that stereotypical whooping sound in our direction as we walked by. Our few remaining friends warned us when they heard of other students' plans to harm us. We had a small circle of young Lakȟóta friends from our community who took it upon themselves to stand with us—literally, like bodyguards. They knew we were being threatened and offered to protect us. We never asked them to do this, and I don't think we ever truly thanked them, but they didn't expect a thank-you, which is so different from Western society today. In our family, if someone has to ask you to help, it is considered shameful. To this day, we are still grateful for the Lakȟóta who stood guard on our behalf. Given the threats we were facing, we were terrified, and their added support made it much more bearable.

"Wólakȟota" means *peace, balance, coming together . . . It is a sacred way of life.*

THAT FIRST YEAR protesting, we were young and inexperienced. We didn't know how to protest, so we copied what we saw on television. People always had signs at the protests we saw, so we made signs too. We were influenced by the memories of the American Indian Movement of our mother's time. Our signs read "Is respect too much to ask?" We sat near the front and to the left of the stage during the "ceremony" and conducted a silent protest and held up our signs. It was just us and a few family members who came to stand with us in support. During the protest, Emma remembers, "I felt, on the one hand, both resolute and tough. I also felt angry that these people we grew up with, whom we respected and cared for, refused to even try to understand our point of view. On the other hand, I felt very sad, alone, and afraid. Although I knew that I wasn't alone, it was a heavy burden to carry the weight of other people's anger and hatred."

The homecoming "ceremony" continued on around us, despite our silent protest. Since the "ceremony" was in September, we had to endure the hostility of the faculty and the students for the rest of the school year. Many of our friendships were never the same, and the school staff only spoke to us when necessary. We were still shunned in the school and community, but we tried to focus on figuring out where our lives would lead us.

At the end of the school year, our graduation ceremony was held in the same auditorium as the homecoming "ceremony." The auditorium was filled to the brim with beaming parents and supporters of the graduating class—three hundred in total. Our family came to watch and support us. The principal would call out the students, one by one, to come to the stage and announce the scholarships they were awarded. Both of us were awarded four scholarships each, so our names were called many times—more than any of the other students. Each time our names were called, the whole crowd, who clapped for all the other students, remained silent. Only our family cheered. We failed to win over the community for our cause, but we never let their social exclusion silence us. We vowed to return year after year, until this racist "ceremony" was abolished.

Also, at the end of our senior year, the CSAP mentorship group we were a part of gave us plaques for our involvement in the program for the full four years. We were the only two to stay in the program the whole time. On the plaques, the organization had given us Lakȟóta names that read "akíčhita wíŋyaŋ," which translates as *woman warrior*. We may not ever play "warrior princesses" in some stupid and racist "ceremony," but we are honored to be recognized as warrior women in our traditional language by members of our own tribe.

SECOND YEAR

After graduation, both of us moved to the Twin Cities in Minnesota for college, which is what most of the students and school faculty at Bennett County were hoping we would do so we would never come back. Despite our personal sacrifices, they still didn't understand how determined we were to win. They also couldn't understand that we felt called from a higher level of spiritual understanding. It was a calling bigger than us, although we were not able to put this feeling into words at the time. We just *knew* we were supposed to make this change, so we came home from college to continue our protest.

Soon others in the Lakȟóta community started to hear about what we were doing, and an organization called the Lakȟóta Student Alliance offered assistance. These were students at the Oglála Lakȟóta College, who also had connections to the American Indian Movement. Both groups were highly trained in protesting since the Wounded Knee Occupation in 1973. Our grandma, aunt, and one prominent Lakȟóta Student Alliance member, Robert "Beep" Quiver, plus a few other members from the alliance, met up with us at our grandma's home, where we planned our second protest around the kitchen table. Beep spearheaded the protest organization. Martin Park was the official meeting point for the start of the protest, and upon our arrival, we were joined by almost seventy-five other protesters. We addressed the group to remind us of our purpose, give thanks, and pray. Then we led the march down Main Street, past the onlooking police officers, toward the basketball auditorium. Sarah was carrying her first son, Aarron, with her.

Members from the Lakȟóta Student Alliance formed a perimeter around the protesters and watched for any threats to our safety. According to our creation story, the Lakȟóta people are said to be buffalo people who emerged from Mother Earth. The circle around the protesters was reminiscent of how the buffalo protect their females and young offspring. When a predator catches the herd by surprise, the buffalo create a multilayered circle of protection, with the females forming around the young and the males around the females.[6] We felt just like the young buffalo, supported by the other members of our tribe.

"Wičháša wakȟáŋ" means *holy man*, *medicine man*, or *healer*. Medicine men often receive visions that guide them to become trained as spiritual leaders.

Peacefully, we entered the auditorium, circled around the perimeter of chairs in the center of the basketball court, and clasped hands to close the circle. During the "ceremony," the royalty walked through the center aisle, toward the stage that displayed a tipi and fire. It was dark and the crowd was silent, until we began chanting to disrupt the proceedings. Furious over our protest, the whole audience started yelling at us. We chanted louder and louder, and then began to sing over the audience's screams. The people onstage gave up on continuing the "ceremony" and walked off the stage. The police were there in full force, equipped with firearms. They couldn't prevent us from entering a public building, but they made sure we didn't stay long and ended up kicking us out of the auditorium while the crowd continued to yell at us. But we successfully managed to stop the "ceremony" that year.

After the second protest, the school board invited us to speak with them. They wanted to know if we would compromise. One board member asked, "How about we rename 'medicine man' to 'little chief'? And how about we make it more authentic? The women can braid their hair and we can have them wear moccasins." The school board had bought into the idea that this tradition was somehow honoring us and the Lakȟóta people—even though the "ceremony" was all fiction. A lie. None of this was accurate and everything about it was wrong. If this were any other minority group, this would not be okay. Blackface is not okay, so why would a bunch of white people playing Indian ever be okay? But we thoughtfully listened to their request. We asked our elders and we talked to community members. There was no way to make this "ceremony" authentic. Ultimately we, at the time only eighteen years old, made the final decision that there was no compromise that could make this charade palatable. It was not okay to pretend to be Native American. PERIOD.

"Itȟáŋčhaŋ" means *chief* or *leader*. Traditionally chiefs are chosen through culturally recognized achievements for helping their people or through lineage. Although today, chiefs are also elected.

22

They were mad and tried to shame us. "Why can't we compromise? Why can't you meet us halfway?" they complained. We were viewed as the problem, while they were unable to see the failings of their own Eurocentric thinking. Despite our refusal to concede, the school board went ahead with their changes for authenticity and continued to try to convince us to give up our protest—but we remained firm. There is no compromising our culture, our spirituality.

THIRD YEAR

By the third year, our protest doubled in size to one hundred fifty people. Both the Rosebud Sioux and Oglála Sioux tribes passed resolutions in support of our protest. Elder Nellie Two Bulls came to speak at our forum. Having the support of the tribal councils and an elder went a long way to win support within the tribal community because, as Lakȟóta, we respect and listen to our elders. More and more, our fellow Lakȟóta were realizing this "ceremony" was wrong and that it should stop. They joined us in taking a stand and faced the same risk of ostracization that we had the past three years. We were grateful to win them over and bring awareness throughout the reservation.

Going back to the Doctrine of Discovery, Native Americans were murdered in record numbers as an attempt to erase our existence and take hold of our resources. The Europeans who founded this nation employed the tactics of genocide against the many Indigenous nations

Maria Yellow Horse Brave Heart, a mental health expert with a PhD in social work, was the first to develop a model of historical trauma for the Lakȟóta people based on the similarities she saw between the Lakȟóta and Holocaust survivors. She defines historical trauma as "a cumulative emotional and psychological wounding over the life span and across generations, emanating from massive group trauma," that is usually accompanied by unresolved grief.[7]

that existed here already. Historical events—like the Battle of Wounded Knee, which killed a group of three hundred mostly women and children; the Indian Relocation Act of 1956, which incentivized colonization in urban areas; the Indian Adoption Project of 1958, which sent 25–35 percent of Native children to white families; the forced sterilizations of Native American women through the 1960s and 1970s;[8] or the legacy of Indian boarding schools separating whole generations of children from their family, culture, language, and spirituality—have all left deep trauma scars across Native American communities.

"Kill the Indian, save the man," the slogan created by Captain Richard H. Pratt, who founded one of the first Indian boarding schools, Carlisle Indian Industrial School, in Pennsylvania in 1879, is proof of the intention to shatter everything that makes our people strong.[9] These schools' sole purpose was to assimilate Native Americans by erasing our languages and cultures, and to teach us to be ashamed of our Indigenous heritage. We are still dealing with this historical trauma today—both on individual and collective levels.

Historical trauma has taken away traditional healthy coping mechanisms and our ability to trust others. We minimize our pain and suffering; we push it deep within our hearts, souls, and beings. We pretend we can forget these traumatic life-changing events, but our secrets make us mentally, physically, spiritually, and emotionally sick with shame, guilt, anger, and sadness. It is a continual struggle to love ourselves. As a historical survival mechanism, we have learned to shut down our feelings and emotions, and in an attempt to numb our pain, we use unhealthy coping methods such as alcohol, drugs, negative behaviors, and so on. But when depicting Native Americans, contemporary media leaves out the trauma legacy we inherited. As we previously mentioned, yes, we suffer from high statistics that paint a grim picture of Native Americans, but when we leave out the historical trauma and context that go with it, we only receive half the picture—one where the reader fills in the holes with stereotypical representations of us.

Stereotypes of, dehumanization of, and racism against Native Americans contribute to historical and intergenerational trauma by impeding the healing process. These demeaning and stereotypical depictions compound our lack of self-worth and contribute to the killing of our spirits. In popular media, Native Americans have been grossly underrepresented and thus symbolically annihilated. Conversely, when we are lucky enough to see ourselves depicted in the media, it is almost always a stereotypical historical representation as "noble savages" wearing headdresses and buckskins,[11] much like the costumes for those homecoming "ceremonies." These historical depictions confine us to the past, thus annihilating any chance of the general public becoming familiar with contemporary Native American voices. Further, it shuts out Native voices from accessing the same platforms afforded to members of the dominant culture.

> **According to Dominic Strinati, symbolic annihilation is the way "cultural production and media representations ignore, exclude, marginalize or trivialize" a particular group.[10]**

Worst of all, a lack of positive contemporary Native American role models in the media communicates to the world that we do not belong and we will never be successful in a number of achievement-related fields like business, medicine, and law, among others.[12] This lack of representation makes the possible seem impossible and contributes to Native Americans feeling as if they have no place in the modern world. This is why stopping racially inaccurate and harmful stereotypical portrayals of Native Americans—like the homecoming "ceremony"—is so important for healing within our communities.

At the time of our protest, the awareness around these issues was still in its infancy. Through our efforts, we spearheaded one of the first mascot protests in the country and raised awareness around these harmful depictions to our tribal community at large. We are forever thankful for their joining us in this fight, for without them, we would not have been able to stop this racist ceremony.

Just a few days before the planned protest of the homecoming "ceremony," we held a rally and march on Main Street. We asked elders to come speak and pray. The protesters were to meet at the end of Main Street, and from there we planned to march all the way up to the school. Beep had been organizing in the Lakȟóta community and told us more people were on the way.

Emma says, "I remember parking there with my sister and cousin Lisa. The day was very still and quiet, and I was praying more people would come. Our cousin Lisa, a traditional Lakȟóta dancer, had the brilliant idea that either Sarah or myself should march in her traditional dress so we could show the townsfolk what a real traditional Native American looks like. Sarah and I argued over who should wear it because neither of us wanted the increased attention that would go along with it. We had both had our fill of negative attention from the years of protesting, and the dress—a beautifully hand-beaded red buckskin leather dress—would be sure to get the wearer plenty of attention. The decision was made: I would wear the dress."

Beep went to a sweat lodge ceremony to pray prior to the protest and was given a prayer stick with a feather at the end. Beep asked Emma to carry this as she walked at the front of the march, as this would protect us. Suddenly a lot of cars loaded with Lakȟóta people pulled up. We were all smiling at one another and overcome with happiness. A drum group got out and got their drums ready.

"Mitákuye oyás'iŋ" means *we are all related* or *we are all connected*. It is the Lakȟóta amen and is said at the end of every prayer. Mitákuye oyás'iŋ reinforces a connection to Tȟuŋkášila, the Great Spirit, as well as to the two-legged, four-legged, and winged beings and the earth.

Emma says, "I never felt so much gratitude for my Lakȟóta people as I had in that moment. It was a beautiful sight to witness as Beep organized everyone into march formation. I walked with the prayer stick in front of the march, followed by the drum group, then all of the protesters. Many Lakȟóta men walked the perimeter wearing red armbands on their upper arms, indicating they were there as protectors for the participants. I remember breathing a huge sigh of relief and I silently thanked Tȟuŋkášila. Safety was so important to me, and I felt unafraid with them present. The drum group began singing prayer songs and we started marching down Main Street. A silence settled over the whole town. It felt like all of creation was listening and watching. It was so still and quiet, all one could hear was the prayer song. I walked slowly with the prayer stick in hand and my head bowed down in prayer. Tears welled up in my eyes in overwhelming gratitude to Tȟuŋkášila and to my Lakȟóta people."

People came out of the businesses and stores to watch. Lakȟóta people from the LaCreek community, who had previously not chosen a side, came from the sidewalks to join the march. In total, there were over three hundred Lakȟóta people marching with us.

FOURTH YEAR

The next year, as we prepared to protest the "ceremony" for the fourth time, the school board asked us a few days before to attend a meeting held in a small building off of Highway 18. Beep came with us. The school board informed us of their decision to immediately discontinue the "ceremony" and to phase out the Warriors mascot. All three of us were relieved and overjoyed.

After four years of continuing our efforts and facing the unending discrimination directed at us, we were exhausted.

In Lakȟóta culture, four is a sacred number and Emma intuitively felt from the beginning that it would take us four years to achieve our goal. The school board held firm to their promise and stopped their homecoming "ceremony"; however, the Warriors mascot still remains. The racist depiction of an Indian man can still be found embossed on all of the team's jerseys and T-shirts today.

AFTERMATH

After the George Floyd protests, the brotherhood and sisterhood of people of color thankfully brought a major NFL name change from the Redskins to the Washington Commanders. We credit the many organizers who said "Black and Indigenous" over and over when referring to issues of police violence and mass incarceration.

Though our protest story is more than twenty years old, the Warriors mascot still remains, and every so often we hear from family members of a petition to reinstate the original homecoming coronation "ceremony." It is apparent that there is still much healing and education needed in this small town as well as the rest of America. If they ever do bring the "ceremony" back, we will return and mobilize again, but now we are stronger. Indigenous communities are reclaiming their culture, their power, and their voices.

Ours would become one of the earliest mascot protests in the country, and it was led by two seventeen-year-old Lakȟóta women. More than twenty years later, we wish we could say this is past history, but it's not. There was a high level of entitlement from the non-Native community, who did not understand how appalling the hypocrisy actually was. The expectation that we *should* feel honored by this charade supports this. But these stereotypical representations—just like other cartoon depictions of "savage" Natives—essentially tell the world today that all of our people are dead and we have no contemporary relevance.

Au contraire, our Indigenous communities, complete with our original stories and teachings, are key to addressing contemporary issues ranging from healing to climate change. Globally, if you tally all the diverse Indigenous communities together, our population is 370 million.[13] We are still here, and our expertise can be a vital tool in protecting this planet we all call home. Already Indigenous communities are responsible for the care of 80 percent of the world's biodiversity[14] and 11 percent of the world's forests;[15] what's more, conservation efforts that include Indigenous peoples' access to land rights do significantly better than lands not under their stewardship.[16] Why does the general public have no knowledge of this, or the many strengths and wisdom our cultures offer?

Mascots meant to cultivate team spirit and foster feelings of belonging are actually creating harmful psychological impacts for those of us who are misrepresented by these derogatory depictions. The mental harm has real-world consequences for Native American youth, for whom suicide is the second leading cause of death and occurs at a rate 2.5 times higher than the national average.[17] School boards need to stop trying to "honor" us with phony, racist ceremonies and mascots. Instead, teach the real history of our people in your schools—that would be the real honor.

Today, scientific research shows that identity is the key to self-compassion, self-love, and healing for all racial groups. Anecdotally, we see this every time a major Hollywood film comes

A 2014 report by the Center for American Progress shows that racist and derogatory mascots of Native Americans create an unwelcome and hostile learning environment.[18] Even the American Psychological Association, also in 2014, adopted a resolution recommending the immediate retirement of Native American mascots, images, symbols, and personalities by all schools, athletic teams, and other organizations.[19]

out with non-white leads. For example, when *Black Panther* premiered, many major publications ran headlines heralding the film as revolutionary.[20]

Likewise, interviews with the cast and crew of *Crazy Rich Asians*, as well as the author of the book on which the film is based, go in-depth about what this movie means to Asian Americans who haven't seen a film with an all-Asian cast since *The Joy Luck Club* was released in 1993. The message is clear: accurate, non-stereotypical portrayals of three-dimensional characters is necessary, regardless of which social or ethnic group one belongs to. Having positive role models from a group is empowering and validating for other group members.

Yet somehow Native Americans are still waiting for accurate representation in film and media. Movies like *Dances with Wolves*, *Thunderheart*, *Wind River*, and *The Revenant* are all movies about Indigenous peoples, but all star white men and are told from their perspective. When this happens, stereotypes become normalized and important truths are left out.

Even more disturbing is the fact that there are non-Natives portraying Native people in many movies, which has been a long-standing practice in Hollywood. In 2020, the Twitter hashtag #Pretendian trended in Canada and the United States, exposing alleged "Pretendians" by highlighting individuals in film, philanthropy, and academia who have claimed to but do not have a connection to a tribal community. Some tribes even sent out statements exposing lack of tribal identity and authentic storytelling. This complex issue has stirred trauma for many individuals around ancestry and identity.

Identity issues also stem from "Cherokee Indian princess" stories that glorify a distant family history connection. In the twentieth century, it was common for Cherokee men to refer to their wives as "princesses" as a form of endearment. Many believe this is how "Cherokee princess" came to be a popular ancestry myth. Others speculate this myth originated as a way to overcome prejudice and racism surrounding interracial marriages. Many Native people have heard the same ancestry story so often, they find it laughable.

Tribes have the right to determine their own tribal membership. Many tribal communities have a generations-old method of identifying their members. They will ask: Who is your family, where are you from, and where did you grow up? These questions help to identify belonging, ascertain cultural knowledge, and provide community safety. Many Native people have been disconnected from their heritage because of the Indian boarding-school era, forced removal to rural reservations, and urban relocation. Not to mention that in the South, most thought it was worse to be Native than to be a slave, so many interracial children were not told of their tribal identity. If you combine the historical and contemporary racist attitudes with the historical and contemporary survival methods, you'll find self-esteem at an all-time low for those who have been isolated and for those still living in those environments. Add to all this the varying government tribal identification procedures and you will find mixed messages, cultural disconnection, and imposter syndromes.

"I don't know one adoptee who hasn't at some point in their life believed they are ugly." —Sandy White Hawk, Sičháŋǧu Lakȟóta Adoptee, Director of First Nations Repatriation Institute

Many tribal communities just want you to be honest about your background. Sometimes those who have been disconnected feel like they are imposters returning to tribal life, but many tribes are willing to have welcome-back ceremonies. The individual just needs to spend intentional time in the tribal community reconnecting, learning, and gaining trust. Just be honest about where you are in your journey to reconnect.

MANY YEARS AFTER the protest, Sarah moved to San Diego and, through social media, reconnected with her high school friend Kathy. Previously, they had been close friends in middle school and most of high school. Kathy was the "warrior princess" our senior year—that first year we protested—and Sarah and Kathy stopped talking entirely as a result. Since that time, Kathy moved to Newport Beach and became a lawyer.

Sarah says, "We couldn't believe we had lived so close for so many years. We had both become young mothers at eighteen years old and fought our way through college to be in Southern California. Here we were, miles away from that rural farm town, out for a swim together, reminiscing and catching up on life after high school as the sun set. All the while, I was carefully avoiding the homecoming topic. It was not a happy topic for Emma and me. In fact, we were still traumatized by the experience."

Of that incident, Kathy told Sarah, "If I could do it over again, I would do it differently."

The topic Sarah was delicately evading had arrived. She sighed heavily, remembering everything. Sarah says, "I didn't want to argue or ruin our reunion, but I couldn't help myself commenting quietly, 'It felt like everyone hated us.' I felt a pang in my heart and looked down quickly."

"Not everyone hated you," said Kathy. "I didn't hate you."

Sarah nodded as tears filled her eyes, still looking down into the turquoise water. She remembered how painful it was to lose so many friends and to feel their hatred.

"Not everyone hated you, Sarah," Kathy said again, louder, and she forced Sarah to look at her. "I didn't hate you, and I would do it differently now that I know."

They smiled at each other from across the pool. Sarah and Kathy shared a moment of reconciliation and healing, and for the first time, Sarah felt like she was able to bridge the divide between our tribal community and the white townsfolk from our small town. Healing had occurred with a simple acknowledgment. These small wins are what sustain us and keep us reaching out to educate the dominant culture about the true history of how this country was built, and to bring to light the oppression and cultural erasure Native Americans have faced since the European migration.

Emma says, "I do not regret my decision to protest the 'ceremony' and Warriors mascot twenty years ago. I had hoped people would have the knowledge and understanding to hold respect for a people who had already suffered too many injustices; however, I understand now that healing needs to come from within each individual—from a place of compassion, humility, respect, and love. I still hold out hope we can get there, because we need to. We have the next seven generations looking to us for guidance and we need to heal for their sake, if not our own.

"When I return home to the reservation, some of the people we grew up with and the older generation still treat us with a bit of skepticism over what we did. However, I see, in the younger generations that have come after us, a growing awareness and a desire for things to be better. This brings me hope for the future and makes me feel all the hardship we faced was worth it."

Lakȟóta Laws

*(Living cultural values through action is how
Lakȟóta people live in integrity)*

"Wówičakȟe" means *holding honesty and truth
with yourself, your higher power, and others.*

"Waóhola" means *to be respectful to people/things,
have regard for others, be polite.*

---

7 WAYS TO BE AN ALLY

For many years, we didn't tell this story because it was too painful to reflect on how the community harmed us as young women with their ignorance. Today we tell this story because so many are inspired by it, and our intention is to help others find healing. Many Native Americans suffer in silence due to historical trauma. Many non-Natives have no idea about the actual physical harm they are causing by refusing to listen. We can move toward healing to free ourselves from pain and suffering. We can all heal our historical trauma so our children and the next seven generations do not have to suffer. It is not easy; it is a process to work through each aspect of healing, individually and collectively.

1. **Learn about your local and regional tribal nations.**
   - Spend time in your local tribal community, getting to know the people by attending local events like wačhípis, or *powwows*, where everyone is welcome. Learn about regional tribal history and the contemporary issues that local tribes are facing, as well as the story behind each type of dance style.

34

- Share truth. Amplify and sponsor educational events in your workplace and community, like the blanket exercise, which educates about history and Indigenous issues.
- Don't expect immediate acceptance. Most tribes have been decimated by outsiders through genocide, land and resource scalping, or their elders were forced to be colonized at Indian boarding schools. It will take time to build trust.
- Acknowledge when you don't understand and ask questions with humility.
- Advocate for Indigenous worldviews, Indigenous rights, and Indigenous equity at the community, local, state, national, and international levels. Find local organizations working on these issues and include them in ongoing meetings to build lasting relationships.

2. **Support truth, healing, and justice in your local community and beyond.**
   - We need justice for the dead. Many churches are now finding hundreds of unmarked graves of children who died far away from their families, often abused and neglected. Support repatriation of their graves and the return of their bodies to their tribes for sacred burial by giving to local Native-led organizations.
   - We need justice for the living. Our elders now have suffered sexual and physical abuse, many times at the hands of trusted religious leaders. Some churches actively lobbied for twenty-year statute of limitation laws in every state to avoid being sued. Our elders are only now able to talk about the suffering they endured. Advocate for overturning these statutes of limitations.

3. Rethink patriarchal and linear structures by understanding how colonization is embedded in laws. Ensure that our perspectives and voices as the original people of this land are at the table, from your local community to regional and national levels. We are not tokens: invite more than just one of us for representation.

4. Identity is complicated and complex, but don't appropriate our culture. If you did not grow up with a specific tribal worldview and/or with the community, there are safeguarded cultural protocols and understandings only taught by tribal leaders. You are not honoring us by distorting our cultural and ceremonial practices.

5. Give land back. Many countries were founded by stealing our resources and claiming our sacred ancestral lands.
   - You, as an individual, can give land back to the tribes after you pass on.
   - You can also advocate for your religious community to give stolen land back, especially if it's not being used!

6. Don't just give us a seat at the table; give us equity everywhere. Indigenous voices have been silenced, invisibilized, and killed since the founding of countries.
   - Give us our equity in amplification now! The world needs our collective healing and thinking now.
   - Partner with Native Americans to help us tell our stories. Allow us to lead.

7. Share land acknowledgments by honoring your tribe or tribes in your community at every gathering, even at the end of films in end titles. If everyone learns how to share this historical connection to the land they live on, then

honoring Native people will be normalized and racism will not live on generationally.

- Encourage your local retreat center to give Indigenous groups at least 20 percent to 30 percent of space now.
- Encourage your local radio and television stations to give at least 20 percent to 30 percent of airtime now.

JOURNAL PROMPTS TO HONOR YOUR HEALING

- We often experience challenging issues during our lives that impact the core of who we are as people. Was there a time when you yourself experienced a challenging issue that changed the course of your life? If so, how did it impact you and change you as a person?

- Have you witnessed someone with a differing background from yours facing a challenging issue? If so, how did you try to listen and understand? If you didn't try to understand, how has this impacted your belief system?

Emmy love, mommy love, iná.

We miss everything about you
since the day that changed our lives.

But you still have the same raspy voice
and rambunctious laugh.

The same chokecherry eyes always dance
to a joke you just made,

and we laugh too.

Your memory of the days before may be a little bit fuzzy;
ours is too.

I know it hurts to remember what could have been.
It hurts for us too.

Yet we see the same bright smile today
and we thank Tȟuŋkášila we still have beautiful you.

—SARAH EAGLE HEART

CHAPTER 2

Happy New Year

BY SARAH

ON NEW YEAR'S EVE, 1985, Mom was out all night working her shift as a police officer on the Rosebud Indian Reservation. Fearful of drunk drivers on the road so late at night, Mom spent the evening at the station after her shift. My siblings and I usually stayed at Aunt Mabel and Uncle Leonard's house in Parmalee, South Dakota. Mom would pick up our brother Benny, Emma, and me in the morning to bring us home to Wanblee. Despite Mom's extra precautions, her fear came to pass. That morning after she picked us up, we were run off the road by two drunk drivers who were racing each other down the highway. That accident would change our worlds forever.

The drunk driver's car struck our car on the driver's side. At the time of the collision, I was asleep in the passenger seat and Emma and Benny were in the back. On impact, I woke up from biting my tongue. I looked over at the driver's seat and saw that Mom was unconscious, with her face turned away from me. I turned around to look in the back, and both my brother and sister were unconscious as well. We all had shards of glass embedded in our hair and bodies. A few minutes later, a white car pulled up, and all I remember thinking was *Oh, thank God!* before I passed out. Next, I woke up in the back seat of a different car. I could hear a police scanner in the background, then passed out again.

The next thing I remember is waking up in the waiting

room of the nearby hospital. My auntie was with me and she led me into a hospital room where both Emma and Benny were staying. While they had their own room, they weren't alone. All of our family was there and it felt almost like a family reunion. We were crammed into Benny and Emma's room, and despite the circumstances, the mood seemed happy and joyful. All the kids were playing, laughing, and running around. I felt jealous because both Emma and Benny had casts and I didn't. I wanted to have one too. Benny was four years old and Emma and I were seven when the car crash happened. It was the 1980s and seat belts seemed like more of an after-thought than a necessity. My last memory before the crash is seeing Benny standing up behind the driver's seat, a favorite spot of his when he was in the car. Emma broke her arm and Benny broke his leg and had to spend the next few weeks in a pelvic cast from the waist down.

After a while, I noticed that the room was emptier, and I realized that the adults were slowly disappearing. They were sneaking out of the room one by one and I decided to follow the last one, so I slipped out without the other kids noticing. As I turned the corner, I saw them going down the long corri-dor, then entering another hospital room. I walked up to the door and, with a little hesitation, opened it and walked into the middle of the room. Mom was sitting up in bed with her iná (mother), Uŋčí, three sisters, and two brothers gathered around her. I could see that Mom's head was heavily bandaged and I started running toward her shouting, "Mommy, Mommy!" But as I ran toward her, I heard her say in a cold voice I didn't recognize, "Who is this little girl? I bet her parents must be really worried about her."

I stopped dead in my tracks and stood there in shock, mouth agape, thinking, *What just happened?* One of my aunties grabbed my hand and said, "Come on, Sarah. Let's go back to the other room now," and she led me back to where my siblings were.

That whole walk back all I could think was *I must have done something wrong. Why doesn't she remember me?*

My auntie and I were greeted by waves of laughter when we entered my brother and sister's room. It was the complete opposite vibe from the room with my iná. One of our cousins was signing Emma's cast. I looked around and saw how happy everyone was and I thought, *I'm not going to tell them Mom doesn't remember us.* I didn't want my brother and sister to feel how I felt at that moment. Years later, Emma told me, "Even at seven years old, you were protecting us," and tears ran down our faces as we acknowledged that memory together.

Trauma victims often blame themselves. Trauma specialists say it is a defense against the extreme powerlessness felt in the wake of a traumatic event. Self-blame continues the illusion of control, but may prevent the ability of working through feelings to heal.

AFTER THE ACCIDENT

Because the drunk driver's car struck our car on the driver's side, Mom suffered the most from the impact. She underwent severe brain trauma right behind her left ear and the brain damage was permanent, unfortunately, but it would take us many years to fully understand just how much it completely changed her. The obvious impacts of her brain trauma were related to her memory loss. She suffered from anterograde amnesia, which meant she struggled to make new memories after the accident. I could tell Mom a story and she would have absolutely no recollection of it five minutes later. Worse, she couldn't remember us, her children. Most of Mom's memories seemed to be from when she was young and from before she had us. Aside from the memory loss, there were much less obvious changes to Mom as well. Her personality changed. She became cold, impulsive, and acted like a teenager. She dressed differently. Some of these changes we noticed right away, and some took us years to realize: all are symptoms and behaviors consistent with brain injury. Our mother currently lives with a cognitive disability.

Immediately after the accident, Mom was in no position to care for her three children. For many months after, Mom would oscillate between moments where she recognized and remembered everyone, and those where she forgot again. Forgetting usually led to Mom breaking down and sobbing, then she would scream at the top of her lungs and try to hit whatever or whoever was nearby in frustration—basically having panic attacks. Mom was living with a nurse then, and I remember that the nurse would take Mom into the other room to inject her with something, and she would calm down and fall asleep. It was heartbreaking to see my mom like that, and since I was a young girl it was also scary. We knew this was our iná, but she couldn't remember us and she wasn't behaving like an iná.

Before the accident we lived next door to Wanda. Wanda was our iná's childhood friend, confidant, and neighbor. We would play with her three kids on the swing set atop a sandpile in the backyard. The two friends created a large shared garden and would often cook family meals together. Our aunties say our mom was a hippie mom, always feeding us fresh vegetables from the garden. Our iná married Wanda's ex-husband's cousin, Randy, who is our little brother's father. Wanda recalls, "I remember Emmy like it was yesterday, with her sultry, sexy voice, chokecherry eyes, and laughter. Your mother adored, loved, and lived for you children before the accident. Emmy was so affectionate and loving toward you. I saw a mother who hugged, kissed, and cuddled her kids all the time. She was a doting mom to Benny. When she came to me after the accident, I held her and let her cry. She had so many stitches in her head. You were so lucky, your ancestors did not let you die. I lost my Emmy that night. Somehow she found me, but that light was not the same. I knew your grandma would provide strength and help."

She was right. Lucky for us, we come from a big supportive family that includes four aunts, two uncles, a grandma, and Old Grandma, who stepped in to look after us. Together, the brothers and sisters agreed to be there for us as parents. It was a tumultuous period of our lives because we moved around a lot among the different households. For a few weeks, Emma and I were split up, but our family saw how hard that was for us and reunited us. We lived with our auntie Mabel for a few months, then with Grandma, then with another auntie. It was a revolving door of houses.

During that time, we were confused about Mom's condition, and the idea of living with Mom scared us. Mom focused on getting better, and our grandmas and aunties would tell us she was improving based on what the doctors told them. Despite the chaos, we were so grateful and so fortunate to have the love and support of our extended family.

Our moving around went on for almost two years until, eventually, some of Mom's memory came back for good and it seemed like she was at least semi-okay again. It seemed like she could remember her children, at least, but it is hard to know for sure if her memory of us returned or if she was pretending. When I ask my aunties if Mom's memories of her life from before the accident are accurate, they say no. Over the years, I have noticed Mom is good at faking like she remembers.

After some of her memory returned and she was somewhat functional again, Mom wanted to take us to live with her. She could no longer be a police officer; however, she did get a job working at a factory making arrowheads. The doctors told us that Mom would get better and that the nerves in her brain were going to grow back together over time. We thought that meant that she would be the mom we once knew. Our family didn't understand how bad Mom's injury really was, or just how limited her recovery would be. On the surface, it seemed as if Mom was ready to look after us. She got a nice trailer house in town and set it all up for us to live with her, and off we went.

Unfortunately, Mom's condition was much worse than we all realized. Oftentimes I would come out of my room or home from school and Mom would be sitting in the living room in the dark, with all the lights off and the curtains drawn, with a blank look on her face, just staring off into space. She had problems with migraines and light bothered her eyes. She became depressed.

Later in life, we came to understand that sufferers of traumatic brain injuries can also become more impulsive because of impairments to the reason and impulse-control mechanisms in the brain. She dressed for attention, in tight spandex, tube tops, and animal prints. She was like a little girl in a grown woman's body, and we began to feel like Mom wasn't in her "right mind." Just to give you a sense of her thinking, she bought Emma and I high-heeled gray snow boots one winter. We were in second grade. In South Dakota—where snow drifts and black ice are the norm for half the year. Despite our cool new (completely inappropriate) snow boots, Emma and I never felt safe. We never knew what was going to happen.

Worse, Mom began drinking alcohol to cope with her condition. In grade school, we lived in a house not far from Main Street and local bars. Our home became the go-to location for house parties. I remember feeling afraid having all these drunken strangers coming into our house. At nine years old, I knew what rape was. Sometimes men would come wandering through the house and I would lock Benny, Emma, and myself inside our bedroom to hide from them. One night, the knocking wouldn't stop. I woke up Benny and Emma to tell them we had to leave. At 3 a.m., we climbed out the window and walked one mile to the nearest telephone, which happened to be right outside the liquor store. I called Grandma to come and pick us up. She did.

Living with Mom didn't provide any stability, and so we still moved around frequently. Mom's drinking got worse as time went on, and she had a revolving cast of husbands—many of whom enabled her drinking. Further, her condition made her an easy target for abusive men. We would live with Mom for a bit, then go back to Grandma's when things at Mom's got too intense. Sometimes we didn't know where Mom was—if she was alive, if she was safe, or if she was off on a binge somewhere. Over the course of our lives, we became accustomed to the cycle: Mom would disappear. Then, Mom would clean up her act a bit and fake like she had things together for a few months. She would come around to Grandma's and say she really wanted us back. We would go off to live with her again until something else happened and we returned to live with Grandma. From ages seven to fourteen this was our life until, finally, I had enough.

LEAVING MOM'S FOR GOOD

At fourteen, we lived in a house next to the gymnasium where we would later protest the homecoming ceremony. Right next to it, there also happened to be a Legion, an athletic building, with a bar inside. During the day, Mom sat in the dark, depressed, and at night she partied at the Legion with her then-husband, and they would bring home half the bar to our house after-hours. I would regularly lock me and my siblings in the attic, trying to keep us away from potential danger, from what already seemed like an out-of-control situation.

One day when I woke up to go to school, I came downstairs to the living room and saw strangers passed out on the floor, empty liquor bottles cluttering the floor and table. I hit my breaking point with the whole situation. Not surprisingly, all of the instability and trauma was starting to impact me. I was tired of being scared at night and disgusted at the living environment I was in. At that moment, I thought, *That's it, I'm not doing this anymore. I can't do this anymore.* I called Grandma and asked, "Grandma, can we live with you? I want to live with you for good."

This was a pivotal decision in my life—a significant turning point. So far, our childhoods had been defined by moving back and forth between households, and I couldn't do it anymore. I knew I never wanted to live in that house with Mom again. I was done trying to clean up the mess. Mom had been good at presenting well and acting as if she had everything together for a bit, but in the end, things always fell apart. And I felt angry at Mom. I felt angry that she couldn't be like a regular mom. That she couldn't remember birthdays or Christmases. That I could bring her a report card full of straight As and she would just say, "That's nice, hun." I was angry at seeing my mom not treated right. Seeing her be verbally and physically abused by men. Men who were violent and disrespectful toward her, men who took advantage of her. In my fourteen-year-old mind, I thought Mom kept choosing men over us, and I couldn't keep choosing her while waiting for her to choose us.

As a child, I was always getting my hopes up. The first time we moved back in with Mom, I thought, *This is going to be great. We're going to have the house with the picket fence, and we're going to have support and money for basketball shoes and new clothes.* Men

47

were always wanting to marry our iná because she is beautiful, but she always picked the same kind of enabling man who nevertheless always brought promises of stability and financial security. For my siblings and I, who grew up poor, those things sounded like a dream come true. At the time I just wanted to be doing the things my white friends were doing: playing basketball and participating in extracurriculars. Our Native friends were all in the same boat as us though—none of us ever had anything. Moving back in with Mom after the accident, it really felt for a moment that this dream was possible, but at fourteen I understood that Mom wasn't really healthy for us. It felt as if we had to let her go to protect ourselves.

Living with Grandma came with its own challenges. Grandma had a single income from being a cook and money was always scarce. Living with her meant I would have to give up basketball because Grandma couldn't afford the shoes or even the five dollars we would inevitably need for the dinners during away games. Those things were secondary to the care and support we received at Grandma's house, and we realized if we wanted any of them, we would have to make them happen for ourselves. That's how Emma and I both started working at age fourteen at the local café.

BECOMING THE HERO CHILD

When Emma and I were little girls, Old Grandma shared with us the significance of what it means to be a twin. She told us, "In our culture, being a twin is considered auspicious because it is thought that twins are reincarnated elders." It is thought that Lakȟóta twins are born with memories and pre-knowledge from their previous lives. Thus we are considered sacred.

Having a twin sister has always been a source of strength and a rare social support that both Emma and I have found invaluable over the course of our lives—especially given the context in which we grew up. However, being a twin also comes with a lot of unwanted attention. People are always asking us what it feels like to be a twin. Worse, they often compare Emma and me to each other. I know that Emma finds this annoying and dislikes the comparisons, but I took the traditional Lakȟóta story of what it means to be a twin to heart. For me it's always been a source of strength and sacredness.

The word for *twin* in Lakȟóta is "čekpápi" (pronounced *chay-kpah-pee*), which finds its root in the word "čekpá" (*chay-kpah*), meaning *belly button*, because being a twin represents a deep connection to the other, similar to the connection of the umbilical cord.

After Mom's accident, I did everything I could to be perfect. I got good grades in school; I tried my hardest at basketball and cheerleading. I became a type A overachiever and just kept pushing myself beyond any limits. I became a "hero child," a common role assumed by the eldest child in families where addiction is a problem. The hero child tries to bring honor back to the family's image through overachievement. I am the eldest child—even if only by fourteen minutes—so I still felt that responsibility to try to protect myself and my siblings, since our mom struggled with alcoholism.

Further, the stories Old Grandma shared with us as little girls instilled in me a deeper purpose and sense of responsibility to my people. I really felt that we had to live up to the stories that were passed down to us, that we had a special duty to grow up and be good Lakȟóta women who represented our values and culture as best we could. Our traditional values have gone on to shape me the rest of my life. They have always reminded me that I am connected to something greater than myself.

"Wakȟáŋ" means *sacred*, *holy*, *spiritual*.

CONNECTION THROUGH KINSHIP

Both Emma and I have virtually no memory of our childhoods from before the accident. I am not sure why, but I think it might be for our own protection that we can't remember. We believe that our brains are somehow shielding us from painful memories of our mother because it would be too hard emotionally to remember her love before the accident. I do not have any prior reference to compare Mom to since I can't recall what she was like, or what life was like, before the accident.

I may not have many childhood memories, but all our childhood pictures show the care and love we received. For example, we have photos from when we were toddlers during our naming ceremony. In the photo, Emma and I are sitting on star quilts that were handmade by our grandma, wearing matching traditional dresses with breastplates and beaded moccasins that Auntie Mabel made. Sitting in our laps are embroidered pillows—more handmade gifts from our grandmas—sewn with real sinew. Those photos, and the care we received, tell me everything I need to know about how beloved we are to our family.

Prior to our births, one of our aunties had lost four babies to hydrocephalus, a condition where cerebrospinal fluid builds up around the brain. Emma and I were the first two babies to be born healthy within our family, so our whole extended family doted on us and were quite protective over us. Our grandma said, "As soon as one of you two made even the slightest noise, all of the family would come running into the room to make sure you two were okay."

The car accident was not the first time our family had to step in to help raise us either. Our father left our iná when Emma and I were just babies. We never knew our father, and aside from one random Christmas card we received at Grandma's when we were teenagers, we had no contact with him growing up. Grandma told us about how she remembers picking us up from our trailer home in Batesland, South Dakota. Mom was sitting on the front porch surrounded by all our belongings, with one of us in each arm. Grandma took us home to live with her and her two sons (our uncles), who are only a few years older than me and Emma. Old Grandma lived there too.

We never knew why our father wasn't in our lives until much later. When we were teenagers, we met our father's brother Richard at a powwow. He apologized that our father wasn't involved in our lives. He seemed very genuine but gave us no real explanation, and we were left confused. We had heard stories of our paternal grandfather (and former Oglála Sioux Tribe's President) Al Trimble attending our baptism, so we knew we were acknowledged and valued. Yet the fact that none of the paternal family members had ever reached out to us was confusing because Lakȟóta society places such a high value on extended kinship. In our late thirties, Uncle Richard would return to tell us that the reason our father wasn't in our lives was because he is schizophrenic.

Despite not ever meeting our father and having a mom who was unable to care for us, Emma and I never felt like orphans. Our extended family stepped in to fill the parental absence because they have always practiced and upheld the Lakȟóta values of kinship bonds by supporting and caring for each other. They do this without even thinking about it. Our aunties became our surrogate moms along with our grandmas. Our uncles became father figures. Years later, we would discover that our extended family made an agreement to be there for us after the accident no matter what happened, and they have more than lived up to that promise.

Lakȟóta families are structured differently from a typical nuclear family because of our kinship bonds. Our relations, the way that we treat one another, go back seven generations. Our grandma's sister would be like our grandma, for example, and we do not have second cousins or great-uncles or anything like that. We treat them all like they are first-generation family members. In this context, Lakȟóta kinship bonds bind us to a duty of care that extends well beyond our immediate family members.

"Thiwáhe" means *immediate family*. However, in Lakȟóta culture, this "immediate family" includes your great-grandparents, grandparents, aunts and uncles, cousins, and parents. Your aunties and uncles are considered your parents, too, and your cousins are your brothers and sisters. As such, you must always be there to help one another and honor those relationships by calling one another kinship terms.

We were raised mainly by our uŋčí, great-uŋčí, aunties, and uncles, and the customs and traditional wisdom they passed on to us profoundly shaped how we look at the world. They were our constant. Looking back, I thank God we had Auntie Jan and Auntie Mabel there. I thank God we had a grandma and a great-grandma who were there to help us understand not only who we are in our cultural identity but also what our responsibility to our community is.

We still struggled, of course. We had this crazy, turbulent childhood that had us moving back and forth, back and forth, between households, with an iná who wanted to be a good mom but didn't know how, whose head was spiraling because her brain was not working, so she was trying to do right by everybody but she didn't know how, and we were in the middle of it—back and forth, back and forth.

Despite all the turbulence, we had moments of happiness and stability that our aunties and grandmas provided. Our auntie Mabel took us to powwows and sundances. During Christmas she would load all of us—Sarah, Emma, Benny, Lisa, and Jason—into her car to drive around the neighborhoods to look at the Christmas lights. She was the one whom we excitedly shared our good report cards with. Some of my first memories are of Auntie Mabel telling me in her most serious voice, "You're Lakȟóta wíŋyaŋ. You need to act like a Lakȟóta wíŋyaŋ." I knew she meant I had to act differently because I represented my family and my community. Not abiding by the customs of our people was not an option in our house.

I know that having their support and having them teach us their values saved us. We learned all the protective factors embedded in our culture from them. The cultural customs and kinship bonds passed down by multiple generations of our family rooted us in our identity and gave us a sense of belonging. I see a lot of people struggle when they don't have a support system, and we were fortunate not only that we had one but also that it didn't limit us. Our family never told us *Oh, you can only do this* or *You're not smart enough*. That encouraging foundation is why we grew up secure in who we are, and why we were able to survive the massive amounts of trauma we experienced.

Still, after the car accident, I don't think we had a true childhood. We were too worried about what was going to happen next. We became busy with trying to take care of ourselves, trying to care for our iná, and representing our family to the best of our abilities. You would think I'd resent having missed out on a childhood, but to me there is no point in feeling that way. It is what it is. We are very lucky in some ways and very unlucky in other ways. The gratitude I have for my extended family far outweighs any resentment. Also, growing up on the reservation, I saw so many other children in the same situation as us. Resentment was a luxury that we couldn't afford.

We were lucky because we had our kinship bonds to provide the anchoring we needed to grow up into strong Lakȟóta women. But not everyone is so lucky, and we know what it takes to come out on the other end of so much trauma: a lot of healing, time, energy, and resources. Many parents and older generations are still struggling with the intergenerational and historical trauma from the boarding-school era. Our grandma was forced to attend a boarding school. Having access to all of the spirituality, cultural connections, and kinship bonds around us gave us the protective factors we needed to survive. But even within our family, hugging and saying "I love you" were infrequent growing up. A lot of other children growing up in similar situations lack these protective factors.

The Lakȟóta word for *pitiful* and *poor* is "unšíča," but it also means *to be deprived of belonging and home*. I know that I come from this pitiful background that many Native Americans come from. We call it "pitiful," but it actually doesn't mean *pitiful*; "unšíča" means *humble* too. When we pray, we ask Tȟuŋkášila to pity us because we are humble human beings on this earth. I'm grateful for coming from a humble background because without it, I wouldn't be who I am today. I know Tȟuŋkášila was there helping us; otherwise, why did we have all that support at that time? That doesn't happen normally. It did for a reason.

According to the Indigenous Lifecourse, protective factors for Native children include: cultural connection and connectedness, family connectedness, community control, spirituality and ceremonies, extended kin bonds and networks, healthy traditional food, and youth self-efficacy.[1]

SEPARATION DOESN'T LAST FOREVER

As a young girl, I was constantly dreaming of what was going to happen or where I was going to go when I grew up. Emma and I began to imagine ourselves attending college off the reservation, and we started to do everything we could to make that dream come true. At fourteen years old, when Emma and I went to live with Grandma for good, I distanced myself from Mom until about the age of twenty-five. I couldn't function if I let myself feel all of the pain that was going on with my iná; instead, I handled it by shutting down my feelings and going into survival mode. Plus, I knew if I was going to go to college, I needed stability that Mom couldn't provide.

No one in our family had ever left the reservation to go to college, and we had never heard of *anyone* doing so. College was a big dream for people like us, and our family thought our ambitions were both crazy and brave, especially since we were on our own in figuring out the process. We knew that not even our guidance counselor would be of any help. In fact, when we asked him for help with getting into summer camps, he told us we would never succeed because we didn't have the grades. The fact that he wouldn't help us made us angry and determined. Of course he was wrong and we got into the University of Minnesota with several scholarships.

Our family contributed what they could, which wasn't much. Just before Emma and I got on the bus to head off to college, Grandma gave us each fifty dollars. We knew nothing about money, since we never had any, and Emma spent most her funds on snacks for the twelve-hour bus ride. We'd never even ridden the bus before. When we arrived in Minneapolis, we were definitely fish out of water. We had no idea how to get from the bus station to the campus—and remember, this was before cell phones!

Emma went on to obtain bachelor's degrees in educational policy and community studies and American Indian studies, plus a master's in counseling. I completed a bachelor's in communications, a bachelor's in American Indian studies, and a master's in business administration. During this time, Mom wasn't really in our lives so much. There were many times where we didn't even know where she was, who she was with, or if she was alive. Every so often, Grandma or a family member would call me to say, "Your mom's drinking too much and she is with someone who is beating her" or "She was out drunk driving" or "Mom is living under a bridge in Rapid City."

Receiving these calls was always challenging because I had tried so hard to distance myself from Mom to maintain my own mental health. For many years, I didn't understand why our family called me or Emma when she was struggling. I thought, *She is not our mom.* Mom was never there for us. She never chose us. She had never taken care of us, but now they expected us to take care of her because now we were the adults. Now we were the inás.

As her children, we always held on to the hope that she would be who we wanted her to be, but she was always making countless promises and never following through on them. Growing up, we thought, *Why can't she be like a regular mom? Why is she like this?* In our minds, she was not our mom, but more like a distant auntie. We had to cut off all emotional ties to her. We didn't understand her brain injury at all, and we didn't understand addiction.

The doctors told our family that Mom's condition would improve over time. They told us the nerves in her brain would grow back together and she would be better. We thought that meant all-the-way better—back to her old self—but that wasn't to be. It was extremely difficult for us to reconcile that our iná was not, and would never be, able to be our mom. It took us until our mid-twenties to realize that, and by that time Emma and I had both started families of our own. I was married and had two sons and we were living in Pensacola, Florida. Emma was married and had a son and was living in Wisconsin on the Oneida Reservation, where her husband is from. I received another phone call from the family. "Your mom got another DUI. We don't know what to do. Can you do something?"

MOM'S INTERVENTION

By this point in our lives, we had almost given up on Mom because she had only gotten worse over the years, but we were also scared of getting a call telling us that Mom was dead. I called Emma and said, "We need to have an intervention for Mom. If something happens to her, I want to be able to say at least we tried." Emma and I had a very honest conversation about how we felt. The intervention would be kind of like our last-ditch effort to try to help Mom. We called up the rest of the family to ask them to show up. Emma drove fifteen hours from Wisconsin. I drove thirty-plus hours from Florida back to South Dakota for the intervention because plane tickets were out of my budget at the time. We held it at an Indian Health Service behavioral health center in Rapid City near our reservation.

Many family members were worried about our iná and assisted with providing information regarding their concerns with Mom being a harm to herself and others. Grandma, Auntie Mabel, Auntie Deb, Auntie Jan, Emma, and I were there. It was the first intervention our family had ever held for anybody. It was also the first time that we sought out help for Mom together.

As we all filed into the conference room one by one, Mom was sitting alone on one side of the room. All the other chairs were formed in a talking-circle style for the family on the other side. It seemed like everyone tried to sit the farthest away from her. Emma was the last one to come in and had the closest chair to our mom. If looks could kill. Emma's head whipped back at everyone else as if to say, *Why am I the one closest to her?!* Mom was furious at us. She didn't want to go into treatment at all. The Lakȟóta ATODA (alcohol, tobacco, and other drug abuse) counselor came in and asked our mom, "Lakȟóta iyá he?" (Do you speak Lakȟóta?) Our mom glared at him angrily and said, "SLOWAYASHNI!" (I DON'T KNOW!) He blinked twice at her with a confused look on his face. We all tried to hide the small smiles on our faces. We had all grown up with fluent speakers of the Lakȟóta language in our home.

Each family member shared our concern for her and how her alcoholism had affected us. We each had our individual stories, but hearing them all together gave us the full sense of how much Mom's behavior was impacting everyone else. She was so angry, but over the course of the intervention, she forgot how angry she was and agreed to enter treatment. (Later, she would credit treatment with helping her fight her ongoing addiction issues. She now says treatment was the best thing that ever happened to her.)

With the help of the counselor, we learned her problem with addiction was a form of self-medication. In her attempt to self-medicate, she had become addicted, and the addiction was a disease. Through these new understandings, we began to realize that the iná who we knew before the car accident was a completely different person and that she would never fully recover from her head trauma. The iná we knew died in that accident, and we'd never get a chance to have her back. Grieving this loss was not obvious to us, because it is grief for the living. More than that, we are grieving the loss of an iná we do not even remember raising us, and who doesn't remember raising us either.

When you shut down one feeling, you shut down all of your feelings. "Shutting down" could also be described as "psychic numbing" or "emotional detachment." This is a component of the historical trauma response as defined by Maria Yellow Horse Brave Heart.[2]

For a long time, I had to separate myself from Mom because of all the expectations I had of her to fulfill that role. I had to shut down my feelings for Mom to survive, but that day, I was ready to feel again. This time, instead of suppressed anger, I felt loss. Instead of silenced resentment, I felt sorrow. Instead of hidden irritation, I felt compassion. I was finally beginning to open my heart to her again and that was enough for empathy to take root.

ACCEPTING WHAT MUST BE

After the accident life was never the same. Iná was always in search of her notebook to write down her thoughts, and our family continued to pick shards of glass from our hair and bodies for decades to come. The damage was done in an instant, but the recovery would take a lifetime. We all slowly learned to love again by accepting the reality of her head trauma.

For a time, our mother had a boyfriend, Art, who showed her unconditional love. I remember lying in my tent during the sundance and listening to them talk in the early hours of the morning. They would drink their coffee and talk about the future. "Well, where will I work?" Mom said. Art said, "Probably in a nearby town at a hotel." (Mom would often work as a cleaning lady over the years, one of the few jobs she could successfully hold.) "I wish I could work too," said Art. "Well, you have a bad back so you can't," said my mom, and they both laughed. Art was disabled and in a wheelchair. I found it so touching to hear both of them talking about the future, of taking care of each other, even though they both struggled physically and mentally. Our mother became very stable in that relationship, attending powwows and sundances with Art. Even though it didn't last beyond a handful of years, I believe that love helped her to see another way of life, and she began to love herself enough to stop drinking.

Currently, Mom lives with Grandma. She used to be so angry and frustrated for not being able to remember, but now she can joke about it. Recently I sat around a table with my auntie Deb and Grandma and we were discussing a family friend who had seemingly gone to "looney town." Without missing a beat, my mom said, "I've been there!" We all started laughing and in that moment I could see healing and love.

I have a lot more empathy for her now, and we know that she will need someone to look after her for the rest of her life. At times, I must play the iná role with her. Grandma will call every so often to say, "Your mom was out all night doing such and such" or "Your mom isn't helping around the house," and I'll have a tough-love talk with Mom. My eighty-five-year-old grandma can say it, but my mom knows she doesn't really mean it. My mom now spends a lot of time with her brothers, Uncle Ike and Uncle Howard. A couple years ago, my now-deceased uncle Howard drove her to vote while my other uncle served as a poll watcher. It was so cute to see all of them together talking about voting. I know that brotherly love is also helping her heal. Even Grandma now teasingly calls Mom her "maške," meaning *female friend*, which signifies that she sees their relationship as different from a mother-daughter one. That's how I know Grandma is healing too.

And now, Mom is learning how to be in a relationship with us. I think that for a long time she felt guilty for not being able to be there for us, and she was avoiding that pain because she could sense that we were angry with her. As Emma and I have worked toward our own healing over the years, we have been able to be in a relationship with her and accept her for who she is instead of who we wished her to be. Now we try to give her encouragement and be there for her in the ways our extended family was there for us growing up. She tries the best she can, but she really is like another kid to us. I have reached a point where I don't expect things from her anymore, but she does try to show me, in her way, that she loves and cares about me. I even got a birthday card in the mail for a recent birthday— the first in forever.

Her long-term memory has improved since she stopped drinking. She tries to share more childhood memories with us.

I think some things are coming back to her, but I really don't know to what extent. Before we understood the full impact of her brain injury and that addiction is a disease, it was hard to know where her alcoholism ended and her brain injury began. We believe the alcoholism and additional associated traumas have compounded her head trauma. But I think now that she is not self-medicating with alcohol as much anymore and is instead using cannabis, we are starting to be able to distinguish one from the other.

Alcohol and cannabis use on the reservation is taboo in many circles, but I know many individuals who have utilized cannabis successfully for pain management. For our mother, the difference between her using alcohol versus cannabis is like night and day. While both substances affect individuals in differing ways, the main differences are that she is no longer placing herself in violent situations and cannabis is better for her overall health. She has become stable enough to help care for her own mother.

Before, Mom's memory span was a maximum of thirty seconds, but now it seems like it could even be thirty minutes. A few years ago, I talked to her over the phone for fifteen minutes about the same subject. She usually never calls me. It was Christmastime, and we didn't talk about any of the things a mom would usually ask about, like how the kids are doing, for example—but we did have a fifteen-minute conversation about my dog and cat. She laughed about Zuzu and Abu's antics. It was the longest conversation that I had ever had with her since the accident. After we hung up, I was overwhelmed with emotions as I remembered what it felt like to have a mother.

Looking back now, I don't know that we would have changed anything. Through our own reflections and spiritual meditations, we have come to peace with an understanding that there are certain choices in this life that you don't have, or that your iná doesn't have. Sometimes things are predestined.

At one of the ceremonies we attended over the years, a spiritual visionary told us our iná had sacrificed half of her spirit so we could be who we are today. She said Iná's sacrifice was part of the bigger things we had to do in this life. Our iná was only sorry because she didn't know how much it would hurt us. This was something that was determined by the Creator. It was not something we or anybody could control. Now my sister and I can accept this reality as part of what we needed to experience to become the people that we are, and to do the work that we need to do.

"Waúŋyaŋ" means *to offer something as a sacrifice*, or *to make an offering*. The Lakȟóta practice of offering may take the form of gifting food, sage, cedar, tobacco, and even flesh in some ceremonies.

When my mom's old friend reached out to me over social media last year, she reflected, "All those years I prayed for my friend Emmy to heal and live a good life . . . for you kids to flourish and be loved and cared for. Congratulations, you came so far . . . I wish you kids love and happiness and every single thing you need and may the gods give you double because that would only be fair . . . and the same for my friend Emmy Eagle Heart." Wanda added, "It's really healing after all these years to see you and Emma doing so very well and I am relieved, so relieved. We are from the strongest people. Our ancestors and Tȟuŋkášila help us endure and overcome and thrive! We are the pté oyáte [buffalo people] and we endure. I sang for your family as a sundancer for many years. I never forgot you."

Lakȟóta Laws

*(Living cultural values through action is how
Lakȟóta people live in integrity)*

"Wówičakȟe" means *holding honesty and truth
with yourself, your higher power, and others.*

"Waóhola" means *to be respectful to people/things,
have regard for others, be polite.*

---

7 WAYS TO BE A GOOD RELATIVE

Being a good relative means we honor our thiwáhe (family) always. Our mother's siblings, Auntie Mabel and Uncle Howard, recently left us to the spirit world, and the void they left in our family is deep. They behaved like our parents by loving us like daughters. They connected us to belonging in a way that meant we never felt alone or unsupported, even in the most difficult of times. Losing a parent is one of the hardest experiences a person has to endure. There are many different types of loss: death, disappearance, illness. We were so confused for most of our childhood because we didn't understand our mother's mental state and we didn't have access to child psychologists to help us process what happened. Instead, we were mentally and physically jolted by witnessing our mother disappear. Collective love healed us. Love from our thiwáhe, for us and our mother. Even though our family also had little knowledge of our mother's traumatic brain injury, they still loved her enough to always find her when she drove down the wrong road searching for her lost notebook. Love truly does heal us all, even in its glorious imperfection.

Understand:

1. If you have cultural knowledge about your tribal community, you have a responsibility to pass on teachings so we don't lose them.

2. Kinship bonds are critical for the survival of Lakȟóta people and many other tribes. Understand your own responsibility as a relative to your extended family on both your matriarchal and patriarchal lines.

3. Respect cultural protocols by asking a trusted community leader or several members of that community for advice. There is knowledge everywhere, even in urban areas.

   - For the Lakȟóta people, you must greet each other according to your relationship to each other. In fact, female relatives are expected not to talk to their male in-laws, but instead to go through their female relatives.
   - Generosity is a prized value. It is customary to bring a meal or a small gift to gatherings.
   - During meetings or talking circles, it is expected to wait for the eldest person to speak first, then the next eldest, and so on. This shows respect for their wisdom. Lakȟóta people also don't speak just to be heard. Listening is more important, unless you have a necessary point to make.
   - In the wašíču world, to be corrected is shameful. In the Native world, to be corrected is to know someone cares for you.
   - It's important to show up for one another, especially for ceremonies, giveaways, or funerals. It's a sign of respect for the family to be there for them in their time of need. Even if it's last-minute. Making the effort means a

lot to the family. Remember: "mitákuye oyás'iŋ" means *we are all related or connected*. It is our Lakȟóta amen. It reminds us of our responsibility to the two-legged, the four-legged, the winged beings, Mother Earth, and the spirit world. It reminds us to help one another, always.

4. **Don't impose hierarchy and patriarchal rules. Reinforcing colonial paradigms can happen often in our community, but the more we indigenize our systems, the more alignment and healing we will see in our communities. Learn about intergenerational trauma or historical trauma in your family or community.**
   - Share your insight with your friends and on social media.
   - Research the Indian boarding-school era by visiting the National Native American Boarding School Healing Coalition's website.

5. **Learn about your family lineage. There was and is strength in your ancestors, so knowing who they were and what they did will help you to connect to them and know your own community responsibilities.**

6. **Lakȟóta people teach that each tribal member's actions represent their family and tribe. Understand how your individual actions are in alignment with the values of the tribal community.**

7. **We have to continue to gather in order to support our people's healing. The separation of our peoples, through adoption or child removal via Indian boarding schools, is a collective wound, and we have to have collective healing.**

JOURNAL PROMPTS TO HONOR YOUR HEALING

- What was your childhood like growing up? How did your childhood impact who you are today?

- What beliefs do you hold?

- What teachings or lessons have you learned about healing that you hope to pass on to your loved ones?

- How do you show compassion and empathy through action?

Our littlest love is our misúŋ; the sun always radiated from his round little face.

Our little brother was always game to play anything we dreamed.
Sometimes he was grass dancer,
sometimes he was the race car driver.

Our little circle of three danced and raced around the little rez house,
sometimes in joy and
sometimes in fear.

Our little dancer stomped down the tall plains grass,
sometimes to sleep,
sometimes dreaming of how he once swept his little body around the wačhípi circle.

Our little race car driver would later escape by racing to the tall trees,
sometimes to forget the bad dreams,
sometimes to build new ones.

It was another kind of forced family separation.

Our littlest love forgot that you can't forget the bad without forgetting the good.
We cradled his sweet little heart in the palms of our memories.
His little circle was always waiting for him to fly home.

Our little love, misúŋ, was never alone.

—SARAH EAGLE HEART

CHAPTER 3

Wašíču Išnála or *White Man Stands Alone*

BY EMMA

MISÚŊKALA (MY YOUNGER BROTHER), BENNY

Our misúŋ (little brother) was our čhépa (chubby) baby doll brother when we were kids. He was named after our kaká (grandfather), Benjamin Black Hawk, and we called him Benny. He has always been so sweet, loving, and kind. He would've done anything for us and we would have done anything for him. We loved him so much. If we could've protected him from the harsh world, we would have. Benny is three years younger than Sarah and I. He has a different father than Sarah and I, but we don't think of him as a "stepbrother." He has always been our little brother. His father committed suicide before Benny was even one year old. I don't have any memories of his father. He and our mom weren't in a relationship when he died, as she was studying at the police academy in North Dakota when it happened.

Benny was a big sweetheart and he would just go with the flow and let us do whatever we wanted when he was young. One of my fondest childhood memories is of Sarah, Benny, and I playing, a couple years before the car accident. We lived in the teacher housing near Crazy Horse elementary school in Wanblee, South Dakota. My sister and I were in kindergarten and my brother was just two years old at the time. Sarah and I were friends with a little girl about Benny's age who lived across the street from us. We used to dress both her and our brother up and pretend one was the bride and one was the groom. Sarah and I would marry them and instead of saying *Your lawfully wedded wife*, we would say "Your awfully wedded wife." Then we would pull Benny and the little girl around our yard in the little red station wagon.

Our stepfather was a shop teacher at Crazy Horse high school. My sister and I would play jacks with our friends during class recess. There was even a swimming pool and we had swimming lessons. (This was huge on our reservation, as there are almost no swimming pools!) My sister and I were constantly in competition with each other. I learned how to ride a bike before my sister did, and I recall riding the bike down the hill near our home, looking back at her gleefully. I was so happy.

I remember watching Mom put her makeup on in the bathroom. She would wear false eyelashes, blush, eye makeup. She had gorgeous brown skin, perfect teeth, and chokecherry eyes. I thought she was so beautiful. For most of my life I could not reproduce anything from before our car accident. I have almost zero memories, even fewer good ones of my mother. I don't recall what kind of mother she was, but she was never the same afterward, and I think the trauma of losing our beautiful mother and remembering was too painful. Perhaps my brain is trying to protect me from further grief over what was lost. Over time, I've learned to not be so hard on myself if I can't remember things from childhood. I know that when I need to remember, or when I am ready to, the memories will come back.

AFTER THE CAR ACCIDENT

Benny was four years old and Sarah and I were seven when the car crash happened. We were in a brown station wagon, with my mother driving and Sarah in the passenger seat. Benny and

I were in the back with the seat down flat. I was asleep. My last memory is seeing Benny standing up behind our mother in the driver's seat, a favorite spot of his when we were driving. I woke up to my broken arm and a scar on my forehead. Like Sarah shared in the previous chapter, that accident upended our lives completely. Our happy world fell apart.

During Mom's recuperation, we were fortunate enough to be cared for by our aunties and grandmas. Once Mom appeared to have recovered, we were eager to have our mom back. But we didn't understand that she was a different person from the mother we had always known. Her traumatic brain injury combined with her alcoholism created a tumultuous and unstable childhood for all of us.

Shortly after the car accident, I recall waking up in our home to the sounds of arguing and crying. I remember peeking around the corner to see what was going on. I saw our stepfather, Lee, yelling at our mom. She was drunk, crying, and crawling on the thin carpet. She had crawled under the kitchen table for protection as he was pushing chairs, the ironing board, and other household items over on top of her. She was so drunk there wasn't any way she could protect herself from him. She finally started to crawl past me into their bedroom. Lee said to me, "Look, this is your mother! This is your mother!" I didn't understand what he meant when he said this, but this phrase would continue to haunt me throughout the years.

I think Lee tried to stay in the marriage but ultimately realized she was no longer the woman he married, so he left. I don't remember ever seeing or hearing from him again.

Sometimes I think about the messages we would get from adults, spoken and unspoken, about our mother after the car accident. Most often they were not good. As though she were someone we should not aspire to be like. There would be this sense of shame. I think it was too easy for others to judge her on her shortcomings after the car accident. Their judgments were not based on the truth and did not demonstrate compassion: She has a traumatic brain injury. She is mentally disabled. Many of her behaviors are classic for a traumatic brain injury. She is a little girl in a woman's body. A shell of her former self. It was not her fault.

She is guilty of being this beautiful woman-child of whom too many have taken advantage. It makes me so angry when I think of how some people would use her. My husband will remind me of how much of a survivor she is, and that is true. He says if the world were to end by some kind of catastrophe, our mother would survive. I think he is right.

Sarah and I often did not feel safe living with our mom because we never knew what was going to happen. We even ran away a couple times. After the accident, Sarah unconsciously took on the role of our mother and caregiver. She always tried to protect us. She tried to shield us from the harsh reality that our mother as we knew her was gone. I believe Benny would, at times, project his anger upon Sarah as the unspoken mother figure because he couldn't express his anger toward our mother. Benny recently shared with us that anger was his go-to emotion.

Anger is a very common emotion for those who have experienced trauma. Even more so if the person has trauma involving betrayal, exploitation, and violence. Sigmund Freud developed the concept of projection in his work on unconscious defense mechanisms as a means of protection against anxiety. Projection is when an individual displaces their feelings onto another individual, animal, or object to avoid anxiety. Other defense mechanisms are denial (inability to realize or accept the reality behind truth and/or lived experiences), repression (blocking painful memories or thoughts), regression (behavior or emotions regressing to a previous developmental stage), rationalization (justification of problems or mistakes), displacement (displacing an emotional response from one person to another), reaction formation (expression of the opposite behavior or emotions that the individual truly feels), sublimation (redirecting unhealthy urges into a healthy activity), intellectualization (intellectualizing an upsetting incident rather than feeling one's emotions), and compartmentalization (placing difficult events into separate compartments to avoid feeling contrasting emotions). These defense mechanisms are not fundamentally "bad," except when they are used too often over long periods of time. I sometimes used repression and compartmentalization.

I would later come to understand that we had developed codependent behaviors. Codependency can be described as when people feel dependent upon loved ones and feel responsible for the emotions and behaviors of those loved ones. They will often sacrifice their own needs to save the others, rather than allowing natural consequences to occur. Some other signs of codependency include trouble with decision-making in a relationship; trouble identifying emotions; trouble with relationship communication; trouble with placing the value of approval from others higher than yourself; difficulty trusting yourself and low self-esteem; holding abandonment fears or needing approval from others; and depending on an unhealthy relationship even at your own expense.

We knew what rape was at age nine. During one of Mom's all-night parties, a stranger kept knocking on our locked bedroom door. Sarah said worriedly, "We have got to get out of here." Sarah opened the window and ushered Benny and me out. It was around 3 a.m. and we walked a mile through the cold dark night through our tiny town to the nearest pay phone in front of the liquor store, to call Grandma and ask her to pick us up... again.

After a few months, Mom would sober up and get things together enough to seem like she was okay again. Whenever this happened, she would turn up at Grandma's, ready to take us back to live with her. Mom was good at presenting well, or faking like she was functioning, when in reality she was far from it, and so after a few months living back with Mom, the other shoe would inevitably drop, and Sarah, Benny, and I would find ourselves at Grandma's again. Or Auntie Mabel's. We continued to move around often between different family members, seemingly never staying at a place for more than a few months. I remember on a particularly chilly autumn day, we were at Grandma's again for a few months when Mom showed up and started yelling at Grandma, "You're keeping my kids away from me! They belong with me."

Grandma wasn't sure what to do. I think on the one hand she knew that it wasn't safe for us to go with her, but on the other, she didn't understand the full extent of our mother's brain injury. Grandma felt guilty that Mom wanted us and so she let us decide where we wanted to live. Sarah and I finally refused to go back with Mom. We were afraid of going back to the all-night parties and the strangers coming into the house. My brother was only ten or eleven years old at the time, and a bit of a momma's boy, so he wanted to be with Mom. Before the car accident, he was the baby of the family and was doted upon by all, especially our mother. He always wanted to be with her and I don't think at his young age he understood how different our mother was. "See? He wants to go with me," Mom would say, using this as a justification to take Benny back to live with her.

Our family was trying to protect us the best they could. I believe they felt helpless with my little brother being so little and wanting to go. I felt that our grandma carried a lot of guilt and heaviness back then. I think they felt the same as we did. They desperately wanted her to be the daughter and sister they had always known. We all slowly realized more and more that she was never going to be the same. When I think back to how hard it was for us as her children, I also think how hard it must have been for them to have to grieve the loss of a daughter and sister, as well.

Mom's been married many times. Sometimes it is hard to recall them all. At the time Benny went to live with Mom, she was married to an awful man—one of the worst that I can ever recall her dating. We didn't know at the time that he was physically, verbally, emotionally, and psychologically abusive. He was addicted to cocaine. Because Benny's dad committed suicide, every month Mom received Social Security money from the state for Benny. Since Mom received regular income for Benny, this was likely a strong motivation for her wanting to take our little brother. But she was an easy target to others, not only because of her brain trauma and disability but also— even more so—because they could use her as another financial source to feed their own alcoholism and addictions. At the same time, she would become hyperfocused on the lifestyle of each guy she was in a relationship with—her whole identity would come to revolve around him all the time. Completely codependent.

Two years later, on a cold October morning, Mom and her husband left the house with Benny and never came back.

REUNITING WITH BENNY

After they left, no one in the family heard from Benny, Mom, or her husband for several months. Nobody knew where they were or how to reach them. They completely disappeared. Auntie Janet, one of the aunts we lived with over the years, was worried and went looking for them in Pine Ridge. She went door-to-door asking, "Do you know so-and-so? Do you know where this little boy is?" At 2.1 million acres, Pine Ridge is huge, so trying to find someone out there is no easy feat. Filing a missing person's report with the tribal police wouldn't have been much use either, given their limited resources. Fortunately, we have a very determined auntie, and after a few months of door knocking she finally found our baby brother.

It was springtime—maybe April—when she found him, and she brought him home to Grandma's house. It was the first time we had seen him in months, and he looked terrible. He was so skinny and gaunt that his clothes hung on him and were worn, dirty, and tattered. Underneath his clothing, Benny's body was covered in sores. He told us that he had tried to find where our mother was in Pine Ridge because he knew he would at least be able to sleep and feel safe. When he couldn't find her, he slept in drainage ditches next to roads or sometimes in abandoned cars. And when that became dangerous, a friend told him about this safe camping place. But Benny got poison ivy bad while walking through fields, so he left to find our mother. He collapsed and was unconscious on the porch of the place where a friend told him she was. When Mom found him and took him to the emergency room, the doctor said it was the worst case of poison ivy they had ever seen. A week later at Grandma's, we got him cleaned up and let him get settled back in, and we began to find out what happened to him. In total, he was missing for roughly six months during the cold South Dakota winter. He was living in squalor in a squatter's house on the reservation. There was no electricity, phone, heat, water, or food. There were other people squatting there too. Mom and her husband stayed there with Benny initially, but her husband suggested they leave him there with twenty dollars for food while they went off, who knows where.

Benny was emanating joy and gratitude when he was reunited with us. A spoiled cousin was complaining about the meal Grandma Rose had whipped up last-minute with commodities. Benny said, "I will never complain about food again. I went for days without food." He survived off the food that he could manage to steal from the grocery store. He told us he had makeshift weapons he built to defend himself from other neighborhood kids and/or adults. He had begun drinking alcohol and smoking marijuana to cope with his deplorable living conditions. He said, "I wanted to go to school, but I was too embarrassed to go, because I couldn't wash my clothes or take a shower." He had been going to school at Wolf Creek elementary school a few miles east of Pine Ridge.

At fourteen years old, I was in disbelief. In Lakȟóta, the word for *child* is "wakȟáŋheža" (*wah-ky-yeh-jah*), and the root word is *sacred* (wakȟáŋ). Yet here was my younger brother living all alone with no protection. He couldn't go to school. He had no running water. He couldn't shower. There wasn't even any heating, and this was over the course of a South Dakota winter, where average lows of ten degrees Fahrenheit are common. I just kept thinking about how scared and alone he must have felt.

I felt incredibly angry at the time; part of me still does. I felt like I failed him, too, and I should have done more to protect him since I was the older sister, even if only by a few years. Growing up, we were taught the importance of Lakȟóta kinship bonds and all that upholding them entails. We were brought up to believe that family is more important than anything else, and that to have family is more valuable than any of life's riches; yet here we had failed to protect our brother. I remember feeling so helpless and angry. I asked myself, *Why didn't I go look for him? Why didn't we know this was happening? Why didn't we find him sooner? Why didn't anyone from the school go and see what happened?*

Benny had a hard time adjusting when he first came back to living at Grandma's. I think it was hard for him to try to live like a regular kid, considering all he had endured. He had a stereo player and played the same sad song on repeat. He was so angry. He would say things like "Why didn't you make me

77

stay with you all?" and "Why did Grandma let me go?" But Grandma hadn't really known that things were so bad with Mom. I think the family knew that she was different, but they didn't know just how much she had changed. Grieving for someone who has suffered a brain injury is not easy because it is grief for the living. Mom is still here, but she's gone at the same time.

Benny could get angry, but he was still really sweet. Despite everything that happened to him, and despite his anger, he was appreciative and grateful to be home and reunited with us all. At the end of the day, he's the kind of person who would do anything to help anyone. He really would. He is very selfless in that respect. I just think he didn't know how to cope with his trauma, and our family didn't really know how much he had been through. Benny didn't, and still hasn't, told anyone the full extent of what he endured during this time period. I know we tried to help him, but we couldn't undo the harm already done.

He recently told us that anger was his default coping mechanism. He began to seek healing through counseling when he became a father and husband because he didn't want his anger to affect his family. However, the therapists he met were not trained in cultural sensitivity to Native American people. One non-Native therapist told him he was "the worst case they had ever encountered" and then retired! Benny eventually found a Diné (Navajo) therapist a few years ago who was trained in Eye Movement Desensitization and Reprocessing (EMDR) therapy. Our brother credits this therapist and EMDR for helping him understand and begin healing from his trauma. He recommends that others interview their therapists because this is what he had to do.

As a psychotherapist, I think about how the first therapist my brother met did him a great disservice in telling him he was "the worst case they had ever encountered" before retiring.

What message did that send to my brother? The therapist could have instead referred him to another therapist who was trained in trauma work and had cultural-sensitivity training. I also think of how much trauma Native Americans endure and how difficult it is to trust someone with their deepest pain. I know that's how it was for me. I would not have sought therapy unless it was a last resort because of how much shame I held.

The Indian Health Service (IHS) is often the only medical and behavioral health resource for members of federally recognized Native American and Alaska Native people, and it is historically underfunded, despite being under the branch of the United States Department of Health and Human Services and part of the treaty agreement with the federal government for tribal land and resources. During that time on the Pine Ridge Indian Reservation, there was only a smattering of resources for trauma and social support, including one IHS behavioral health program and one domestic violence program, Čhaŋgléška Inc., established in 1989. What was available was far from sufficient because the reservation, as I mentioned, is massive. It can easily take one hour to drive from one end to the other. There wasn't even public transportation available at that time. Now there is, thankfully. Still, we need a drastic increase of mental health services out there to combat the epidemic of trauma and resulting mental health problems. Because of the severe shortage of helping professionals, it was next to impossible for someone like my brother to go to behavioral health therapy or receive any counseling at the time.

Benny also suffered from abandonment issues. First, from his dad dying, and then from his mom abandoning him. He was left alone with no one to protect him. He had to take care of himself. This is another trauma. What breaks my heart is that almost everyone who lives on reservations has similar issues and difficulties trusting anyone. A lot of Native Americans just don't feel like there is someone they can confide in or open up to. Without establishing and maintaining healthy relationships with others, healing and finding support becomes increasingly difficult.

BENNY'S ADDICTION

Our mother finally left her husband that summer, a couple months after we found Benny. Mom arrived on Grandma's doorstep at 2 a.m., severely beaten and shaking with fear. As soon as Grandma let her in, Mom closed the door and locked both the deadbolt and the chain. She told Grandma, "My husband is going to kill me because I stole his car so I could leave town and get away from him." She was badly injured and scared.

Because we lived in a small town in a rural area, the gas stations did not open until 6 a.m. so Mom had to hide out until she could gas up and leave. She stood by the door until the sun came up, visibly terrified that her abusive husband would turn up to kill her at any moment. As soon as the sun rose and the station opened, she was gone. She fled to Colorado to live with her sister and her brother's families. She didn't come back to South Dakota for many years.

Benny continued living with us until he entered high school. He was so behind in his studies with everything that happened to him. Eventually he quit school and went to Job Corps, then went to work out of state for a couple years, and then he decided to move to Colorado to be closer to Mom. Even with everything that happened, he still wanted to live close to her. That natural inclination to look for support from a parent never really goes away. For most of our lives, my siblings and I always held on to the hope that Mom would become the person who we wanted her to be—who we *needed* her to be. We understood neither brain trauma nor addiction then. We always wanted to believe in the countless promises Mom made but could never keep. It took many years until I stopped asking, *Why can't Mom just be like a regular mom? Why is she like this?*

I think Benny was still in a hopeful phase when he moved to Colorado to be closer to Mom. Our mother had remarried again, for the sixth time, but became addicted to amphetamines (speed) and methamphetamines. Our brother soon became addicted to methamphetamines as well. He met his girlfriend and together they had a daughter. He was able to stop using meth cold turkey in order to be a good father.

CHILDHOOD TRAUMA LEAVES A MARK

In the previous chapter, Sarah shared that the Lakȟóta word for *poor* is "unšíča," and that it signifies something much deeper than a lack of material wealth. More accurately, the word means a combination of *pitiful* and *to have compassion and empathy*, and in Lakȟóta society, no one is considered more pitiful than those among us who lack kinship bonds, connection, and a sense of belonging. It is important to have this compassion and empathy for people. To help others in need. Benny, Sarah, and I come from humble beginnings. We lost our fathers before we could know them, and lost our mother, too, in the car accident. We were orphans. As much as our family tried to protect us, there were just too many risk factors out there for us growing up, and sadly, they were unable to shield us from all of them.

After years of being a practicing psychotherapist, I have become all too familiar with the long-term impacts of childhood trauma on mental and physical health. One tool that clinicians use to screen for childhood trauma is called the Adverse Childhood Experiences (ACEs) score. It was created by Dr. Vincent Felitti and Dr. Robert Anda and their colleagues in 1990 during a groundbreaking study they conducted to determine the impact of childhood trauma on leading causes of death in adults. Felitti and Anda narrowed in on ten adverse childhood experiences that captured what they considered to be markers of abuse, neglect, and household dysfunction. The ten items cover a gamut of experiences, including recurring emotional abuse, physical abuse, sexual abuse; divorced parents; living with a parent who has a mental illness or has attempted suicide, or a parent who has an addiction; having a parent go to jail; or seeing physical altercations that involve your mother. Each item equals one point on the score, for a total of ten. A score of four or more is considered high.

Felitti and Anda's research demonstrated a clear link between childhood adversity and poor health outcomes. Further, they established a dose-response relationship between ACEs scores and poor health. What this means is the higher your ACEs score, the worse your health outcomes will be. A person with a score of four or more, for example, is twice as likely to develop heart disease and cancer, and three and a half times more likely to develop chronic obstructive pulmonary disease than a person with a score of zero.[1]

Since that original study, ACEs scores have become a hot topic in trauma research. In 2018, the surgeon general of California, Dr. Nadine Burke Harris, published a fantastic book on the topic titled *The Deepest Well: Healing the Long-Term Effects of Childhood Adversity*.[2] In her book, Harris compares our body's stress response to a thermostat. A functioning thermostat regulates the heat in a building, much how our "stress thermostat" regulates our stress response. For example, when we experience something stressful, our bodies release stress hormones that activate the fight-or-flight response needed to react to the threat. However, our stress thermostat can work a little too well, even to the point of breaking and resulting in a dysregulated stress response, or more simply what Harris calls a "toxic stress response."

Childhood adversity increases the risk of a toxic stress response developing in a child, and this has a snowball effect over the course of the child's life.[3] The impacts of toxic stress over a lifetime are profound. It causes havoc throughout the body, from the immune system to the hormonal system to our brain structures. Toxic stress can result in increased rates of viral infections, autoimmune diseases, cardiac diseases, obesity, migraines, depression, aggression, ADHD, drug addiction, teen pregnancy, and lack of impulse control, among many other negative outcomes. It can even impact the way our DNA is read and transcribed through epigenetic markers that can be passed down from parent to child along with DNA. We are just starting to unravel the significance of what it means for the child to inherit these epigenetic markers, but some avenues of research are revealing a potential relationship between these epigenetic inheritances and the legacies of historical and inter-generational trauma that Native Americans have endured for centuries.

My ACEs score is six and I imagine Benny's and Sarah's would be high as well. Fortunately, there are numerous protective factors that can go a long way to helping mitigate toxic stress—the most important being having a close connection to a caregiver. We were incredibly lucky to have family who practiced kinship bonds and stood in our mother's and father's places to raise us; however, I cannot help but feel that the time Benny was separated from Sarah and I shaped him in a way that did not shape us. He was only eleven at the time, and I feel how the neglect he received then contributed to his toxic stress response. The aggression, dropping out of school, strug- gles with drug addiction, isolation—all of it makes sense when I view my brother through this lens.

Sadly, I think what happened to my brother isn't that uncommon on our reservation, or many other reservations, for that matter. A lot of people on Pine Ridge are living in poverty, and there's so much alcoholism. People sometimes sell their food stamps for cash to get alcohol and other substances. Being raised by a parent who is involved in violence, substance abuse, and the criminal justice system is all too common out there. Roughly 60 percent of the children on Pine Ridge live in substandard and overcrowded housing—many without electricity, running water, insulation, sewage systems, or kitchens.[4] My heart aches thinking about how many children on Pine Ridge are marginalized and at risk of toxic stress as a result.

In my work with adolescents and teens over the years, I have found it difficult to help them begin the healing process when they have to go home to the same unhealthy environment. Oftentimes, I am assisting them with psychoeducation to identify triggers and healthy coping skills to manage their emotions on a daily basis.

BEFORE MY WEDDING DAY

Despite Benny being quick to anger due to his issues with toxic stress, he has always been loyal and fiercely protective of his family. For example, he was very close to our cousin Jason, who is half Oglála and half Sičháŋǧu (Rosebud Sioux Tribe). My aunt and uncle were divorced, so Jason would travel back and forth from his mother's home in Allen on our reservation to his father's home in Parmelee on the Rosebud Reservation. There were families with huge rivalries that functioned similarly to gangs. One night, Benny and Jason were hanging out together when a bunch of guys came after Jason to beat him up. One of the guys had a crowbar and went to hit Jason with it in the back of his head, but Benny saw what was about to happen and stepped in the way to block it. Benny took the impact of the crowbar to the back of his head just to save our cousin. Luckily, no one died. But like I said, he was very selfless, and I have the feeling he would do it again for our cousin, whom we considered as close to us as a brother or any other loved one.

In August of 2003, ten days before my wedding, I left for work early in the morning and shortly after I backed out of my driveway I saw a white owl fly in front of my car. I blinked my eyes several times and stared in disbelief. I thought, *I did not just see a white owl in broad daylight.* For Lakȟóta people, a white owl symbolizes the impending passing of a loved one. I didn't want to believe it, so I shook my head and dismissed what I saw.

The entire day was very surreal. Sarah called me in the morning and we excitedly discussed final wedding details. She was my official wedding planner. I think she took on the role without either of us having much discussion about it. It was one of those unspoken agreements we had. We talked about how weird the day had been for both of us. It was very hard to explain, but I felt as though my spirit was not in my body. I couldn't shake the feeling. I tried to dismiss it. We still needed Jason's measurements for the tuxedo and it was the last day we could order it. We talked about how we were all going to coordinate with Uŋčí and Tȟuŋwíŋ Mabel to get his tux measurements. We had a plan in place. Sarah rang up his mother to tell her to tell Jason to stop over at Grandma's house. He did come by, but only for a short moment to say, "You can take my measurements when I get back." Grandma gave him a hug and said goodbye, not knowing he would die an hour later.

Jason was driving from the Pine Ridge Reservation to Rosebud Reservation to pick up his sister's paycheck from the casino. Nobody knows exactly what happened, but he slammed on the brakes and got ejected from the car and died instantly.

I had wanted both of my brothers, Benny and Jason, to stand up in my wedding, but at the time had heard that Benny was still addicted to meth. I remember thinking, *I don't know if he is using. Can I really count on him?*

Sarah said that the day before the accident, she'd seen a papier-mâché mask of Jason's face when he was a young child at Auntie Mabel's house. She thought, *He's going to die on the Rosebud Indian Reservation in my car.* The thought was so jarring, she said to herself, "That's crazy! Why am I thinking that?!" The next day he began his journey to the spirit world exactly as she foresaw: on Rosebud Indian Reservation, in her car that he borrowed to run an errand for his sister. Sarah knew she had been notified so she could be prepared to help the family with funeral arrangements, and she ended up being the liaison between the families.

Everything surrounding his passing felt significant and deeply connected to our spiritual ties and our Lakȟóta belief system. I didn't find out Jason had passed until after I was done with work for the day. Sarah tried to call me all day to break the horrible news but couldn't reach me.

We had his funeral before the wedding. Benny hitchhiked from Colorado Springs back up to the reservation just so he could be there for the funeral. He had no money to his name, but was determined to be there. Benny was a pallbearer for Jason's funeral. Our auntie Mabel would talk of how grateful she was that our brother could be there for my cousin that one last time.

We held a three-night wake with the burial on the fourth day. Every single night, the skies lit up with lightning. The wakíŋyaŋs were with us as we laid our little brother to rest. The lightning and rain surrounded us, but we never got rained on, not once. It rained off in the distance, all around us. During the funeral procession, with the cars driving slowly, the world fell completely silent aside from the thunder. Everything was so quiet and filled with heavy spiritual undertones. Jason had been a gift to us. He had only

"Wakíŋyaŋ" means *thunder*, *thunder being*, or *thunderbird*. They are considered spiritual forces of nature and are therefore sacred. We honor and revere the wakíŋyaŋs.

been with us for a little bit of time before he had to go back. His father would later talk about the spiritual numerology of Jason's life, with his birth date on April 13, 1982, and his death on August 20, 2003. There were four months between April and August, seven days between the thirteenth and the twentieth, and twenty-one years with three cycles of seven. For Lakȟóta people, four and seven are sacred numbers.

My husband and I still had our wedding as planned. It was supposed to be the happiest day of my life, but I felt angry at having to pretend I was happy when I'd just lost a brother. Tȟuŋwíŋ Mabel told us that Jason would have wanted us to hold the wedding. Despite the circumstances, it still turned out beautifully. Everything fell into place. We all wore blue ribbons on our dresses to honor his memory, and we never did end up filling Jason's spot in the wedding. We felt as though we couldn't replace him. When we looked at the photos later, there was a bright light in every photo where he would've been standing. It gave us comfort to know he was there.

FOR LAKȞÓTA PEOPLE, a year of mourning is customary, but Jason's parents decided to mourn for four years. Other Natives back in the community thought it was unhealthy for them to mourn for so long, but my aunt and uncle were adamant and said, "No, we loved him so much, so we are going to mourn him for four years." There was a "wiping the tears" ceremony for the family after the four years.

> Elisabeth Kübler-Ross, a Swiss American psychiatrist, defines the five stages of grief and loss as denial, anger, bargaining, depression, and acceptance. But there is no one "right" way to grieve.

"Ištámniyanpi-thačhánku Wašígla" means *wiping the tears*. It is a Lakȟóta ceremony to let go of grief, usually a year after someone you loved passed away. During the ceremony, the person leading it takes a feather and wipes your eyes, mouth, and ears, then the feather is touched to your heart as a symbolic gesture of wiping away the grief held there. It involves a big memorial feast and a giveaway to honor the life of the person who has journeyed to the spirit world.

Our aunt and uncle have land next to each other on the Rosebud Indian Reservation. This is where they laid Jason to rest, where he grew up and where his father raises his horses. His father was in deep mourning when he built the cemetery. He shared with us that he sat down crying and asked, "Am I doing the right thing in building this cemetery here?" When he looked up from crying, all the horses were surrounding him and the fence of the cemetery he just built. He knew their presence meant that Tȟuŋkášila and Jason were telling him it was okay.

FAMILY MAKES YOU STRONG

Jason's death was extremely hard on Benny. They had been so close. Benny already wasn't doing well at the time and continued to spiral into addiction. He wouldn't begin to heal until much later, when he met his wife-to-be and they started a family of their own. When his girlfriend became pregnant with their first child, Benny knew he couldn't be there for them if he was an addict and managed to overcome his addiction. I believe having this family connection helped center Benny's life and ground him. The neglect and abandonment he experienced as a child left deep scars within him and he felt like he didn't belong or fit in anywhere, until he had a family of his own. He finally found something greater than himself worth surviving for.

I experienced this as well the night I first met my husband purely by chance. I was in Wisconsin, reluctantly attending a friend's graduation party. The relationship I was in had just ended. I wasn't heartbroken. I just felt nothing. I was very depressed and did not see a future for myself. I did not know how to move forward. I didn't think my life had any meaning. I know my sister saw and felt this within me, which is why she talked me into going to Wisconsin for our friend's party. I really did not want to go. She said, "You might just meet the man of your dreams!" We laughed very hard. We had never been to Wisconsin and imagining "the man of my dreams" seemed witkó (crazy). But I met him the night after we got there while we were out dancing at Club Oasis. While he walked me to his car, I had a premonition that he was my person, my life partner. I recall feeling shocked when this knowledge hit me. I quickly dismissed it because I was so surprised by the idea. But when I think about it now, I realize the spirits were trying to show me that I had a future. He grew to be a source of strength, support, and unconditional love.

When we became expectant parents of our first child, our son, all I could think was *My son needs me.* It made my personal healing that much more important. When I was feeling sad or depressed or overwhelmed, I reminded myself I had someone else who needed me to work on myself and to heal. Having children gave me the strength to push through my own unresolved traumas and to be the parent who could do all the things that our mother couldn't for us growing up. I don't think I would still be alive if it weren't for my children and husband. I think it is the same for Benny.

I am not surprised that Benny has turned into such a loving family man despite all the hardship he's had to carry throughout his lifetime. He's always been full of so much sweetness, and has always wanted unconditional love. Now he receives and reciprocates that with his wife, children, and grandchildren.

I've been deeply moved to watch my brother begin to heal from the traumas of the past and develop new coping skills. I know it takes immense inner strength to keep moving forward and to even take another step. My brother has been through so much, and because of that, to me, he will always be one of the strongest people I know.

HEALING OUR KINSHIP BONDS

Benny, Sarah, and I lost our childhoods to trauma and circumstance. Looking back now, I feel deep gratitude to Sarah, with a twinge of sadness, because she lost her childhood just a little bit more than Benny and I. Sarah was still a child herself, but I think with her taking on some of the caregiver role, Benny feels she should have helped protect him too.

When Benny had his first grandchild, he called Sarah excitedly and said, "Sarah, you're going to be a grandma!" Benny could call Mom, but it isn't quite the same. Of course, she would be very happy and excited. She would probably say, "Ah, yes. That's excellent." His calling Sarah confirms her role as a mother figure for him.

Sarah replied, "Benny, I know we haven't talked in a while, but I want you to know that I love you and I'm always here for you. I just cannot deal with the drama."

Benny said, "Yeah, I get it. I know I am a bit of a hot mess." They both laughed.

Sarah said, "Benny, I think sometimes you are mad at me for stuff that happened to us when we were kids. I was only a few years older than you and I was a kid too. There was nothing I could do. I am sorry for everything that happened, but I had no power."

Since then, Benny and Sarah's relationship has grown stronger. For Sarah, it was important to vocalize her own lack of power in the situation and to express her love for him despite everything that happened to all of us.

BENNY RECEIVES HIS INDIAN NAME

My great-grandma Emma, whom I am named after, didn't speak any English, only Lakȟóta. We were fortunate to have grown up with her in our young lives. She pledged at the Bear Creek powwow to give us our own Indian names when Sarah and I were four years old and Benny was still a toddler. Receiving an Indian name is no easy task; there is a whole process. The family must first make a pledge and has a year to prepare the community dinner and giveaway for the naming ceremony. When the family makes the pledge, they also ask an elder, in this case Old Grandma Emma, to select the Lakȟóta name. You can make the pledge during community gatherings, such as a wačhípi (powwow), inípi (sweat lodge), wiwáŋyaŋg wačhípi (sundance), or other sacred ceremonies.

"Čhaš'úŋtȟuŋpi wičhóȟ'aŋ" means *naming ceremony*. The Lakȟóta people have long held naming ceremonies to provide a solid foundation in Lakȟóta society. The child or adult is gifted either an eagle feather (for males) or an eagle plume (for females) fastened to a quill medicine wheel representing the four directions. A person is selected to tie the feathers on, usually a person of honor or high regard whom the parents pray the child will grow up to emulate.

Old Grandma Emma gave me the name Waŋblí Wíyaka Wiŋ (Eagle Feather Woman), and Sarah received the name Waŋblí Šiná Wiŋ (Eagle Shawl Woman). Now when I look at the naming photo of us as young girls, I know we were beloved. In the photo, our grandmothers are standing behind us as we sit on chairs. We are dressed in matching dark blue traditional dresses, breastplates, beaded leggings, and moccasins. We are sitting on handmade and hand-quilted star quilts, holding handmade pillows on our laps at the giveaway. The fact that our humble family went through so much trouble to gather the giveaway items and dress us traditionally demonstrates that we were beloved children through this honoring ceremony.

Benny is half white and half Lakȟóta. Old Grandma Emma named Benny Wašíču Išnála (White Man Stands Alone). Since he first understood what it meant, Benny has not liked his Indian name. On a recent trip back home, one of our aunts and Sarah spoke to our grandma Mary Rose. They said, "He is really upset about his name. Maybe we should have another Indian name for him or do something different?"

However, our family is spiritual, and the naming ceremony holds deep significance to our people. Uŋčí Mary Rose believes he should feel lucky and honored that Old Grandma Emma gave his Lakȟóta name to him. In the year leading up to the ceremony, Old Grandma Emma would pray while she beaded and quilted. She would ask the spirits to guide her as to what name was suitable.

I think his name reminds him of what he lacked growing up, of how he felt separate from the rest of us. But I also feel his name suits him in a sense because he has spent most of his life separated from our family. He has been on his own with his own family. He has appeared guarded to everyone most of his life. He rarely, if ever, calls us for help. He never seems to need anything from us. Even though we don't see him or talk to him every day, he'll be there if we need him. He wants to be closer and he wants to have more of a relationship, but I think he is still working on himself and trying to heal.

Despite Benny having the same mother as us, his life turned out much different than ours. In the end, I know Sarah and I had a bit more support through it all—and that additional support made a world of difference. First, Sarah and I had each other—we are twins, after all, and no bond is quite like the bond between twins. Second, we had the love and support of our big extended family, who were able to shelter and protect us from some of the worst traumas. Third, we had CSAP when we were in high school, which gave us access to counseling, coaching, and resiliency tools. Our brother never recovered from his time out of school during the months he was on his own, and that left him feeling like he was always behind, which resulted in another major blow to his self-esteem and self-worth. Social support is an important lifeline for dealing with the tumultuous ups and downs of being a human on this planet. Without support, we have nothing.

While Sarah began healing later in life when she started working on her codependency with a therapist, I found myself increasingly drawn to healing professions so I could try to make sense of what happened to us. I wanted to understand trauma and help others heal. Further, I knew I had to use my experiences, my story, and the lessons I have learned along the way to help others like me. Other young Native Americans have stories so similar to ours but never get to hear, read, or see these stories. So many youth across the reservations with broken hearts, trauma, and toxic stress, who feel alone and forgotten. Most of all, I want them to know they are not alone. It is the reason I do what I do. Most of our childhoods were defined by surviving one day at a time. As adults, we no longer need those survival mechanisms and can now move into healing. We can learn to heal from toxic stress and release ourselves from pain and suffering. We can find peace in our hearts again and begin to love ourselves, and then we can teach our children to do the same, thus breaking the legacy of historical and intergenerational trauma. I could have eternally condemned myself for all the ways I failed my brother, or my sister, or myself—but then where would my three children be? Where would my capacity for love be?

In order for me to heal, I needed to honor myself and the life given to me by the Creator and my ancestors. I needed to choose to live my life. I needed to forgive those who hurt me and be forgiven by those I hurt to end the cycle of despair and self-hatred. And in turn, I knew I needed to use my gifts and experiences to support others in their healing journeys. In the next section of the book, we will begin to unpack the tools and modalities that have helped us heal from a lifetime of trauma.

Lakȟóta Laws

*(Living cultural values through action is how
Lakȟóta people live in integrity)*

"Waúŋšila" means *to have
compassion, kindness, or mercy.*

"Wáȟwala" means *to have humility*
or *to be peaceful.*

---

7 WAYS TO LOVE YOURSELF

We often seek love in all the wrong places, when what we really need is to ask for help from the loved ones already near us. Tȟuŋkášila helped me realize I have had sources of unconditional love even if I felt I was alone. When I experience difficulty, I look at my life and see the unconditional love of my hasáŋni (husband), čhiŋčápi (children), thiwáhe (family), thióšpaye (extended family), and tȟamáškeku (friends). How did all these beautiful people come into my life at the exact-right time that I needed them?

I also loved myself by learning how to eat healthier and prioritize my own self-care. Often our anxiety or moods tempt us to fuel our body with caffeine or alcohol or even other drugs. Simple changes to your diet—like increasing your vegetable intake, cutting out processed sugar and foods, getting enough rest, cutting back on red meat, and increasing probiotics—can be life changers! Being mindful of what you put in your body during times of stress or mourning is critical to support your healing.

1. **Understand Native American trauma research and education.**
   - Learn more about the Indigenous Lifecourse and Native youth protective factors developed by Indigenous scholars Dr. Karina Walters, Dr. Michael Yellow Bird, and Dr. Rosalee Gonzalez.
   - Research and compare Adverse Childhood Experiences scores and long-term health among different racial groups.
   - Understand attachment styles.

     Attachment theory was first developed by John Bowlby, a psychoanalyst who studied the impact of separation between infants and their parents. Bowlby's research indicated infants will react according to the following four behaviors: secure attachment, anxious-resistant attachment, avoidant attachment, and disorganized-disoriented attachment.[5] Secure attachment is when an infant was distressed when separated from their parent but was able to be soothed quickly. Anxious-resistant attachment is when infants displayed increased distress when rejoined with their parents. However, they appeared to want to be soothed and reject the parents at the same time. Avoidant attachment is when the infant appeared to display no distress or little distress when separated from their parents or disregarded the parents upon return. Disorganized-disoriented attachment is when an infant's behavior was unpredictable upon reunification. These attachment style behaviors are believed to be intuitive and based upon the early care the child obtained. A secure child is one who obtained love and support from their parents/guardian/caregiver. The child who obtained varying levels of care or neglect is prone to increased anxiousness with parents/guardian/caregiver. It is also believed that what people have learned about attachment as a child will affect their future relationships as adults. We see this in many Native American people who have experienced childhood abandonment or trauma.

2. **Prioritize your mental, emotional, physical, and spiritual health.**
   - Let go of what is not serving you. This could be unhealthy friends or relatives. It could also be self-limiting beliefs.
   - Understand what negative self-talk is and how to change this to positive self-talk with the use of mantras or affirmations.
   - Find places where you feel the everyday sacred in your life. I often find healing by water—like lakes, rivers, and oceans.
   - Take a food-sensitivity test to find out what your body needs or doesn't need in your diet.
   - Learn how to cook traditional meals, like bison or root-based plants. Eat red meat sparingly like our people did back in the old days. Eat healthy foods and notice the difference in how you feel mentally, emotionally, physically, and spiritually.
   - Try to exercise to release healthy endorphins and raise your serotonin levels, which will reduce depressive and anxiety symptoms. At least thirty minutes a day can do wonders for your mood and your health!
   - Learn more about spirituality, traditions, rituals, ceremonies, and kinship-bond terminology for Lakȟóta people and other tribal nations.
   - Get an emotional support animal! My own igmú (cat) and šúŋka (dog) are sources of unconditional love that taught me how to play again and are excellent healthy coping mechanisms.

3. **Seek unconditional love in all aspects of your physical and spiritual life, from your friendships to your romantic relationships.**

4. Surrender to your individual healing process. Understand that it will take time.

5. Learn how to hold self-compassion by being kind and gentle to yourself as you are healing.

6. My grandma loves to spend time around the kitchen table drinking wakȟálapi (coffee) with friends and family. We give family updates and she gives advice. When she hears someone did something they shouldn't have done, she says, "Huh-huh," and we all laugh. Spend time with healthy friends, relatives, and elders to have fun. Laughter is medicine.

7. Practice healing exercises, including:
   • Mirror work. You would be surprised how difficult it can be to tell yourself "I love you" in the mirror.
   • Breathwork. One technique I use is to breathe in slowly for seven seconds, hold for four, and breathe out for seven seconds. Do this four times. I like to imagine I am breathing in love and light and breathing out negative energy.

JOURNAL PROMPTS TO HONOR YOUR HEALING

• Who has been your source of unconditional love?

• How do you practice self-love?

• How can you truly incorporate self-love and unconditional love into your life on a daily basis?

• How can you teach others/loved ones to practice self-love?

I had a beautiful dream.
I was sleeping under the sundance arbor where the sundancers rested
and was awoken to the beautiful singing of the male sundance leaders
calling the sundancers to get ready.
I hurriedly wrapped the shawl around my waist
and put on the sage bracelets, anklets, and crown.
I lined up behind the women walking into the sundance arbor.
As I looked out in front of me, the sundancers' attire
became swirls of the sacred colors of red, yellow, white, and black,
moving clockwise around the sundance arbor, around the sundance tree.
I woke up as I entered the circle.

—EMMA EAGLE HEART—WHITE

CHAPTER 4

Reclaiming Spirit

BY EMMA

THE PINE RIDGE RESERVATION is beautiful and peaceful with its seemingly never-ending prairies, Badlands, and Black Hills. The Lakȟóta people hold a vast knowledge of their culture, history, and spirituality, and I feel an immense gratitude to Wakȟáŋ Tȟáŋka (Great Spirit). The Lakȟóta way of life is one I love and one I work to instill within my children. Our Lakȟóta belief system, extended-family system, traditions, values, and worldview are things I don't take for granted. I feel so fortunate to have grown up with my uŋčícilas, tȟuŋwíŋs, and lekšís (uncles). I appreciate how fortunate I truly was because the knowledge, lessons, and teachings have carried me through some of the darkest days of my life.

But historical and intergenerational trauma embedded in our history means we have a lot of healing to do as well. Our grandmother, great-grandmother, aunties, and uncles did their best to shield us. We have a friend/sister who lived across the street from us, and we laugh sometimes because both of our families were very protective, and we weren't permitted to leave our fenced-in yards. At night, we were not to be outside due to the Lakȟóta belief of negative energy/spirits being out at night, including in the form of people who are not in a healthy mindset. Even as we grew into teenagers, we knew the reservation wasn't always safe at night. There was the use of alcohol and drugs, fights, stabbings, and home invasions. If you went anywhere, it was common knowledge that you needed to have your "backup" with you due to unexpected fights.

As a young girl, I observed how people treated others. I wanted to always be kind and compassionate to those around me. I tried my best to follow the seven Lakȟóta values of prayer, respect, compassion, honesty, generosity, humility, and wisdom.

"Čhaŋkú Lúta Ománi" or *Sacred Red Road* is a Lakȟóta belief and worldview for living a good and spiritual way of life.

LOSS OF SPIRIT

My decision in sharing the truth of my sexual assault has solely been to help other survivors of sexual violence to not feel alone. I felt so alone for so many years until I met other survivors who gave me the strength and courage to share my own experiences. I don't want to call my sexual assault a story because I feel it takes away from the devastating reality. For survivors, to be able to voice their sexual violence is a means to taking their power and spirit back. To finally begin the healing process. Unbelievably, twenty-eight years later in this day and age of media, I have quickly learned the world STILL isn't safe for survivors. This saddens and angers me. It breaks my heart for all of the survivors who are here and, sadly, yet to come. This isn't the complete story I wanted to share. It is the story that is "safe" to tell.

After completing the first year of our protest, I wanted to feel like a normal high school student. I was trying to cope with the staggering amount of racism I was enduring, not only in my high school, from students, staff, and teachers, but also in my hometown. We couldn't walk into the grocery store or gas station without being verbally attacked. These people did not want to hear our side and were only interested in their perspective. I tried to be strong, but it was a heavy burden to carry.

When my childhood friend Naveah called me at home to ask if I wanted to hang out with her and some of her cousins on a chilly October night, I didn't hesitate. I had known her all of my life, so I trusted her and felt safe being with her.

Powwows are gatherings among Natives where we meet, socialize, sing, and dance. There are different traditional dances performed with regalia and music, and even competitions with prizes. There was a dancer there I thought was handsome. He was a few years older and lived in another community, so I would see him around from time to time. I decided to go out with them because I felt safe knowing a few of the people who would be there.

The powwow dancer with the beautiful eyes picked me up in his car filled with my cousin and two other guys. We drove to a dirt road outside of town, way out in the boonies, in between some farmers' fields. Everyone was smoking and drinking except for me. I had signed a Center for Substance Abuse Prevention (CSAP) agreement to not use alcohol or drugs. We were standing outside together just a few meters from the car. The air was crisp; we could see our breaths condensing as we exhaled. We were talking and joking around when the powwow dancer came and put his arm around my shoulders. I thought he was very handsome, but I had a boyfriend already. We had been dating for three years while he lived on another reservation, so we were attempting a long-distance relationship. When the powwow dancer started talking to me, I was of two minds. One part said, *You have a boyfriend*, but the other said, *He's here and your boyfriend isn't.*

I had a crush on the dancer, and I liked the attention he was giving me. Given his age and his skills as a dancer, I was surprised he was interested in me. He pulled me in closer and started kissing me; against my better judgment, I started kissing him back. He suggested, "Why don't we sit in my car?"

"Okay," I said.

I got into the passenger side while he got into the driver's seat. He put on the radio and for a while we were just talking,

102

then he started kissing me again and I could smell the alcohol on his breath. I wanted to stop. The smell of alcohol became scary and sickening. Quickly, everything seemed to be going too far and I didn't know what to do. I cried, "No! Stop!" I tried pushing his body off of mine, but he was a lot stronger. The tears streamed down my face. I couldn't breathe. I froze and couldn't move. I could feel my spirit leaving my body in this moment just to be able to cope with what was happening to me. He didn't care. My tears meant nothing. The music was playing in the car, and I could hear the others still laughing, talking, joking outside. I remember lying there completely frozen in terror; I couldn't even scream for help. I couldn't say or do anything. I think my mind went to a different, faraway place.

After he was done assaulting me, he didn't say anything. He just got out of the car and I thought, *Oh my God, what just happened?* I immediately started to blame myself and ask, *Why am I even here? I don't even drink and I have a boyfriend!* For a long time, I thought it was my fault because I was there and knew I shouldn't have been. I blamed myself because I had a crush on him. The shame spiral began and would continue relentlessly for many more years. The negative self-talk began as well. I called myself every name in the book: "whore," "slut," "cheater." I think the others knew something was going on, but they didn't know the full extent. We all left shortly after.

I later learned about the four types of trauma responses called "fight," "flight," "freeze," and "fawn." The flight response includes running or fleeing; fight involves aggressiveness; freeze is when one is unable to move, respond, or react; and fawn is when one attempts to avoid conflict by pleasing a person. These trauma responses are often developed in childhood. Another common defensive trauma response is called "tonic immobility" (TI). It is a defense reaction to a predatory attack where resistance and escape are impossible. TI is an involuntary response due to intense and inescapable fear. The person becomes paralyzed and is often unable to speak or cry out for help.[1] TI is so common in sexual assault survivors it was initially labeled as "raped-induced paralysis" in research literature.[2]

I went home that night and cried. I couldn't understand what had just happened to me. I felt like it was my fault. I felt completely alone. I felt ugly, dirty, and dead inside. This experience changed me and my life. Looking back, I'm saddened to realize that even if I had attempted to press charges and reported it to the tribal police, absolutely nothing would have happened. Who cares about a young Lakȟóta girl who was just raped? They would say that I asked for it. That I wanted it.

For a rape survivor, making that decision—to report or not to report—is very personal. Only a rape survivor understands what the repercussions might be. It is one of the most difficult decisions they will make. This is why I don't hold judgment, because I know the reality of this decision for survivors. For myself, I couldn't report that rape knowing it would only lead to more pain and suffering and, worse yet, retaliation from him and his family members against me. Physical violence is very real on my reservation. Lakȟóta families are huge. We believe in extended family to the seventh generation and treat one another as first relatives. Physical violence is a perfectly acceptable response to resolving disputes between families out there. I worried about not only my own personal safety but also the safety of my family. I didn't want to risk anyone else getting hurt.

The next day, Naveah came over and said, "He says to tell you he is sorry about last night." I looked at her in shock. I wondered, *Does she know what he's apologizing for?* I never said anything to her and instead backed away from our friendship.

Years later, my twin and I told our family we were writing a book. Two of our tȟuŋwíŋs were the first we told. I mentioned it when I was visiting them and saw a look pass between both of them. I smiled to myself because I could tell they were wondering what we had to write about. But our family has always unconditionally loved and supported us. They just said, "Oh, okay." Then I asked them to sit down. I finally decided to share my sexual assault with them. One tȟuŋwíŋ became really sad and said, "He has been in my house!" I just nodded. The other tȟuŋwíŋ became very visibly angry. They came to hug me and say they were sorry they hadn't known. One tȟuŋwíŋ told me as she hugged me, "My girl, you are very strong." I'd never thought of myself as strong and I had to think about it, but I can see it now. Carrying this burden is very heavy. A few days later, my čekpá called me to tell me a friend had asked her about the sexual assault. She asked me, "What do I say?" I immediately felt the old, familiar fear of retaliation against myself and my family creep in again. I knew one of my tȟuŋwíŋs had said something. I felt a sense of anger, like I wasn't being believed. I said, "Tell her it happened and if she has any questions, she can call me." One tȟuŋwíŋ said she didn't say anything. My other tȟuŋwíŋ later apologized and said she was angry about what had happened. I forgave her because I understood how she felt.

I had always wondered if Naveah knew what he had apologized for, but I discovered she didn't have any idea why he apologized. But when she found out about me, she believed me. She told my čekpá that another victim had told her the same thing. She didn't believe them, but because we grew up together, she believed me. When he "apologized" after the sexual assault, my spirit was so dissociated from my body that I don't think the apology registered. I recall thinking in a very faraway corner of my mind, *Maybe I was the only one. Maybe it was a mistake. Maybe he is really sorry.* Either way, it didn't matter because I felt so dead inside. When I heard about the other victim, I felt a sense of survivor's guilt. I realized the apology was only a ploy so I would not report the rape. I see that now. Statistics show that perpetrators are often repeat offenders.[3] If I had known this when I was younger, I might have felt differently about reporting the crime. But I also know this was the right decision for myself at the time, as I couldn't have imagined that there would be others. I was barely functioning. I was trying to bury the rape in the back of my mind, but it was always there. Then I was trying to make sense of something that made no sense. It only made sense to blame myself. I hated myself. I felt so much guilt, shame, and fear—it became a never-ending cycle of self-hatred. I compared my rape to others and thought, *Well, mine wasn't as bad as theirs.* I thought I didn't have the right to feel victimized because it wasn't "as bad." It would take me nearly fifteen years to understand I had the right to feel my own sadness, my own despair, my own anger at this rape, and to recognize everything that was taken from me that night—my spirit, my sacredness, my self-love. Now I know that a sexual predator knows exactly how much risk is involved. It's not a "mistake." He only apologized so I wouldn't report the rape. He counted on my shame and my silence.

I would run into him every so often—usually at powwows. Every time I passed by him, my body would freeze again, and I was overwrought with the most repulsive feeling. Powwows became triggering, to say the least, and I avoided as many as I could. Especially in South Dakota. Eventually, I stopped going to them altogether.

The following summer, I went off to university and escaped any potential run-ins with him. While away, I longed for my Lakȟóta people, for my reservation and all

Historically tribes did not have domestic violence. There were societal safeguards in place, such as males being expected to live within the family circle of their in-laws. This practice therefore eliminated the potential power imbalances between couples, as the female was surrounded and protected by her extended family. Additionally, anyone breaking the tribal society code of conduct was banished from the safety of that tribe.

its beauty, and for the sacredness of the Black Hills. I missed the long, hot summer days. I missed my thiwáhe, my thióšpaye, my family. But ever since that night, home no longer felt like home. It was a catch-22. When I needed to go home, I would become more hypervigilant and go into a shame spiral. My anxiety and fear would wreak havoc on my mind. Especially when my husband, who made me feel safe, wasn't able to come with me. But I used my spirituality and prayers to give me strength and it helped to ease the fear.

UNIVERSITY

My first years in university were some of the most challenging and traumatizing of my life—I barely know how I survived. But like so many survivors before me, I carried on as best I could. That first year, though, I was trying to forget everything by distancing myself from the traumas back home, including the backlash and bullying from the protest.

The summer after Sarah and I graduated from high school, we participated in a summer program for minority students at the University of Minnesota. We stayed in the dorms on campus and took summer classes while Sarah was pregnant with her first child. The program allowed us to get oriented to the campus and provided us the opportunity to meet and interact with a diverse student population. The campus was massive and spread out over two cities. It was so big and overwhelming; I felt like just another number lost in a throng of students. I never felt close to anybody there.

Many survivors of sexual assault try to forget that anything even happened to them—and I was no different. Immediately after the incident, I started minimizing the assault and trying to forget about it, but I couldn't. I blamed myself constantly. I couldn't comprehend that I was assaulted, that what he did was not okay. I didn't tell anyone, including my sister. Years later, I would realize that trauma cannot be repressed and forgotten; the more you try to repress it, the worse it gets.

Before the assault, I never drank because I was part of the CSAP program, but after it happened, in my moments of struggle and sadness, I would binge-drink to self-medicate and numb the pain. I was attempting to get through my first semester of university, but I was failing most of my classes, and I remember thinking, *I can't really get it together here.* On top of everything else, I felt like a failure.

Somehow I managed to stick it out and finish the school year, and then I worked as a summer youth camp counselor on campus. I did what I needed to do for the position, but outside of that, I wasn't functioning. The smell of food was nauseating; I ate only crackers and diet soda. I didn't even notice I was shedding pounds until a fellow camp counselor looked at me in astonishment one day and said, "Wow, you lost a lot of weight!" I looked down and realized my clothes were too big and hanging loosely on my body. I didn't feel anything.

When I look back on it, I was really depressed. At the time, I didn't realize I was grieving—grieving for a piece of my spirit that I'd lost. I backed away from everyone and became increasingly distrustful of people. I felt alone, isolated, and like nobody cared about me. It would be many years until I found out I was suffering from post-traumatic stress disorder (PTSD), depression, and anxiety. The hypervigilance and fear were crushing.

After two years of silence, I finally told my čekpá. I knew she was wondering what was going on. Sarah and I were on the highway heading back to South Dakota for a visit home when she asked, "What is going on with you? Why have you been acting so weird?"

I didn't want to say because I thought she wouldn't understand what I was going through. Worse, I was afraid she might tell someone. Rape was one of the worst things I could ever imagine happening to me. My trust in everyone had been violated beyond comprehension, and I was living with so much shame that I was terrified of anyone finding out. This was one of the first secrets I can remember keeping from her. But I reminded myself, *She is my twin sister. If I cannot trust my sister, then who can I trust?* On that car ride home, I began to tell this story for the first time. I just cried and she cried with me.

Now I am able to freely share this story with others. I hope other women out there find comfort, solace, and healing in these words. I will never stop advocating for the health and safety of Native women because we have already had too much taken away.

Eventually I was able to compartmentalize my assault enough to continue with my studies. It was a monumental task, and I ended up transferring universities four times, but I eventually finished. I even completed a master's degree in counseling. I continued to rely on my spirituality heavily during this time, and I never questioned, for even a second, that the Creator was watching over me and giving me the strength to push forward.

A shocking 84.3 percent of Native women experience violence over the course of their lives, with 56.1 percent reporting sexual violence, 55.5 percent reporting domestic abuse, and 66.4 percent reporting psychological aggression from a romantic partner. A whopping 39.8 percent reported experiencing violence within the last few years alone.[4]

AFTERMATH: TRAUMA RESPONSES

Trauma, even if survived, tends to stay with us. Try as we may to forget. As we continue our lives and face even more traumas, our trauma responses revert back to how we handled our original hurts. For survivors, there often is no one there to explain and label the experience. For many of us, complex

PTSD, dissociation, paralysis, and thoughts of suicide become part of our new normal, which leaves lasting reverberations after the original hurt has subsided.

Through my career as a counselor and my self-healing journey, I have learned that our ability to handle distressing events is related to how we first encountered trauma and how we coped with that original hurt. When the assault took place, I reverted to using the same coping mechanisms as when my mother had her brain injury. I just completely shut down, detached from life, and distanced myself from my emotions. In my mind, I made up beliefs to give meaning and sense to what happened—even if the beliefs were wrong. This time I believed that I was a slut, a whore, and I deserved what happened. Worse, after the assault I found myself paralyzed by memories that were triggered by things like the smell of alcohol. I could feel myself holding my breath. I had to remind myself to take deep, cleansing breaths. Remind myself I was okay. I was safe. I wasn't alone. I had to learn how to return to my own sense of power by overriding my trauma responses and calling my spirit back. I began by examining how my reactions came to be and how they functioned. Below I will unpack some of the latest research on these responses and how we can counteract them.

A recent study looked at a large clinical sample of women who had been raped within the last month. They found that during their assaults, 70 percent of women suffered from significant paralysis and nearly 48 percent suffered from extreme paralysis.[5] Further, another study found that survivors of child sexual abuse or adult sexual violence reported the highest frequency and intensity of paralysis when compared to individuals who experienced other types of non–sexually related traumas like natural disasters or physical violence.[6]

PARALYSIS AND PTSD

Whenever we experience something terrifying, our natural stress-response system kicks in. This involves the sympathetic nervous system, which controls our fight-or-flight survival responses by regulating the adrenal glands, which release adrenaline and prepare the body for action.[7] But survivors of sexual assault usually cannot fight back or flee because it may be unsafe to do so or they may be prevented by their perpetrator, thus overriding their fight-or-flight response. Once this response is overridden, the only way a person can cope is through tonic immobility, which I previously touched on.

Tonic immobility has become a hot topic within research communities because it goes against the common misconception that a survivor would fight back in an assault situation. It raises many red flags for the justice system because victims undergo intense questioning to determine how much they resisted their assaulters in order to classify their assaults as rape. A court can rule that a victim gave passive consent if they did not resist enough; however, the research on paralysis suggests that what might be interpreted as passive consent is actually an involuntary and normal biological reaction to a threatening situation. And since sexual assault survivors experience more severe and frequent paralysis than victims of other types of trauma, there is a good chance that a survivor will find themselves unable to resist or cry for help.

Yet many survivors still feel they should have been able to resist their attackers, leading them to harbor feelings of shame and self-blame. This reaction manifested for me. I questioned why I had even been there, and I thought it was my fault because I'd liked him. It took me years to process that I was not at fault. Not surprisingly, these increased feelings of shame and self-blame are associated with higher rates of PTSD and depression.

A study found that, six months after an assault, PTSD prevalence was almost twice as high in women who had experienced extreme tonic immobility when compared to women who did not experience tonic immobility. Women who had experienced TI were also three times more likely to have severe depression after six months.[8]

To sum up: (1) sexual assault survivors experience involuntary paralysis with greater frequency and intensity than sufferers of other types of trauma; (2) paralysis exacerbates feelings of guilt and shame, thus increasing the risk of PTSD and depression; and (3) paralysis during sexual assault increases the risk of experiencing paralysis during PTSD flashbacks, hence further triggering PTSD symptoms. This is a vicious cycle that many survivors find themselves trapped in. Is it really all that surprising that many survivors find themselves overwhelmed by their feelings of guilt and shame, becoming depressed, distrustful, and isolated, and struggling with thoughts of suicide? I am living proof of the consequences of such a trauma, and I would never wish what I went through on anybody—not even my worst enemy. Providing education on paralysis as a normal trauma response to sexual assault could go a long way toward stopping feelings of guilt and shame in survivors, as well as providing the additional benefit of reducing PTSD symptoms.

TRAUMA MINIMIZATION

I spent most of my twenties minimizing my trauma, telling myself it didn't matter, that it wasn't a big deal. I had encountered Native women who were not only sexually assaulted but also terribly beaten and hospitalized. I thought, *Who am I to complain about what happened to me?*

Minimizing the trauma burden is one way of lightening the load by giving survivors a sense of control and agency over the horrific experience. It also, however, normalizes the trauma as a feature of this oppressive patriarchal society while rein-forcing dominant narratives around rape culture, like "rape is just sex."[9] Fortunately, women (and some men too) are coming forward to share their own experiences with sexual assault and to demand a reversal of this normalization. All of us survivors know it really is "that bad," and the #MeToo and #TimesUp movements are long overdue, revealing the mountain of injustices women have stored within their bodies for too long.

After I completed my master's program, I became a domestic violence (DV) advocate working with victims and survivors of domestic abuse and sexual violence. My workplace also dealt with stalking, harassment, and restraining orders, attending court hearings with victims. At times I served as a lay advocate or expert witness. We facilitated eighteen-week domestic abuse psychoeducational support groups for survivors. We often encouraged victims, after completing one program, to return and complete another program, because there was often another aspect of their healing they could work through. I loved working with survivors. We often attended trainings and gave presentations at conferences. Inadvertently, we would often work through different aspects of our own traumas as well. In one of the presentations with other domestic abuse and sexual assault advocates, one presenter said something that resonated with me. She spoke of how sexual assault survivors minimize their trauma. She said, "This trauma is the worst thing that has happened to you in your life." At that moment, I took in a sharp breath and tears welled in my eyes, because I could feel a deep pain in my heart; I wept silently as I realized

> Minimizing our trauma has long been a coping mechanism for survivors because typically when we share our stories, we aren't taken seriously or believed, or worse, we are blamed. Consequently, we develop strategies to carry this burden of trauma within us while, at the same time, preventing it from sinking us.

she was right. It was the worst experience that ever happened to me, and I needed to start honoring the young woman whose spirit and sacredness was taken from her. Finally free from my prison of trauma minimization, I was able to continue the journey toward healing.

SUICIDAL IDEATION

After the sexual assault, I thought a lot about suicide, and I contemplated jumping off a tall building or bridge. The only thing preventing me was a story I heard two years earlier from one of my CSAP counselors. He said, "Those who commit suicide aren't able to get to the happy hunting ground"—a place Lakȟóta people long for their spirit to go to when they die. It is like our version of heaven. He also said, "Spirits are all around us, and when we pray and ask them for help, they get excited and think of ways they can help you. When you're having a hard time, pray and the help will be right there." Praying became my lifeline as I continued my battle with depression, post-traumatic stress disorder, anxiety, and suicidal ideation, and I credit this story with saving my life.

A large majority of my clients have contemplated suicide. Since Native women are two and a half times more likely to be sexually assaulted than women of any other ethnic group in the United States,[10] it is not surprising that we see an epidemic of suicide and suicidal ideation within our communities. The numbers on Pine Ridge Indian Reservation are even more dire. On public health surveys, the majority of teenage girls report they have been raped, and suicide epidemics plague the community every few years.[11]

In my work as a psychotherapist, I have almost a sixth sense in identifying clients' suicidal ideation because I have been there before myself. Often it is just an indescribable feeling. When I work with a client contemplating suicide, I share with them that I understand suicide on a deeply personal level. I know what it is like to be in this deep, dark space. To experience an upsetting incident or relive the memories of past traumas. It feels as if all of those old pains are coming together and slamming forward. It becomes very painful and overwhelming. The first thought is suicide because they are trying to find a way to escape from all of the pain. Some say suicide is a selfish decision for a person. It is not. This person has been trying to overcome all of their traumas, many times on their own, due to the stigma of mental health. I tell people that when someone says they are suicidal, they should believe them, help them, so they don't feel alone. Together, we must work on developing better coping skills, as well as learning about available resources, support groups, trauma counselors, and spiritual healing ceremonies. All are important steps to counteracting the feelings of isolation, self-blame, and dissociation that entrap sexual assault survivors and lead to suicidal thoughts.

> At a national level, 33 percent of all female rape victims contemplate suicide and 13 percent attempt it.[12]

THE IMPACT OF INTERGENERATIONAL TRAUMA ON HEALING

Our legacy of trauma was inherited from the Native American boarding-school era. The evidence is in the colonial mismanagement and racist policies of those schools, which magnified the hurt and disconnection we see across our communities today. For example, many of the individuals who operated and worked at those schools were perpetrators of sexual abuse who preyed on Native students.[13] Unfortunately, we see this abusive pattern in our health systems as well. These actions dehumanized and traumatized our people for generations.

I had the privilege of receiving facilitator training as part of the Mending Broken Hearts program offered by White Bison for healing professionals. The aim of the course was twofold: to educate Native Americans on the legacy of intergenerational trauma, and to utilize traditional cultural ceremonies and teachings to facilitate healing.[14] One of the program trainers, a survivor himself, taught me that we can trace our current epidemic of sexual abuse within our communities all the way back to the boarding schools. Based on the work and facilitation I have done over the years, I see the validity of his words.

Historically, Native Americans didn't have a lot of the struggles that we have now. We knew how to love one another and nurture our children, we had healthy relationships, and we thought of our children as sacred. Then treaties were broken

---

"We want to begin with a simple proposition—the proposition that the character of Indian people has been deformed by the sustained assault on Native cultures. To take our lands, non-Indian people had to convince us we were something other than what we were. To kill our ancestors and take our lands, they had to define us as something less than human. To colonize or exterminate a people, you must first define them as a weed. You must transform them from a person to a pestilence. Once objectified, they can be killed without thought or remorse. But this process is even more insidious. The ultimate evil inflicted on Indian people was teaching us to hate ourselves so deeply as a people that we began killing ourselves and killing each other. This was the legacy of the boarding schools. More than religion, more than industrial skills, many of the children came out of it all with a sense of self-hatred that poisoned their very beings." —Don Coyhis, White Bison Inc.

---

and there were invasions of our land. Then boarding schools happened. People lost their language, their culture, their spirituality. They lost their identity and a sense of who they are.

Parents never learned how to be parents in these schools; instead, they ended up mimicking abusive patterns they learned from the teachers, nuns, and priests who managed these schools. Abused children become abusive parents, thus transferring trauma to the next generation. And when new trauma happens, many of us lack the proper coping skills to deal with it because of all the disconnection and harm already done to us and our cultures. Thus, many choose unhealthy coping strategies like self-harm or self-medication with drugs and alcohol. The general population holds stereotypical views of Native Americans, assuming we are all alcoholics, drug addicts, and criminals, but they don't take the time to learn the history behind these coping behaviors. They don't ask *why* our people are struggling.

Learning about boarding schools and intergenerational trauma was important to my own healing. I realized my pain wasn't only my own—it was also the pain passed down from my ancestors, the same pain my people struggle to heal from. I began to understand why I would get triggered when certain issues came up while I was teaching. For example, it would make me so angry when I saw a picture of Chief Big Foot dead and frozen in the snow from the Wounded Knee Massacre of 1890. How could publishers put that picture of our frozen, murdered chief in their history books? How is that okay?

This history taught me to be compassionate with myself,

> To date, there has never been a comprehensive study on the impact of boarding schools in the United States; however, Canada adopted residential schools based on America's boarding-school model, and research conducted at those has established the pathway of intergenerational trauma. The Cedar Project found that Native women were 2.35 times more likely to be sexually assaulted in their lifetimes if they had a parent who attended a residential school.[15]

because it's five hundred years of healing that I am trying to accomplish in my lifetime. This is the case for all contemporary Natives—we all have to deal with this legacy of trauma and stop the cycles of dysfunction from being passed on to the next generation. It is an enormous task, and if we stumble along the way, we must remember to be gentle with ourselves and acknowledge that we are healing from more than just our own traumas. When we feel an emotion that is overwhelming, it is because it isn't just our own. Rupert Ross, a white Canadian criminal prosecutor who worked closely throughout his career with Indigenous communities in northwestern Ontario, authored a book titled *Indigenous Healing*. He writes, "Healing must engage in bringing back the traditional Teachings. Those Teachings restore the spiritual centre of what colonization took away." He also quoted the Community Holistic Healing Circle—a team set up within the Hollow Water First Nation to address trauma within the community: "Much of what used to be described as 'healing' is now viewed as 'decolonization therapy.'"[16] In other words, our culture is our medicine, and rejuvenating the traditional ways will lead us back to the Sacred Red Road.

FINDING THE ROAD TO HEALING

For traumatized individuals, small, seemingly insignificant things can reopen old wounds. For me, it's whenever someone asks, "What's wrong with you?" or says, "It's not that hard." It's an old trigger going back to my childhood. As a child with abandonment issues, who couldn't understand why her mother couldn't be a mother or her father a father, I would automatically think, *There must be something wrong with me. This is why I am unlovable and unwanted.* These feelings intensified after the sexual assault because my internalized shame was compounded. It led me to solidify the belief that there really was something wrong with me.

Oftentimes when faced with trauma in childhood, we create negative core beliefs about ourselves, other people, and the world. These negative beliefs can become so deeply embedded that they are difficult to untwine. They might connect with and reinforce other unhealthy thoughts, and feeling strengthened, they might then say, "See! We knew this was true all along!" They become our truth even when they are not our truth. These negative core beliefs include:

1. Helpless: "I am helpless/powerless/weak/trapped/vulnerable/inferior/a failure/not good enough."
2. Unloveable: "I am unloveable/unwanted/not good/ugly/unimportant/undeserving of love. Something is wrong with me."
3. Worthless: "I am worthless/bad/unacceptable/dangerous/toxic/crazy/evil."

How do we change these negative core beliefs? We begin by creating positive core beliefs. The first step is to recognize the cycle: I become triggered, the negative core belief arises, the negative self-talk begins, and then the downward shame spiral commences. Once I understand that, then I can realize I am able to stop this pattern. I begin by seeking truth in my life. If I feel helpless, I ask myself: If I were not good enough or smart enough, how did I earn my college degrees or my job? Unloveable: If I were undeserving of love, why do I have love in my life? Worthless: If I were undeserving of anything good in my life, why do I have good in my life? It's a process. It takes time and practice, but it gets easier. We can create new positive core beliefs. Now when someone asks, "What's wrong with you?" and triggers me, I allow myself to feel it, but then I let it go. The ability to release is key to coping and the start of the healing journey.

Some easy ways to let go when we are feeling triggered include breathwork, meditation, mindfulness, smudging ourselves, and praying to the Creator. In my lowest moments, I would pray to the Creator continuously throughout the day to take away my pain in a kind and gentle way. Visualization also helps me cope. I like to imagine my ancestors' love creating waves of energy throughout my body and carrying away my internal pain and trauma. I also like to be near water, like a river, lake, or bay, because it is healing and cleansing. I pray with tobacco and set it out. When I was younger, I used to think everything had to be done in a certain way at a certain time. Like only praying with tobacco when the sun is rising. I think this was related to perfectionism rooted in trauma. Of course, no one is perfect, and I was setting unrealistic expectations upon myself that I couldn't achieve. That no one could achieve. I tell my clients there is no one right way to pray or believe. All ways are okay. We have to remember to be kind to ourselves because we are simply doing the best we can.

CALLING YOUR SPIRIT BACK

As a survivor, it is easy to think, *People don't understand*—and it's true: they don't. Rape totally and utterly changes you—down to the very core of your being. The way you look at the world is different. Your self-image suffers and negative self-talk becomes routine. A piece of your spirit decides to leave; therefore, when we work on our healing, we are trying to reclaim that piece.

One ritual I like to use with my clients, which I learned from working in the domestic violence field, involves the person calling their spirit back to them. It's simple to do at home. I start with a grounding practice by lighting some sage and purifying ourselves and the space. Next, I ask my client to close their eyes and pray to the Creator to help them with healing. Then I say, "Call your spirit back three times by calling your name three times. You can use your Indian name, or if you don't have one, that's okay. You can also use your given name." The client calls their name, ends their prayer, and opens their eyes. I ask, "Could you feel it?" Usually my client feels an internal shift in energy afterward. Their spirit has returned to them.

It is too painful for our spirits to reside inside our bodies when we go through intense trauma, so they decide to leave, causing us to feel detached and out of sync with life. The medical field's term for this loss of spirit is "dissociation." Dissociation is a common symptom of extreme trauma where a person feels disembodied and detached from the world around them and themselves.[17] These individuals have a hard time connecting to their bodies and visceral sensations, and sufferers feel like they are walking around detached from both the emotional highs and lows of life. But if we do this ritual, our spirits will return, and we will feel more alive, grounded, and secure inside ourselves.

"It is important to acknowledge the spirit within one another. Once the spirit is acknowledged, it can ignite the light within. This inner light is our greatest source of healing." —Deborah Parker, Tulalip/Yaqui, CEO of National Native American Boarding School Healing Coalition

This cultural approach to healing is excellent for Native Americans because we acutely feel the loss of connection to traditional wisdom and culture, which is what makes us particularly vulnerable to dissociation from the world and from ourselves. This ritual helps rekindle our spiritual connection while bringing back some embodied awareness—a key ingredient for combatting dissociation and paralysis trauma responses.

MY RETURN TO SUNDANCING

At sixteen years old, I made a pledge to sundance for the healing of my mother. When one makes this commitment to Tȟuŋkášila, they commit to sundancing for four years to bring healing, plus one additional year as a wóphila (a thank-you year) to Tȟuŋkášila for helping you. But I'd only completed one year. After the sexual assault, I couldn't continue. The shame was so overwhelming and I felt at odds with my own sacredness. It wasn't until my late twenties that I felt ready to renew my commitment.

Sundancing is a sacred ceremony where the community comes together, once a year, for prayer and for healing. It is practiced among the Plains Indian tribes. For many years, the American government prohibited tribes from holding the ceremony, and it wasn't until 1978, with the passing of the American Indian Religious Freedom Act, that tribal communities could lawfully partake in this powerful healing ceremony.[18]

Returning to sundancing was a huge catalyst, beginning my most transformative period. I was praying for help in healing myself, my iná, my thiwáhe, my thióšpaye, my oyáte (people), Uŋčí Makȟá (Mother Earth), and makȟásitomni (the whole world). It was such a beautiful experience while I danced. I could sense the power and sacredness—I felt as if I was directly communicating with Tȟuŋkášila. I also felt like Tȟuŋkášila was bringing people into my life to help me heal. More than anything, sundancing showed me that I am worthy of love, sacredness, and peace on this earth. I share this with my clients who struggle with making a connection to their spirituality. I tell them that when I question this, I remind myself of all the good that has come into my life: the unconditional love of my thiwáhe, hasáŋni, čhiŋčápi. Also: All the gifts of my best friends, who know me and love me. The chance meeting of a person who shares with me their knowledge to help me be compassionate and forgive myself.

Everyone who starts sundancing makes a pledge that is between themselves and Thuŋkášila. We put our prayers into our tobacco ties as we make them. I have often been told, "Don't forget to pray for yourself. Ask Thuŋkášila to help you with whatever you're feeling." So when I make my tobacco tie, I pray for myself too.

The sundance takes place over four days and as part of our four-year commitment, we sacrifice by fasting. The dancers remain in prayer and are sacred during this time. They are not permitted to talk to other people or family. They wear sage crowns and sage bracelets before entering the sundance circle. The sage is for spiritual protection and is considered very sacred and powerful after the ceremony ends.

People who come to pray and support the sundancers are not to be under the influence of alcohol or any other drug when they are there. My mom was only able to come sporadically, but she came when she could. After I finished dancing the fourth year, I went to my uŋčí's house, came to the door of my iná's bedroom, and said, "Mom, I wanted to give this to you." I handed her my sage crown. I said, "Mom, I sundanced for you." With her traumatic brain injury, we think her memory span is close to three to five minutes, but in that moment, it felt like she was there. Like she understood. She said, "I know you did, honey. I know you did. Thank you." We hugged, and I felt enveloped by her presence. Seconds later, her mind wandered off again, but for that moment I thought, *Oh my goodness, she is here.*

Recently our mother shared her own experience of sexual assault. She had been visiting a friend in Colorado Springs and was raped by a friend of a friend. Because she had been a tribal police officer, she somehow remembered and trusted the system enough to go through with the rape kit. A few years later, the police would track her down in South Dakota because they found a DNA match thanks to her. He had also raped other women and was in prison. She was able to extend his sentence with her testimony. It is sad to know sexual assault is a generational experience for many Native women, yet justice was served because she stood up for herself and others.

In my twenties, I felt an isolation and the sense that others wouldn't be able to understand what I had gone through, but by working as a domestic violence advocate and fulfilling my commitment to sundance, I noticed a huge shift in my personal healing. After sundancing, I felt a change in how I looked at myself, and this led to a change in how I treated myself. I no longer minimized my trauma; I owned my story, even the ugly parts. I stopped putting myself down all the time, and I invited self-love and healing into my daily life with greater intention. I welcomed the gifts of my culture, the true legacy of what my ancestors left us—not only the residuals of their pain but also the profound and sacred ceremonies and cultural understandings that have sustained my people for generations.

Not long after I finished my commitment, I had a beautiful dream. I was sleeping under the sundance arbor where the sundancers rested between rounds of sundancing. I was awoken by the beautiful singing of the male sundance leaders. They did this to let all the sundancers know it was time to get ready to return to dancing. I hurriedly wrapped the shawl around my waist and put on the sage bracelets, anklets, and crown. I lined up behind the women walking into the sundance arbor. I stepped in, so happy and full of peace. As I looked out in front of me, the sundancers' attire became swirls of the sacred colors, moving clockwise around the sundance arbor, around the sundance tree. I woke up as I entered the circle.

HEALING IS A LIFELONG JOURNEY

Despite all the work I have done to get to this place, I know there is more healing I need to do. This is typical of the Indigenous worldview because for us, healing is a lifelong journey. A Lakȟóta Sioux spiritual leader called Gene Thin Elk said, "Healing is a way of life for the Native American who understands and lives the cultural traditions and values."[19] Our traditional teachings tell us that our well-being is a balance of physical, mental, spiritual, and emotional factors. We are never in perfect balance, thus there is always more healing to occur. It isn't simply a modality we invoke when times are tough. Instead, healing is imbued in our daily activities with clarity and intention—as a way of life. Therefore, I don't look at myself as if I'm healed. I'm a work in progress, and I think everybody else is too. We can work through a lot of different aspects of our healing, but we can still have remnants of old trauma and become re-triggered. Healing is like an onion, of which we continually peel back the layers. Just when we think we may be done, there is another aspect to this layer we need to work though. I continually keep working toward a sense of inner peace.

When the work gets tough and we feel like we cannot go any further, we must remember we are never alone. When I feel this way, I smudge and pray. Smudging with sacred medicines (such as sage and cedar) cleanses, balances, and purifies not only the energy but also your spirit within. Prayer is also a form of mindfulness. In praying, we are taking this time to acknowledge our feelings and ask for help from Tȟuŋkášila/ Wakȟáŋ Tȟáŋka. We can rely on the Creator to help us carry the burden, leaving it in the Creator's hands, as it were. I don't know or understand why I have had to suffer with this pain in my life. But I do know that if I had not, I would not be able to connect with my clients when they are at their deepest level of pain and despair. I understand them because I have been there before too.

In Lakȟóta we have the phrase "mitákuye oyás'iŋ." It is a very sacred phrase and not to be spoken lightly. We say this phrase during rituals and at the end of prayers to remind ourselves of our relatedness to everything that exists. For us, relations not only include our blood relatives but our plant, animal, insect, and spirit relations as well.[20] We are all connected. Mitákuye oyás'iŋ is the way we should all be, treating one another like we are related, being good to one another, being kind and compassionate, and loving and supporting one another. It is a universal philosophy that, if all of us practiced it, could go a long way to healing the hurts in this world and could decolonize our minds, bodies, and spirits from the residuals of trauma we inflict on one another.

Lakȟóta Laws

*(Living cultural values through action is how
Lakȟóta people live in integrity)*

"Waúŋšila" means *to have compassion,
kindness, or mercy.*

"Wóčhekiye" means *prayer, spirituality,
religion, or belief.*

---

7 WAYS TO RECLAIM SPIRIT

In all of my work as a youth advocate, domestic abuse advocate, and psychotherapist, I've found it is important to hold
compassion and self-love for others, but most important to
do so for yourself. Holding waúŋšila truly means being kind
to everyone, yourself included, in all the ways that you can.
I have always felt so grateful for the kindness others have
shown me, which they may have thought was nothing. I used
to continually struggle with negative self-talk. I used to feel
that I wasn't worthy of love. In many respects, it didn't matter
what others thought of me because of how much self-hatred
I held for myself.

My self-forgiveness began with my work with survivors. I
thought of how I tell them what happened is not their fault.
They were not to blame for what happened to them. No matter
the circumstances. They were also not to blame for the self-
destructive behavior that may have begun afterward, when they
went into survival mode. I believed this wholeheartedly for
my clients. It hit me when I would tell them all of this. How

could I not believe the same for myself? The armor around my heart began to crack and allow self-love to enter. I began to forgive the seventeen-year-old young woman for all she did when she was surviving.

1. **Understand that women hold an incredible amount of strength.**
   - During our moon time (period), we are considered sacred. We are asked to care for ourselves and surround ourselves with women relatives and friends.
   - It's important to keep those relationships with your female relatives who stand with you when you need them. Remember to reciprocate by being there when they need you.

2. **Learn more about PTSD, a horrific consequence for many sexual assault survivors. Sufferers undergo intrusive re-experiencing of the trauma through flashbacks and nightmares, which can lead to the person avoiding situations that remind them of their trauma. In addition, the sufferer will experience increased negative thoughts and feelings, and display heightened arousal (hypervigilance). And if that weren't bad enough, trauma can also trigger dissociation, which consists of feelings of unreality, being detached from oneself, and distorted perceptions of time and place.[21] Quite literally, the survivor doesn't feel real or like a part of this world anymore.**

3. Understand PTSD flashbacks. Experiencing paralysis during an assault not only increases the risk of developing PTSD but also increases the severity of PTSD symptoms. For example, one study found that individuals who reported paralysis at the time of their trauma were also likely to experience

paralysis during PTSD flashbacks. This is extremely important because paralysis increases feelings of lack of control and being stuck for the survivor—both of which maintain PTSD symptoms.[22]

4. Continue to work on loving yourself and stay rooted in unconditional love.

5. Make self-care a priority. I will say it again. Make self-care a priority. We, as mothers, daughters, partners, etc., often place the needs of others above our own. When you are on an airplane, during the safety instructions, you are told to put your own face mask on to breathe before assisting others with their masks. It is the same concept. We are unable to help others efficiently if we can't breathe. Additionally, the COVID-19 pandemic has never made it more clear how important it is to take care of ourselves—emotionally, physically, mentally, and spiritually.

6. Create daily rituals of purification, grounding, and rebalancing of your spirit, such as smudging with sacred medicines, spending time with wakȟáŋheža (sacred children) and huŋkáyapis (elders).

7. Call your spirit back. I learned this in my work as a domestic abuse advocate and I continue to use it in my work as a psychotherapist. I believe your spirit is not in your body when you experience a distressing event or emotion.
   • To begin, pray to Tȟuŋkášila or set an intention for assistance in returning your spirit.
   • Call your name (Native American or English) four times out loud or in your mind.
   • Each time you call your name, you feel your spirit moving down farther and farther into your body.

- Notice the difference in how you feel.
- Give gratitude to Tȟuŋkášila.

JOURNAL PROMPTS TO HONOR YOUR HEALING

- Do you hold any negative core beliefs? If so, what are they? What is the positive core belief that you are replacing the negative one with?

- Are you aware of any triggers you hold?

- What daily rituals keep you centered?

- How do you honor your healing process and how do you plan to continue your healing?

My girl, it is all a part of life.
Loving and learning.
Evolving and transforming.
Lost in the exhilaration.
Hope carrying you to the clouds.
But my girl, seek the sun to know the truth.
The truth may break your heart, but believe the truth
before you are curled in a ball of regret under the palm trees.
It's true, the truth will set you free, like an eagle flying through sky world.
Forgive yourself as you land on Uŋčí Makȟá.
She will heal you as you walk in the center of everything that is.
She will love you, no matter what comes.
Remember to return to the heart.

—SARAH EAGLE HEART

CHAPTER 5

Standing in the Center

BY SARAH

RENEWING MY VOWS

ON A COLD January afternoon when I was twenty-nine years old, I was lying on the bed in the dark, looking at the ceiling, feeling restless with my thoughts but not sure why. I felt lost. This had been going on for a couple weeks and I was oblivious to the numbness I had succumbed to. My husband, Rich, came and stood in the doorway and suddenly asked me a direct, unexpected question: "Are you happy?"

I looked at him, bewildered.

He said, "I don't want to wake up in ten years and find out that you weren't happy." We often talked about what we would do when our sons were out of school in another ten years. I was jolted out of my self-imposed apathy. *Oh my God, he is talking about divorce! No, I can do it. I can tough it out.* I said to him whatever would make him leave me alone again. After he shut the door, I thought to myself, *Why did I think I was toughing it out? Shit.*

Six months earlier, we had celebrated our tenth wedding anniversary by renewing our wedding vows. It was a beautiful Episcopalian ceremony next to the Perdido Bay in Florida. We danced under twinkling lights in a tent next to the beach, with the ocean waves and trees as our backdrop. Since Rich was in the military, our sunset wedding renewal was a full-on US Marine Corps affair—complete with walking under the swords. An Episcopalian priest blessed us while I was adorned in a perfect gold-lace mermaid dress—and I was at my goal weight! (I had struggled with my weight loss for a decade after giving birth to my sons.) It was everything I thought I had missed in our first wedding.

But when I walked down the aisle for the second time, I remembered how I felt when we got married ten years prior. I was anxious and worried about everything and everyone except for him. I thought to myself, *You're supposed to look like you're happy and in love.* There was just one problem: Why didn't I feel it? I was forcing myself to look like I was in love, rather than feeling it.

Our original wedding was in the backyard of a relative's home in Pine Ridge. I was nineteen years old. My grandma made my wedding dress, and I still carried baby weight, since I'd just had my son six months earlier. Our backdrop was a beautiful blue star quilt made by my grandma, and we were married by a Lakȟóta judge. No one forced me to get married, but no one asked me if I wanted it. They just expected me to. Hell, I expected me to. I had found one of the few sober Lakȟóta men, standing at six feet four inches, who had attended college, respected me, and wanted to care for his son.

But ten years later, six months after renewing our vows, we got divorced. As I looked at the carefully crafted life we had built, I realized it was not for me. We owned a home and had the white picket fence I had dreamed of as a child. We also had another son, Brenden. I love my sons and it broke my heart to break up their dream, too, but once I knew, I knew. I could no longer ignore it. I could not continue to play the dutiful housewife alongside the other military wives, who mostly talked about their husbands' careers and ranks. I wanted my own career, and I knew that would never become a priority when we relocated every four years. I also knew I didn't love him the way I should have.

Rich told me that he was surprised I wanted to go to back

to college after having our first son, Aarron. He thought I would prefer to drop out of college, have our son, and stay on the reservation, but I was determined to attend college. So I transferred to Black Hills State University and completed two degrees, and I even graduated on time. My senior year, I carried twenty-four credits during the fall semester and twenty-seven credits during the spring semester. While there, I became president of the college club for Native Americans called Lakȟóta Omníčiye; I often joke that they helped me raise my first son and make it through college! I started college pregnant with my eldest son, Aarron, and graduated pregnant with my youngest son, Brenden. Later in San Diego, I would return to college to obtain my MBA while working full-time. To say I was determined to succeed is an understatement. I was working to prove everyone wrong, especially those that underestimated a young Lakȟóta mother who grew up on the reservation.

After I finished my schooling, I realized Rich and I had nothing in common anymore. He was a homebody when he wasn't deployed, while I yearned for adventure. I enjoyed going out salsa dancing, even attended weddings with friends, but Rich never joined us. I also began falling deeper into my spiritual practices, and Rich was not a spiritual person. There was so much I was doing all by myself; I felt alone even though I was married. Three tours overseas will do that to a marriage.

Wanting more made me look selfish in the eyes of my extended family. They had upheld us as a perfect model of what a Lakȟóta family should be. They loved Rich because he was sober and a good dad, and they were angry at me for leaving him. They assumed I must have cheated, because why else would I leave such a perfect man? One day Rich called me and said, "I'm sorry. Your cousin called me at a bad time asking me if I thought you cheated, and I said yes."

My own family started spreading rumors of my supposed infidelity. I was disappointed in their behavior. I wrote my family an email stating that my relationship was none of their business, and then I cut off communication with them for six months—including my sister. It was an extremely difficult choice because of our close kinship bonds, and being the eldest in my generation meant that I had embraced the role as big sister, mentor, and counselor to all of my younger cousins. But I was angry and I didn't want my children to hear the rumors. Instead, I decided to focus on my sons and on my self-care. That time apart allowed me to build healthy boundaries and break free from the image of being the perfect Lakȟóta wife. I began to start my own healing journey.

Years later, one of my aunts would apologize in her own way: "We acted like he was our husband." I understood, because many of my aunties have been married several times, with many heartbreaks along the way, including men who had cheated on them. These are the same aunties who also taught me to ensure my sons had their father in their life, no matter what. Lakȟóta women take on so much when Lakȟóta men do not live up to their responsibilities.

IGNORING ALL THE WARNING SIGNS

A few months after my divorce, a friend and I went out for a night of dancing. A burly, muscular man with dark features approached me and introduced himself as Dale. He asked if he could dance with me. He wasn't my usual type, but I immediately sensed chemistry between us.

Over the next few months, we went out on dates to restaurants followed by strolls along the ocean. He told me stories about being in the

Intuition is a nonlinear and nonrational way of coming into knowing, and can help guide you. It can be a gut feeling, a warning system, or an extra nudge you feel inside, telling you to go after that opportunity. Messages can be subtle, coming in the form of signs or appearing in dreams.

navy and about his other business, which would often take him out of town. He mentioned he had a home in Tampa, and a boat, and he talked about me traveling from Pensacola to go boating with him. I enjoyed spending time with him because he was always cracking jokes and was just fun to be around— something I was sorely lacking at the time. Every day felt like a struggle. I was juggling being a single mom, trying to emotionally support my two sons' transition with the divorce, while also working at my new job at a small Episcopal church. The attention of a man who was fun and carefree was just the distraction I needed.

On one of our dates, we rented a movie at Blockbuster— back when that was still a thing—and went back to my place. It was a relaxing evening, but for some reason after he left, I had a gut feeling to look at the movie receipt. Upon pulling it out of the trash, I saw that the account was under a woman's first name with his last name. Alarm bells rang out in my mind as I thought, *What is this about?* The next time I saw him, I asked, "Who is this woman on your account?"

"You don't need to worry. She was my ex-wife, but we are divorced. I just keep using the account to maintain my privacy. I don't like people knowing about where I am or what I'm doing," he said.

Of course, I thought that was odd, and I asked him, "Can I see your LES?"—his leave-and-earning statement from the military. I knew if I saw it, I could see whether there was a spouse listed.

"Sure, but I don't have it with me. I will show you later," he replied.

However, later never seemed to come, and every time I brought it up, he turned it back on me by questioning my loyalty and whether I even loved him. As the days passed and he still didn't show me his LES, I began to feel like I wasn't valued. To lessen the pain, I told myself, *What does it matter?*

I don't really care about him anyway. We aren't that serious and we're only dating.

Months and months passed of this ever-so-seductive game of cat and mouse: he loves me, he will bring the LES; he loves me not. I dared myself to wait and see. Finally, he showed me his LES, and exactly what I had suspected was there in black and white: he was getting spousal support. He said, "I am divorced; they just never changed it on my LES. I never corrected them because it ends up being extra money for me from the navy. I swear it doesn't mean anything."

I didn't believe him, but I just kept telling myself we weren't serious, so it didn't matter. As the months dragged on, it became harder to keep convincing myself of this. We would plan trips to his house in Tampa, which I still hadn't been to. He'd say, "Get your bags ready. We're going for a trip this weekend." He loves me, he's going to take me to his house in Tampa. I would leave my sons with their dad and pack my suitcase, do my makeup, dress nice, put on heels, and be ready to leave as soon as Dale showed, but he'd never come. I would spend all of Friday night waiting until he would call me to tell me about some emergency he had with the navy, or that his other job called him and he had to fly off somewhere. He loves me not.

The navy was a perfect excuse because I couldn't just call up his commander and verify his schedule. As the months rolled on, so did his excuses. My suspicions grew, but every time he came back from deployment or wherever, he showered me with love and made me feel special. I let the relationship continue against my better judgment and against a gnawing feeling in the pit of my stomach telling me something wasn't right. *Oh well, I will just distract myself with work*, I thought. *I don't care anyway.* I lied to myself and stuffed the feeling of being unloved deep down.

Prior to dating Dale, I never had a chance to date because I became pregnant with my first son at eighteen and married shortly after. In a sense, this was my first boyfriend as a fully formed adult. When I met him, he seemed to be this well-traveled, successful, and charismatic person. I grew up in the Midwest, where people are usually honest, and I think I was too naïve to see the games he was playing with me. My experience with liars was limited, and so I took him at his word instead of following my intuition—a mistake that would cost me dearly.

TWO YEARS WENT by and I received a big promotion for a leadership role within the church that required me to move to Los Angeles. By this point, Dale and I had broken up and gotten back together many times, yet he requested to be stationed in San Diego so he could be close to me in Los Angeles. He suggested we rent a house together and split the bills. I was so happy at this token of what I perceived as love in the form of stability. As a single mother working to support my children, I thought creating a home together and sharing expenses was ideal. I found us a house and moved my family in, but somehow, he never gave me his share of the rent. Months passed and I felt more and more frustrated as the bills piled up, until we ended it, yet again, and he left on deployment. The signs of our unhealthy relationship were abundant, but I wasn't listening. Upon his return, we reconnected and started this whole dance over once more.

After a few months living in LA, he told me he was going to introduce me to his mother. I'd been wanting to meet her for a long time because of how important family is to me. We drove from LA to New Mexico and all I could think during the drive was *Wow, I'm actually going to meet her*. To me, meeting his mother meant our relationship was real and that he valued me. We stayed at her place in this small mountainous town. She was petite and had very brown skin. She was also sweet, very welcoming, and was happy to cook for us. However, on the first night I was there, I had a dream that his mom's house was on fire. I could see him standing outside the front door talking to his mother, but I was still trapped inside the burning house. I was screaming at him, but he couldn't hear me.

I woke up startled and relieved it was just a dream. As I got out of bed and went into the bathroom, I found myself singing a song: God, *send me an angel* ... It was a tune I had never heard before. I was surprised to be humming because deep down I knew I wasn't happy. I hadn't sung to myself in a very long time. The lyrics in my head were so surprising, I looked them up online and discovered they were from a real song called "Angel" by Amanda Perez.

Once I played the song, I knew that it was speaking directly to my situation. I loved him, but all he did was lie to me. Now I had to leave because there was something I had to do. I knew immediately that this dream was a message showing me where I was at: this relationship was on fire, and I was not supposed to be here. I knew, without a doubt, that the Creator had answered my prayers and was telling me to get out. I cried quietly to myself the whole drive back home. I was overwhelmed with how direct this message was to me and how Tȟuŋkášila answered my prayers. However, by this point, the emotional and sexual hold that he had on me was so strong, and I didn't listen.

One day he told me he wanted to buy a home for us in the beach town of San Clemente, California. We drove almost two hours from Los Angeles to a gated community and, oh darn, the realtor couldn't make it to let us in to the supposed house he had bought. I didn't even flinch because I had already suspected it was all a lie. At my lowest points of shame I thought, I cannot find anyone else. Without him, I will always be alone. He kept telling me these stories about how we were meant to be together, until one day I found out that I was pregnant.

For a brief moment, as we spent a weekend in a San Diego

hotel talking about our future, I felt happy. For a moment, I once again had hope. When Monday rolled around, we were driving in his gold Volkswagen to stop by his command in San Diego. He ran in to check in while I was sitting in his car—like I have a million times before—and for some reason, my intuition told me to look in the glove compartment. I opened it and on top of all the papers was one that stated "Emergency Contact" with the woman's name from the Blockbuster receipt, and in parentheses it said "spouse." This paperwork was from his most recent deployment. I had to know the truth, so I called the number.

When the phone was picked up, I heard a woman's voice say, "Hello."

"Hey, my name is Sarah, and I have been dating Dale for almost three years now. He tells me that you two are divorced. And I just want to know, is it true or not?"

At first, she didn't believe me and accused me of lying. She said, "Who are you? Why are you calling me? What are you doing? Where are you at?"

I said, "I'm sitting in his car right now. Why would I make this up? I'm sitting in his gold Volkswagen."

"Yes, we are married."

"Okay, that's all I need to know." And in a weird way, she began to defend him, and started saying they were getting separated. I told her, "It doesn't matter," and then hung up the phone. All my illusions about him had finally shattered, and I could see him for the liar that he was. While I was sitting in that car waiting for him to return, I wasn't even mad anymore. Instead, I was thinking, *This is who he is. I knew it. Why didn't I listen to the Creator? Why didn't I listen to my gut?!*

I confronted him when he returned to the car, but he had no more comebacks. I had finally learned the truth and was putting together the many lies he had told throughout the years. We went to dinner to talk, but my brain would not stop thinking about how I was pregnant and I didn't even know who this guy really was. I started to contemplate my financial situation, how I worked for a church, and how I had just gotten a new national-level job. I was in a position of leadership representing Native American people on the staff of the presiding bishop. My role required a lot of travel, and I would soon be finding myself away from home 50 to 75 percent of my time. I thought about how the United States was going into a recession. Where would I find a new job if I decided to keep this baby on my own? Then I thought about my two teenage sons who lived with me, and how we were barely making it. In my heart, I knew I couldn't financially afford to have another baby, so I told him, "I have to leave. I need to go home," and then I proceeded to leave without him.

Upon arriving back at the empty home that I rented for us, the one he never paid any rent for, I began to pray. I prayed all throughout the night. The next morning, I called Planned Parenthood. As I waited for them to pick up the phone I thought, *If they have an appointment within the next day, then it's really meant to be.* I had to travel for work in two days, leaving me only a small window. By some miracle, they had an opening the next day.

As I prepared for the appointment, I alternated between praying and crying. I told no one. I didn't tell my twin sister. I didn't tell Dale either. I didn't tell anybody. I kept this shame to myself. I went to the appointment alone and then drove myself home, where I lay down on the bed, covered my head with a blanket, and curled into a small ball in the perfect house I rented for us under the palm trees. I had sacrificed my body, but I knew that without a doubt, it was the right decision. I had to care for my two sons and ensure we had a place to live.

IN MANY INDIGENOUS societies, women have the ultimate authority over their bodies to determine if they carry a pregnancy to term or not. In fact, in many societies all tribal

142

members had knowledge of menstrual cycles and learned contraceptive planning. For example, Iroquois women had access to plant medicines for birth control, and no man was allowed to have control over the decision. However, conservative Christian beliefs have seeped into government, as well as corrupted our traditional Indigenous knowledge systems. Many have forgotten traditional Indigenous medicinal plant knowledge and the right Indigenous women have to utilize this knowledge to care for their bodies.

Some may be shocked to learn that the bodies of Native women have been a target historically *and* in contemporary times. In the six years following the Family Planning Services and Population Research Act of 1970, at least 25 percent of Native American women of childbearing age were sterilized.[1] Procedures were performed either under extreme pressure or duress or without the women's knowledge or understanding through the federally funded Indian Health Service. It was federal policy to sterilize Indigenous women!

In November 2004, Cecilia Fire Thunder became the first female elected as the president of the Oglála Sioux Tribe. In early 2006, South Dakota passed one of the nation's strictest anti-abortion laws called the "Women's Health and Human Life Protection" bill. The bill banned all abortions in the state, including for survivors of rape and incest. Fire Thunder announced her intention to create a Planned Parenthood clinic on her property on the reservation—outside the jurisdiction of state law. However, this decision was met with fierce opposition from the rest of the Oglála Sioux tribal council, who impeached her on June 29, 2006, and then issued a ban on all abortions on tribal land.[2] Even now it is still illegal to obtain an abortion anywhere in the state of South Dakota.

As of 2020, the Supreme Court has a conservative majority of 6 to 3. In 2021, over 500 abortion restriction laws were introduced in 44 states.[3] Native women in Texas are standing up against the US Supreme Court's refusal to block the state's ban on most abortions. They highlight the facts that Native women already suffer from major health disparities, Indigenous women are more than twice as likely than white women to die from pregnancy or related conditions, and Indigenous women also experience the highest rates of rape and sexual assault.

TWO DAYS AFTER the abortion, I traveled to a work event that just so happened to be in the middle of the Black Hills—my homeland. The event was a huge gathering of church people and I was there as a church representative. I felt alone and disconnected. A few hours later I was struggling to hold it together, so at lunch I took my phone and walked away from the campus alongside the highway. I called Father Jeff, my old boss and military chaplain from the little Episcopal church I'd worked at in Pensacola. We had not spoken in months, but he knew about my tumultuous relationship. With the sacred lands of the Black Hills surrounding me, tears streaming down my cheeks, I told him about what happened, including the abortion. Father Jeff comforted me. He didn't shame me or scold me. He was so loving to me in that moment, so kind and compassionate. I know his compassion is not always found in Christian priests. I thank the Creator for Father Jeff being there for me.

I share my abortion story because I believe I am meant to share my experience. I also believe we need to stand up for a woman's right to choose and her right to control her body. We are taught by Christianity that Thuŋkášila will not be compassionate when you make these types of decisions. The pro-life movement says I am going to hell, but Father Jeff didn't tell me I was. Instead, he prayed with me and said he was sorry that this happened to me. Having this spiritual figure embrace me, faults and all, reinforced the message "You are still loved." After we talked, I thought to myself, *Every time I've prayed for an answer, the Creator has given it to me.* From the time that I found the receipt in the trash can, to the time that I saw the truth clear as day on the LES, to the time that I woke from the dream and unknowingly sang the Amanda Perez song.

Another six months later, Dale was deployed again. This time, I would not see him for a while. The space apart gave me a break from the drama of us and allowed me to see how dysfunctional our relationship really had been. I felt depressed that I had been in this crazy, fucked-up relationship with this liar and was still healing from the trauma of the abortion. I finally realized that it hurt to hope, even though I lived on hope. It was a survival tactic for sure. One that I learned from childhood and that got me through times of waiting for my alcoholic, MIA mother to show up. But it was still a dysfunctional cycle of hiding the truth of his behavior from myself. I let him lie to me and I lied to myself, hoping it wasn't true. In the harsh face of reality, I learned true love is about action.

I finally got up the courage to send him a *Dear John*–type goodbye letter. A couple weeks later, he called me to say he received it. I was walking by palm trees under the moonlit skies of LA, and I said, "I think it is better that we stay apart from each other. I can finally hear Tȟuŋkášila again. While I was with you, I always struggled to hear Tȟuŋkášila. Now I know it is time to move on." It hurt to admit the truth—that he didn't love me the way I needed to be loved—but I loved myself by walking away.

I learned from being with him that a relationship can disrupt my connection to the Creator and what the Creator is calling me to do. The drama, the games, the lies—they were all a distraction from me doing the work I am meant to do. The hold he had on me was gone. I had broken free, but I had paid an ultimate price. I sacrificed my body to learn the lesson, instead of just listening to the Creator from the beginning and trusting my intuition. Through the pain of being with him, I learned to trust my intuition and to listen to the Creator again. Further, I no longer felt like I needed a partner to feel complete.

CODEPENDENCY FROM CHILDHOOD

At one point during my marriage, Emma mentioned to me, "I think you might be codependent." My initial response was, "Whatever. You don't know everything just because you're a therapist now." I didn't really know what it meant at the time, but it stayed in my head.

Codependency is "a pattern of behavior in which you find yourself dependent on approval from someone else for your self-worth and identity."[4]

Anyone can become codependent, but there does seem to be an increased risk for those who come from parents who were emotionally abusive or neglectful. It should not be a surprise that I found an emotionally unavailable and pathological liar attractive—and that I wouldn't admit the truth of his behavior to myself! Perhaps this, too, was another inheritance from my unstable childhood, although I think being born a twin might have something to do with it as well. Even in the womb I wasn't alone.

After my divorce, I wasn't sure what to do with myself. I began focusing inward and realized that I still had healing to do. I began to see that many of the choices I was making were not actually meant for me. They were for other people. I decided to investigate codependency more seriously and, being the overachieving, type A personality that I am, I devoured every book I could find on the topic.

I sought out another codependency counselor/priest when I was living in Los Angeles and conveniently, one of the priests who lived in the building next to mine offered codependency counseling. We had our sessions in the Spanish-style court-yard in the center of the complex, next to a fountain, with our two chairs facing each other.

Before our first meeting, he asked me to bring a picture of myself as a child, with no further specifications. During our first session, I told him about my childhood trauma and what it was like growing up with Mom. I cried the whole time and even apologized at one point. He said, "Don't feel bad about it. Think about all the times that you should have cried and didn't. You never gave yourself permission." Instantly, I knew he was right.

At the end of our emotionally charged session, he asked to see the photo. I'd brought a picture of myself from when I was about four years old, smiling big and looking happy. As he looked at it, he asked, "Why did you pick this picture?"

"I don't know," I said.

"Look. You are happy here, and you picked this photo. This is who you really are. You must remember that you can be happy. That you can have everything that you want to have."

My sister and I were processing the fact that the mother we knew before the accident died but we never got to mourn her. We also were starting to put together how weird it was that we had no memories of our lives from before the car accident. With no memory of who she was prior, it wasn't obvious to us to grieve that loss. But the heart still remembers; I remember the loss of my childhood. When the counselor said what he did, it was a big "Ah-ha!" moment for me, because I had forgotten that I was full of joy once. Even though I have no memories from that time, I had picked that picture for a reason.

I remember calling up Emma afterward and saying, "So, hey. How long is this whole healing thing going to take?"

"What do you mean? You want a timeline?" she replied.

"Yeah."

She started laughing and said, "Of course you would want

a timeline for your healing." I laugh at this now, too, and tell people, yes, my type A personality wanted a timeline.

Over the next six months, it became increasingly apparent to me that healing could not be rushed. I grieved the loss of the mother I knew before the car accident. I was crying at home all the time. My ten- and thirteen-year-old sons were worried, and I was open with them: "This has nothing to do with you two. This is me and my stuff. I am working on my healing. Don't worry." Many Native mothers are new to healing and must struggle through their healing process while supporting their children through theirs as well.

I continued going to counseling too. The priest helped me gain some perspective on my need to control things and my desire to be perfect. He told me, "You like to plan things and look down the road for problems. You are the eldest child of an alcoholic. You have learned all these behaviors because you're the hero child and not all of it is bad. These are all things that have also helped you get to where you are at right now." It was true. I was successful. I was a young mother who completed her MBA and always succeeded at work. But as the eldest child, I never allowed myself to feel all the low points that came along. I always kept it together and was strong for everyone else. Plus, I was compensating for the reputation of our family by trying to be the hero child. The counselor helped me recognize that I had this control-freak side that came from a disruptive childhood, but it was important to recognize how my instinct helped me survive that childhood, too, so I could finally start accepting myself. I learned to be aware of my coping mechanisms as well as where and how to utilize them, and came to understand when they were bad or unhelpful. I didn't need to be perfect. I learned to be kind to myself and to stop trying to control everything.

Throughout our sessions, I began to understand my behavior, and understand why I got married. I started to question my connection to my spirituality and what it meant to me. I began asking myself what it was that I wanted—a question I could never ask myself before. I was also beginning to understand that I was in control of my own healing process and that healing is ongoing.

In the beginning, I thought going to counseling for a few months was all I needed to heal myself. Instead I continued to learn my lessons the hard way. After six months I stopped going to counseling, which was also about the time I met Dale. Looking back, I know I would have benefited from more sessions. When I started dating Dale, I felt like all the work I did on my healing went out the window. I was also too trusting of people. I was just so naïve and young, and had no clue what I was doing and, as a result, I would accept less than what I deserved. He was always dangling a carrot over my head to keep me chasing him. Sadly my overachieving nature lured me into thinking he was a prize worth winning. But I think he knew that. These types of emotional manipulators know exactly what they are doing.

I had the abortion within six months of being hired at my new role for the church in California. I was struggling with my shame plus feelings of low self-worth from the toxic relationship. But I was also a brand-new staffer, a team leader, and I was trying to be the epitome of Christian perfection because I felt like I had to live up to that. When you're working for a church, you are in prayer all the time. Basically, your work life is prayer. Plus, we are encouraged to use our intuition. Part of our work was reading passages from the Bible and then reflecting on those passages. My job was to align, which meant I found the parallels in Lakȟóta culture within these Bible passages.

At the same time, I was working on preparing for the 2009 General Convention, where the Episcopal Church would be the first denomination to repudiate the Doctrine of Discovery acknowledging how Manifest Destiny had impacted the genocide and land loss of Native Americans. After the resolution was passed, I developed a theory that we need to have action and healing to move forward. I utilized asset-based community-development training, where we focused on community resources and merged these with healing modalities from the White Bison teachings, which my sister told me about. I helped implement the White Bison training within church communities across the United States. When I first met Dale, I was still early in my healing and it was easy for me to put those lessons aside. After my promotion, I was also a busy executive traveling constantly, so it was easy to keep myself distracted from the truth. However, all this time in prayer, self-reflection, and trainings for work forced me to deal with my own healing again. I could feel all of it building up, the abortion and the shame and being in this toxic relationship, until I finally realized, *Oh crap, all my childhood abandonment issues are still there. I need to face this.*

Looking back, I know if I had had all the tools to understand what happened to me as a child, I would have made different choices as an adult. When I didn't understand my healing process, what had happened to me, or how to cope with it, I behaved in ways that I thought were coping but were actually more self-harming. Like dating horrible boyfriends. Or sacrificing myself for everybody else. I entered relationships that weren't really for me. Even my marriage wasn't for me. It was because my family expected me to do it and because it seemed like the right thing to do. I was trying to be perfect so that I could correct all the mistakes of my past.

I feared being alone because I didn't know how to love myself. Growing up, we saw very few examples of self-love through our mom or the community. Racism was rampant, and the messaging of being less-than because of the color of our skin was reinforced everywhere: at school, when the counselor said that we shouldn't apply for that program because we wouldn't be accepted; at the stores, when someone would follow us around in case we stole something. Indian boarding school left our grandparents worried about teaching us our language, and their own childhood abandonment left them feeling unworthy at times. And with a severe lack of contemporary Native American role models in media, it's hard to imagine being Native American and loving yourself. We really didn't see any examples of self-love portrayed anywhere. Without self-love and respect, it was easy for me to fall into childhood habits of sacrificing myself for others to the point of almost missing out on my own calling. Emma often says, "It all comes down to self-love. Every time I talk to any person in any counseling session, it always comes back to self-love." For me, it was true. Learning to love myself was the most difficult yet most important lesson in my adult life. Only after I accepted myself could I truly begin to see myself in the center of the circle.

SARAH AND KEVIN

Kevin and I met in 2012, literally the day after I left yet another toxic relationship. I had been dating a guy I thought was my Prince Charming for six months, until he backhanded me in the back of a limo while we were at the Democratic National Convention. Sure, there were blatant signs that he was

"Theȟíla" means *to love* or *to hold dear*.

not the Prince. That night it was his excessive drinking and jealousy that I was talking to the driver. I told him I could talk to whoever I wanted, and *WHOOSH!* That slap instantly transported me to a dark place of childhood fear and overwhelming feelings of inadequacy. I burst into uncontrollable tears. In that moment, I became a domestic violence survivor. And the driver did nothing. The next day, I called my čekpá and reluctantly told her what happened. She told me, "Don't pretend this didn't happen. If anyone asks you, you tell them the truth. You have choices now." I could call the police. Instead, I insisted he go to counseling, or I would call the police. In response, Prince Charming, who wasn't charming or sorry at all, wanted me to leave town. I called a friend, who let me stay with them so I could continue to attend the convention.

The next day, I went to an event where I met my current partner, Kevin, whom I'm still with to this day. Back then, Kevin was an elected member of the South Dakota House of Representatives. He would later become a South Dakota state senator and eventually president of the Oglála Sioux Tribe, but I cared more about his almost-fifteen-year commitment to sundancing. His spirituality meant the most to me.

We were friends for a year and a half before we started dating. This was a first for me, as I had never vetted a partner like that before. Initially, I didn't see him as someone I would date, but he was kind, he listened to me, he empowered me. We had many conversations where he reminded me of who I was. It felt refreshing to have a male figure like Kevin behind me, empowering me in work situations where I constantly had to deal with men who were trying to undercut my power and credibility.

For example, my white male bosses at the church made decisions about my diversity team without talking to us. They brought us into a room one day for a so-called consultation and told us, "Okay. We've decided to change your team. What do you think?" We were all looking around at each other like *What are we supposed to say?* They had already made the decision and then told us this was how it was going to be. Afterward, I was strategizing how to tell my bosses that this was far from a proper consultation, stressing over how to approach them. Kevin texted me out of the blue and I mentioned my situation. He called me right away and asked, "Hey, what's going on?"

I vented for forty minutes while I sat in a Lyft on the way to the JFK airport, sharing what horrible decisions my bosses were making as I whizzed past the skyscrapers over the bridges. As we pulled up to the terminal, Kevin said, "Well, just remember you are there for a reason." He knew that I felt called to that position and the work at the church. He continued, "When you go into that room, don't give up your power. Just say whatever it is you need to say, and whatever is going to happen is going to happen." I thought, *Who is this guy reminding me I am a Lakȟóta woman and not to give up my power?* That's when I saw Kevin in a different light, because that was the first time I had a man encourage me and validate my spirituality, my career, and my power.

When we finally did start dating, I didn't know how to be in a relationship that wasn't dysfunctional. At first, it felt boring because there was no drama, but I adjusted when I realized he was the first man to kiss me on my shoulder in the middle of the night when he thinks I am sleeping. He thinks I am the most beautiful woman in the world. And I believe him because I see the genuine glow of love and tenderness in his eyes. It is a stark contrast to the dead eyes of those selfish men lost in themselves.

We don't always agree, but we talk things through, and it doesn't have to be his way or the highway. We each help the other accomplish whatever it is that they set out to do, by extending our networks and knowledge to each other. It was the first relationship where I would give *and* receive support. There was no sacrificing myself for the other person. I know that a lot of young women don't know what it's like to have that kind of support and aren't able to discern the differences between bad relationships and bad behavior with accepting love. For me it always comes back to loving myself first, and then allowing others to love me too.

After all of the trauma, sadness, horrible boyfriends, and the abortion, I still feel worthy. Now I can look back with gratitude because I feel like it's not a path that many get to experience. The Creator still gave me these opportunities despite my getting divorced or having an abortion—things that people told me were horrible, for which they said I would be punished by God and would go to hell. I don't regret having an abortion because I needed to care for my sons, but I do regret not standing up for my own self-worth and walking away sooner from that toxic relationship with Dale. I placed myself in the position of having to make the most painful decision I've ever made in my life. I don't wish that on anyone. I wish I'd loved myself enough to walk away earlier.

I was always looking for love and validation from others because it was too hard to look at my own pain and suffering. The shame I carried was so immense that I hid it behind my achievements. But in not dealing with my own shame, I held on to blind spots when it came to my friendships and romantic relationships, allowing others to mistreat me to the point that I sacrificed myself. I chased hopes and dreams that weren't even my hopes and dreams.

Sometimes we distort what it means to be a Lakȟóta wíŋyaŋ. Sometimes other people distort it for us by saying, "You have to do X, Y, and Z in order to be a good person." But it is about getting to a space where you love yourself enough to listen to yourself and to follow your own guidance from the Creator, your own intuition.

My situation is no different from the ones that many Native American women have faced or will face in their lives. If you live in a state where it is all white men making the decisions, then you're screwed out of reproductive justice as a woman. But Native American women in particular are too often left out of the conversation. Somehow it is okay to sterilize us or take our children away to Indian boarding schools, but it's not okay for us to choose whether or not we can have an abortion?

Kevin was the first person whom I shared my abortion experience with. I told him, "I know that the Creator is with the woman when she's making that choice, because that's what happened to me. I was praying the entire time while I had the abortion." At first, I felt anxious because I thought, *Is he going to understand or accept that I have had to make this decision? We might have to break up.* If he was anti-abortion, it was a deal breaker. I believe in a woman's right to choose, and I know from experience that it is far from an easy decision—especially when neither you nor your family can afford to have a child. But to Kevin's credit, he said, "I always voted pro-choice because I believe men should not be making the decisions for women's bodies." Thankfully, we didn't have to break up.

Kevin also doesn't pressure me to get married. We decided our relationship doesn't need to follow any specific marital rules or societal expectations. In fact, we have lived separately for the majority of our entire relationship! For most of our time together, it's been a Great Plains–West Coast relationship! Maybe someday we will get married, but it probably won't be a Christian wedding. It could be a marriage by the pipe, prayers said by a medicine man, with us surrounded by our closest loved ones in a circle and wrapped by a blanket signifying our commitment to one another. Afterward he would officially move in to my tipi and I could throw him out if he doesn't live up to my standards by simply placing his items outside. In Lakȟóta culture, women own the homes and have the power to determine what's best for us. Sometimes we forget that.

> "Theíč'iȟila" means *to love oneself, to withhold oneself, to value or prize oneself highly.*

From the beginning Kevin accepted me for who I was entirely, faults and all. He loved me despite my imperfections, and over time I continued to let go of my need to be perfect. The person who is ultimately going to love you will love everything about you, including your imperfections. It took me a long time to figure out what made me happy. I discovered I had to spend time alone with myself and with Tȟuŋkášila to find out that I am the prize.

Lakȟóta Laws

*(Living cultural values through action is how
Lakȟóta people live in integrity)*

"Waúŋšila" means *to have compassion,
kindness, or mercy.*

"Wóčhekiye" means *prayer, spirituality,
religion,* or *belief.*

---

7 WAYS TO FOLLOW INTUITION

When I look back at the love story of my life, I see that I didn't always value myself. I followed a pattern of dating people who attempted to control my life, and I stayed in relationships with toxic individuals who valued their needs above my own. They toyed with me using games of manipulation where often I was pitted against another woman, and I fell into the trap of competing for attention and love. I chased men like they were the prize. I didn't listen to my intuition or Tȟuŋkášila, who was flashing red lights at me. I didn't listen to my čekpá, who didn't know them and didn't like them! I learned all my lessons the hardest way possible and in the end sacrificed myself unnecessarily.

Looking back at my younger self, I have compassion for her, because she just didn't know how loved she was. I was fortunate I had others in my life who showed me *through their actions* that I was beloved. If you learn anything from my story, please let it be that you are *always* the prize and that you deserve to be treated accordingly. If their actions don't show you that they love you, then they don't love you.

Now I use intuition in my everyday life to tap into my creativity, find connections, and create opportunities. The church first surrounded me with faithful allies who reinforced my exploration of the unknown. Since then, I have continued to surround myself with spiritual colleagues who trust my leadership and help my visions become reality. Intuition guided by spirituality is the key to following the path you are meant to be on.

1. **Know your own sacredness and power.** Lakȟóta women are considered the most powerful during menstruation and because of their ability to give birth. Long ago, a man who battered a Lakȟóta woman would be shunned by his family and the community because he behaved contradictory to Lakȟóta law. He would no longer be allowed to lead a war party or own a pipe.[5]

2. **Identify your nonnegotiables in love and understand how you want to be treated as a life partner. Know the difference between lust and love.**

3. **Understand the difference between positive and negative energy. Positive energy is life-giving and true happiness. Negative energy is draining and can distract you from your purpose in this life.**

4. **Listen and breathe in truth. Don't lie to yourself or others about your love interest. Sometimes we rely on hope too much and give others the benefit of the doubt when their actions have shown they don't deserve it. Truth is the purest form of love you can give to yourself. It is also the purest form of love others can gift to you.**

5. **Don't rush into love. In mainstream society we are influenced by Christian values of marriage and believe we are only worthy if we are chosen for marriage.**

- Your relationship is no one else's business.
- Often traditional marriage expectations force us to give up ourselves and our priorities for our spouses. True love is balanced and complementary.
- It's okay to have a nontraditional relationship. You get to decide what's best for you and your relationship with your partner.

6. **Learn about your own intuition.**
   - Be still, listen, pray, and reconnect. When I prayed and asked Tȟuŋkášila for help, I could feel my guides on my shoulders. Pay attention to how your body feels; this is called a "gut feeling." I would often feel sick to my stomach when something didn't seem right.
   - Meditation is one of the best ways to let intuition present itself because you allow space for it to show up. Meditation can clear mental clutter by quieting the mind of its usual flow of thoughts, thus releasing your inner knowing. When you focus on your experience in the present moment, intuitive messages can reveal themselves, as they are no longer competing with the noise of daily activities.
   - Dreams can be potent portals to unlocking our intuition because conscious thought takes a back seat while the subconscious takes over. Dreams help us process daily events but in a nonlinear way—perfect for receiving messages from our intuition. If you focus your thoughts on an unresolved problem before going to sleep, this can prime your subconscious brain to work on the problem while you dream.

7. **Identify how the Creator communicates with you.**
   - I have found that often when I don't listen to the Creator's guidance, the Creator will make me listen by initiating a sudden change or an unexpected event. That's

when I know to focus on listening deeply to ensure I am on the right path.

- Prayer and participation in ceremonies are also tools for unlocking your intuition. Whenever I need guidance, I pray or go to the sweat lodge, and usually the answers come if I am willing to listen. Sometimes an issue or problem is just too difficult or stubborn for us to solve alone. At these times, I step back and pray, then leave the rest up to Tȟuŋkášila.

- If religion is not your thing, listening to an astrologer or consulting a set of oracle cards can be a fun, insightful alternative.

JOURNAL PROMPTS TO HONOR YOUR HEALING

- Often those who are codependent replay the same patterns and live out the same experiences with different people. Extreme highs and lows are addicting, but they are not healthy or good for the psyche. Consider: Do you tend to be attracted to toxic people and are you excited to be in their world of instability? When you meet stable individuals, do they seem boring to you? Ask yourself: Are they actually boring or are you just unused to someone with a secure attachment style?

- Do you struggle with aspects of codependency, such as maintaining self-confidence, setting and holding boundaries, trusting yourself, and acting independently?[6]

- Which behaviors of your codependency have you healed and which areas still require work?

"I'm sorry, please forgive me.
Thank you, I love you."

—HO'OPONOPONO PRAYER
FOR FORGIVENESS

CHAPTER 6

Life and Death

BY EMMA

AT ELEVEN YEARS OLD, I woke up at 3 a.m. to a noise coming from outside the house. The rest of the family was still asleep, but I have always been a light sleeper. At Grandma Rose and Old Grandma's house, my bedroom was on the other side of the kitchen, and I heard someone banging at the door that led outside. I groggily padded across the linoleum to see who it was.

Our door had a little chain lock with a knife wedged into the doorjamb, which Grandma made sure to latch at night due to a couple of prior break-ins. I opened the door the width of the chain and I couldn't see who was there, but I could hear a man gasping, "Help me. I need help."

Sensing the panic in his voice, I ran to wake up Grandma Rose, who got up and threw on a bathrobe over her nightgown. When she opened the door, the man collapsed right there in the middle of our kitchen floor. Blood was everywhere, all over him and all over our kitchen.

Old Grandma was standing by her bedroom door, which opened into the kitchen, and I went and stood next to her. The commotion woke up the others and soon everyone was filling our tiny kitchen, trying to assist in some way. Uŋčí Emma, Tȟuŋwíŋ Jan, and I looked on as Uŋčí Rose knelt beside the man who had passed out and pressed a pile of towels onto his chest to stop the bleeding.

I stood there frozen, not sure what to do. I remember watching someone call for an ambulance right away; I think

163

it was Tȟuŋwíŋ Jan. Meanwhile, Uŋčí Rose was trying to do everything she could to save him. Despite our house only being a mile outside of Martin, where the local hospital was, the ambulance took forty-five minutes to arrive. It felt like we were waiting forever, and the longer we waited, the more somber we all became. Growing up, I had always been somewhat aware of racism and what people would say about our reservation. Non-Native people believed that if they came to our reservation they would get shot, killed, or beaten up. They always made it sound so bad and scary, but to us, it was just our community. Yes, some bad incidents did happen. But bad things happened everywhere, not just here.

As the man lay dying in our kitchen, people began gathering on our driveway and porch. Looking out the window, I saw people standing in the glow of the streetlamp—waiting and wondering what had happened. Neighbors came by to see what was going on and some of the man's family members were there. It turned out we knew him; his name was Freddie and he was maybe in his late twenties. We found out Freddie went to a party when a fight broke out and someone stabbed him. Whoever it was, the person cut a main artery close to the heart. People who heard about the fight went and contacted others, and they all gathered outside our house. There were bloody footsteps all the way down the road, up our driveway, going to our door. People kept checking on him and asking if he was okay.

Everyone living on Pine Ridge is trying to survive day-to-day. Everybody is living in poverty, but our family had a little bit more money because our grandma had a side business selling star quilts and worked as a cook at the Oglála Lakȟóta College (OLC) LaCreek District Head Start program. With her extra earnings we could afford a Chevy Malibu, a TV with cable, and most importantly, a working landline phone—luxuries to many in our community. Growing up, we didn't understand the concept of classism. We were raised with the value of humility, to never boast or brag. Much of our clothing came from secondhand shops and thrift stores and family-rummage sales. There were Christian charities that would donate clothing to the districts and we would go to the LaCreek District CAP office to rummage through the clothing. We were happy to live simply. Many in the community knew our house was the only one in the neighborhood with a phone—Freddie included, so he came to us to call for help. Later, Grandma Rose spoke of other times this had happened, listing the names of those who had come before. She was always able to do something to help save the person. She was so distraught that she couldn't save Freddie this time. When the ambulance finally got there, the paramedics pronounced him dead, took his body, and left.

Afterward, I remember standing outside with the neighbors. Nobody really said anything. Everyone was sad and many were wiping away tears. Some cried and others felt it was just another thing that happened. After getting over our initial shock, we began to collect ourselves and take in the ghastly, bloody scene around us. There was so much blood everywhere, on the porch, the driveway, and all down the street. With the help of our neighbors, we washed away the stains of the evening's horrors before the sun rose.

For years after, our family members would say they sensed Freddie's spirit in the kitchen. Neighbors would tell us they saw someone sitting on our porch. We all thought it was him.

BRAINSPOTTING

Since 2016, I have worked at Oneida Behavioral Health (OBH). Most of my clients are Oneida, with the rest coming from the other surrounding reservations like Menominee, Stockbridge, or Brothertown. There are also those who have relocated to the Oneida community from reservations in other states. Out of twenty-two therapists, I am one of six Native American mental health psychotherapists who work there. We have one Native American alcohol, tobacco, and other drug abuse (ATODA) therapist and one Native American social worker. My clients like that I understand Native American culture and the traditional ways.

In 2017, all of the therapists at OBH were given the option to become a certified brainspotting practitioner in phase one of the brainspotting training. The other two Native American therapists I work alongside were already trained in the technique and they loved it. Like me, they also combine our spiritual and cultural practices with psychotherapy. So when they mentioned how amazing brainspotting was and the fantastic results they were having with their clients, I thought, *If they are recommending this, it must be worth checking out.* At the time, the only thing I knew about brainspotting was that it came from eye movement desensitization and reprocessing therapy (EMDR), which is a specific protocol, whereas brainspotting is looser in its structure. This resonated with me because I could more easily combine it with cultural practices like smudging.

Brainspotting was first discovered in 2003 by Dr. David Grand through his work with EMDR, and since then, over thirteen thousand therapists around the world have taken the training.[1] Brainspotting works by utilizing the body's natural self-scanning and self-healing abilities to bypass our conscious thinking processes and unlock our emotional and body-based processes instead. This is an advantage over talk therapy, which activates the surface level of the brain where language is encoded, while brainspotting accesses the nonverbal and somatic levels of the nervous system. Because trauma can overwhelm our brain's ability to process, we can become stuck in our trauma responses and remain unable to heal. Many of my clients have experienced complex trauma, and trying to make sense of it all through talk therapy can become overwhelming for them. Brainspotting circumvents the need to explain cognitions and beliefs through traditional talk therapy by directly tapping into the brain-body, where many traumas get stored. This has made it an invaluable technique when working with my clients.

While being trained in brainspotting, we were required to use brainspotting on ourselves. Safety was an issue for me because I wasn't sure how vulnerable I could be among my work colleagues. Being vulnerable can be very difficult to a survivor of trauma. Ultimately, I decided to be as authentic and open as possible to allow brainspotting to work for me. I volunteered when the instructor asked for someone to demonstrate on because I thought, *Since I experienced so much trauma, perhaps I would be a good example for the others to learn from.* In hindsight, I don't know what I was thinking. But I have always tended toward openness with my trauma and healing process to help others. Many others are often very guarded, and I understand. It's hard to be vulnerable and to feel safe. Especially when one has experienced trauma and even more so when one is asked to delve into that at a place of employment. I attribute some of this fear to a historical mistrust of systems and, in this case, health and employment.

I sat in a chair in front of the class while the instructor sat in front of me and said, "Choose an activation issue you would like to brainspot. It could be a feeling, a memory, or an image. The activation issue chosen should elicit a shift in your emotions or body sensations. Usually, it is a traumatic event."

"I want to know why this memory of Freddie's death affects me so much and why I remember it so vividly," I said. I shared with the group the story of what happened that night to Freddie. Many of the traumas I have experienced are deep and complex, so I chose to brainspot this one because I thought it would be "easy" in comparison; however, this one ended up going deep too. I have to laugh at myself sometimes. *What did I get myself into now?* I thought.

After I chose my activation issue, the instructor told me to give my level of activation a rating from zero to ten using the subjective units of disturbance scale (SUDS)—ten being the highest level and zero signifying no activation. The SUDS is used throughout the session to track a person's progress around the activation issue, with the aim of getting the score down to zero or as close to zero as possible. Less activation from the issue means healing is occurring.

The instructor was demonstrating on me what Dr. Grand calls the brainspotting "outside window" technique. How it works is, while I think of the activation issue, the instructor looks for the associated brainspot by using a pointer to guide my gaze along the different horizontal, vertical, and depth axes of my vision. The instructor was able to determine where my brainspot was by watching my eyes for reflexive cues, such as excessive blinking, while they tracked the pointer. When and how often the client blinks while thinking of the activation issue is a window into the client's mind of where a trauma occurred.

Before beginning the brainspotting therapy session, the instructor asked me, "Where in your body do you feel most calm? This is your resource spot, or safe spot." While scanning my body I couldn't find a calm spot anywhere—most likely another remnant from the massive amounts of trauma I've endured over the years. Instead, I thought about how I can feel my spirit guides and ancestors at my shoulders when I am in prayer, and I used that as my spot. The instructor said, "If you feel overwhelmed, just go back to that area. You can pull your energy back there to ground yourself."

While I processed the brainspot in my mind, I could feel Freddie's spirit present. I imagined us sitting together and talking. I had a flash of awareness about my feelings around safety and how they are linked to the racism I see directed toward my community. In the endless minutes waiting for the ambulance, I had realized this was the bitter reality of racism. I felt so much anger and then sadness. Why did another young Indian man—and many other young Indian women, for that matter—have to die? Why did it feel like the outside world never blinked an eye when this happened? I grieved for him and all the other relatives who have been lost to racism. I thanked his spirit for helping me heal and understand this, and I focused my energy on helping his spirit heal as well. The group watching me had no idea this was happening, and I never told them because I wasn't sure if they would understand the spiritual connection I felt during the healing. During the session, I also discovered that my sense of feeling unsafe goes back further than I realized. It was rooted in childhood aban-donment issues, in how I never felt safe growing up without loving care from my iná. Realizing this brought on an intense rush of emotions, and tears started streaming down my face.

The instructor said, "That's great. Let's see if we can keep squeezing the lemon and see if you can go just a bit further with this."

I looked at her and said, "No, I'm done." I thought, *Do you know how far back into traumatic memories I just went?* It was over-whelming and emotionally exhausting.

After the demonstration was done, my feelings around the memory changed. Now I understood why I felt the way I did and why that memory was so vivid and easy to recall. It was because Freddie's death was one of the first examples of systemic racism I witnessed in my childhood, and because what happened to him was an indication of the disregard that the general population has for Native Americans.

I had thought my sense of feeling unsafe began with my sexual assault. I now know it began with the loss of my iná. With continued work on my healing, I was actually able to recall the exact childhood moment in which feelings of abandonment began for me. It was after the car accident, when I woke up strapped down in the back of the ambulance in so much pain, and I couldn't see my family. I was alone. This makes sense because parents and siblings are a child's first sense of safety.

SYSTEMIC RACISM IN
OUR COMMUNITIES

When the ambulance finally arrived, none of us said anything, but we all knew. The paramedics confirmed our suspicions, placed Freddie's body on a gurney, and left as we all stood by watching. Many wiped away silent tears. We were all thinking, *Why does it take forty-five minutes to drive one mile out of town?* I tried to rationalize what could've taken them so long. It felt like his life just wasn't a priority. They say Freddie died from being stabbed too close to the heart, but I know racism killed him just as much as any knife wound.

While brainspotting, I imagined myself back there as if it was happening again, and Freddie's spirit was there with me too. I remembered how angry I was and the realization I'd had: *Wow, people really don't care about Natives, otherwise they would have come.* Reliving this experience while brainspotting helped me realize two things: One, that this had been my first time directly witnessing how systemic racism costs lives. Two, that I had always assumed my hypervigilance over the years was due to being sexually assaulted, but now I knew it was also because of the real threat that racism presented in my daily life.

There are many behaviors I think I must do in order to feel safe. Not only for me, but to protect my family and create a sense of safety for them. For example, when my children were small, I didn't allow them to walk to and from school or walk to catch the bus alone. I have always felt excessively worried about where they were and if they were safe. Nighttime is another trigger of mine, and I don't feel safe if I'm out by myself at night unless I'm with my husband. Through brainspotting Freddie's death, I realized that my fears are grounded in systemic racism and all the additional threats it poses to me and my loved ones. Every day we face additional threats to our safety, even in something as simple as calling for an ambulance and having to ask yourself, *Will it even come for me?*

While I was processing the brainspot/activation issue, I had flashes from the childhood car accident and saw that that was when my hypervigilance began, as well as my sense of not feeling safe. When we are children, feelings of safety come from having a loving and supportive parent present; I never felt safe because I never had a doting parent.

After the session, I was also able to understand and talk about the Freddie memory in a different way. I understood how it affected me, how to make peace with it, and what the memory was really about. I know that his spirit helped me realize why I felt triggered by racism and safety, and I thank his spirit for helping me work through and heal from this. By understanding these triggers and where they come from, I finally made peace with them, and my quality of life improved. Now I am able to work through my anxiety when I get triggered from taking a walk or going to a grocery store at night.

Whether their trauma is from sexual assault, domestic violence, or child abuse, many survivors struggle a lot on a daily basis—myself included. I think of it as suffering. When people experience trauma, it is always there afterward. We may not be able to think about it every day or have it be a main focus, but it's always there in the background.

As a child, you're not aware of systemic racism; you cannot see it until you are older and you start piecing together all the ways the rest of society treats your community. For example, it wasn't until I was older that I realized people are scared to drive out to our reservation because they perceive Natives as a threat. Only then did I see how real racism is and how it manifests in a myriad of ways that create harm to our community. I began to see how many non-Natives don't really care about Native Americans or our history.

However, our history is also every American's history—no matter how uncomfortable that might be. Native Americans have been positioned as "other," inferior, and savage for centuries. Sadly many Native Americans, myself included, have become conditioned to think this way about ourselves, resulting in our just accepting horrible treatment. We begin to expect bad things to happen to us. Each incident becomes "just another one of those things that happens." Part of it is that we think we do not deserve good things or that good things will not happen for us. For too long, we have so internalized these hateful and racist messages that it has made it difficult for many of us to even imagine things being any other way. This taints how we see ourselves and leads to ongoing trauma.

It's important for all of us to own our history and work to improve. Native Americans have so much to contribute to mainstream society: cultural education, language, spiritual education, and values and wisdom passed down over thousands of years. Through our advocacy and healing work, we have seen more and more people begin to understand that Native American experiences and perspectives can provide valuable guidance in a rapidly changing world. As more people take the time to learn about our issues and our history, we will continue to find more allies that can support us in a variety of ways. The issues we are fighting for, like narrative change and increased visibility in the media, literally mean the difference between life or death in our communities.

BRAINSPOTTING WITH
NATIVE AMERICAN CLIENTS

As a therapist, I feel that I only get one chance for the client to decide if they can trust me. At Oneida Behavioral Health, all of my clients are Native American. Bearing witness to historical trauma, systemic oppression, and genocide has created a massive chasm of trust issues for Native Americans. So I must build rapport and trust with the client in order for us to do this work. Feelings of safety and openness can only come from a foundation of trust between the client and therapist; thus the therapist's main job is to hold a safe and supportive space for the client so that healing can occur.

Because of my upbringing and experiences, I can understand where my clients' trust issues are coming from. I never realized just how much my past helps me connect with my clients until my supervisor said one day, "Emma, you are able to build rapport with people so quickly."

Whenever a new client walks into my office, I can see that they are deciding whether or not they can trust me. My approach is both integrative/holistic and based on cognitive behavioral therapy (CBT). I also share my story and how I healed. When I feel there is a rapport, I will discuss the brainspotting therapy process and share one of my personal experiences with it, usually a car accident I was in. My Native clients can see their own lives reflected in my stories, thus providing a level of safety and trust for us to work together. Many will speak of their trust issues, and I tell them, "I know, because I do the same whenever I meet someone. I ask myself, 'Can I trust them or not? Are they good or bad people? Are they healthy or unhealthy?'" For many of us, our healing is assisted by working with people who have been through similar issues and who come from similar backgrounds.

With brainspotting we are taught to "squeeze the lemon"

and ask our clients, "Can you go a little bit further?" However, I do not push my clients unless they want to be pushed because the majority of them have experienced complex trauma. Often it is hard for them to understand why they feel the way they do, because the traumas become so intertwined and interwoven. Brainspotting is really efficient at helping the client figure that all out, but I know how triggering it can be when dealing with too much at once. I tell my clients they can stop at any time and I will honor that. I also tell them that one of the best parts of brainspotting therapy is they do not have to share everything, because that can be triggering as well. Not everyone will be able to tolerate brainspotting therapy. This is also okay. My philosophy is that everyone is doing the best that they can in any given moment, and we don't always know what they have been through. Given this, I always try to meet the client wherever they happen to be in their healing journey.

Brainspotting has helped many of my clients heal. It is amazing how connected everything is, even when you may think things have nothing to do with one another. For example, a client could brainspot anger, depression, anxiety, a memory, or an image, not thinking it is going to be that serious or deep—but we never know what it is connected to. Other clients may not be able to vocalize the issue at all or what they are experiencing while processing a brainspot and the associated trauma. But one of the biggest benefits of brainspotting is that a client's mind will continue to process the issue for up to seven days. The client will become aware of new realizations within this time period. It is also amazing because the client can process everything internally within their minds. This means the client does not need to share every detail of their brainspotting process with the therapist in order for it to work. This is a major selling point for clients who often have not just one but multiple traumas, or for whom sharing can be very triggering.

Before we begin a brainspot, I always ask a client to take a minute to smudge and pray or give intention to their session. Then I ask them to allow any thoughts or issues related to their activation to come through. I will ask a question to help guide them, like "What is the feeling around the activation issue?" or "What was it you needed at this time?" Often, I am using my own intuition as a guide. As they talk more about it, we try to discover what their core belief around that issue is. For many of them, their core belief is "I am unlovable." I remind them to be kind and gentle to themselves. While we work on our healing, we can become more sensitive to triggers, resulting in negative thoughts and feelings about ourselves. I use these moments to teach my clients the importance of positive self-talk, mantras, and affirmations, as well as how to utilize these in their lives.

For many Native Americans, spirituality informs our worldview and how we view ourselves. Many non-Natives don't understand how that spiritual connection shapes our view of the world. We can feel the spirituality. We know it's there, we know it exists, and we know there's healing available through that connection. The ones who have a good healing experience pay attention to the spirituality and to the impact that it makes on their lives.

At the start of any healing work I do, I begin with smudging and praying. It helps center my clients, releases their negative energy, and offers them protection. I pray to Tȟuŋkášila to help the client with whatever guidance they need in that moment. Time and time again, I have seen spirituality help people heal, especially for those who say they can feel it. At the end of our session, I always make sure the client is feeling grounded, and we will use the "calling your spirit back" exercise from chapter four. I also remind my clients to smudge and pray at home. Spirituality also plays a role while I guide the client because I can feel Tȟuŋkášila and the spirits present, guiding me to the relevant brainspot as well as to the right words that help the client go deeper into the activation issue.

A great strength of brainspotting is that the technique allows us to process trauma a lot faster than traditional talk therapy; however, some might try brainspotting and discover it is not for them. Maybe they don't feel safe or the process feels overwhelming. Fortunately, there are many different healing modalities. I found healing in many different forms, so I know there isn't just one way to do it. Tȟuŋkášila always presents us with opportunities to heal, provided we pay attention and surrender to the process. Since Native Americans carry intergenerational trauma, too, I have found that complementing brainspotting with other modalities can help many of my clients make sense of the legacy we struggle to overcome.

INTERGENERATIONAL TRAUMA

In chapter one, we introduced Dr. Maria Yellow Horse Brave Heart's definition of historical trauma as "a cumulative emotional and psychological wounding over the life span and across generations, emanating from massive group trauma." Historical trauma responses are features of and reactions to massive group trauma and include depression, anxiety, self-destructive behaviors, suicidal thoughts, anger, low self-esteem, and difficulty recognizing and expressing emotions. Her research explores historical trauma across different populations and concludes that what contemporary Native Americans struggle with in terms of historical grief is like what Jewish Holocaust survivors went through because it addresses trauma for a group of people.

My clients want to be healthy and avoid passing on negative behaviors to their children, and whenever I educate them on the legacy of historical trauma, they say, "Oh my gosh, this explains exactly what has been happening in my family." Many

Natives do not even know they are experiencing intergenerational and historical trauma. It is difficult to understand or even put into words until you see the research and realize this is how you feel too. I grew up seeing many negative behaviors in myself and other Natives. We don't realize how dysfunctional these behaviors are because they are normalized and we become so used to seeing them. We are living this pain without understanding where it comes from. But through learning about historical trauma, we can make sense of how it impacts our own lives, and then begin to heal by making different choices for ourselves.

After learning about how historical trauma and intergenerational trauma is passed down through DNA, I paid even closer attention to the issues my family experienced. My iná was an alcoholic, a drug addict, and a sexual assault survivor. If you have addiction in your family or have experienced trauma, it is easier for you to become an addict as well, so I am mindful of alcohol. Many Natives will drink to get drunk, and I can see that tendency within myself.

Even our youth experience the impacts of intergenerational and historical trauma. Recently, my husband and I discovered that our youngest daughter was carrying a pocketknife with her whenever she went skateboarding by herself. We asked her, "Why do you have this knife with you?" She said, "To protect myself." Later she told me, "I have never been raped, but I feel like I have been." I thought, *Is it because of what I went through that she feels this way?* But I know she, too, is feeling the trauma passed on from generations.

Whenever I feel triggered by the past, it helps me to know that the overwhelming feelings of guilt and shame are not only my own but also my family's. I am processing their grief too. To stop spiraling, I focus on my healing and positive coping strategies like smudging, praying, asking the Creator for help, talking to someone, and grounding myself. I also use the Ho'oponopono prayer of forgiveness as my mantra.

DURING MY TIME working as a domestic violence advocate, I returned home to South Dakota to help facilitate a healing program we were doing for the White Buffalo Calf Women's Society shelter. The program was White Bison's Mending Broken Hearts: Healing from Intergenerational Trauma and Grief, which can be done in a group setting or individually. White Bison Inc. was founded by Don Coyhis from the Mohican Nation, and the organization has been working with Native Americans and healing since 1988. They offer a multitude of healing programs focused on sobriety, recovery, wellness, and intergenerational trauma.[2]

Part of the program includes a documentary that White Bison created, called *The Wellbriety Journey to Forgiveness*.[3] The creators traveled to different reservations to document the stories of survivors from the boarding-school era and to see how historical and intergenerational trauma still affects Native Americans today, as well as to explore different ways we can begin to heal.

I still use the documentary and materials with my clients receiving counseling today. A lot of the Natives I work with do not understand their negative coping mechanisms, their family issues, or how to begin their healing. The documentary and its curriculum explains to them why there is such a massive loss of our languages and Native speakers, and also helps explain why our communities are deprived of nurturance, why so many Native American parents struggle with basic parenting skills, alcoholism, and addiction.

We also implemented an educational program in Martin, which some of our family members attended—including our grandma. Prior to Uŋčí Rose attending the program, she told Sarah and me, "For me, boarding school was good because they taught me a lot of skills." She didn't understand why other Natives said negative things about the boarding school because her experience was okay. After attending the program and watching the documentary, she said, "I understand now how it negatively impacted my family." The documentary includes many elders sharing their experiences at boarding schools, including some well-known Native elders like Ben Nighthorse Campbell, who was a Colorado representative and state senator.

Seeing the documentary made Uŋčí Rose realize the things she lost from going to boarding school. She has a hard time saying "I love you," and her capacity to nurture was impacted because the students were raised by school administrators who were, at best, indifferent toward the children. She had difficulty showing affection because that just did not happen there. Hearing others share their stories of abuse also helped Uŋčí Rose recognize some of the abuses she faced herself but had normalized.

Here on the Oneida Nation of Wisconsin reservation, where I live and work, only a small handful of fluent language speakers remain. On Pine Ridge there are more, but a lot of the speakers are elders. Uŋčí Emma only spoke Lakȟóta and she taught Uŋčí Rose. However, Uŋčí Rose often spoke English to her children or grandchildren because of her time at the boarding schools. My tȟuŋwíŋs and leksís understand Lakȟóta but have trouble speaking Lakȟóta. Uŋčí Rose thought we would have a better chance of surviving in this world with only English. Many of the Lakȟóta elders never taught the next generation because the boarding schools tortured them for speaking Lakȟóta. Now it's causing a language crisis on our reservation and everyone is concerned we will lose it altogether.

Our family has a picture, from years back, of all the fluent speakers left. They were the elders and were being recognized as the language holders. When the photo was taken, there were maybe thirty-five fluent speakers left on the entire reservation. Not every fluent speaker was there, but many were. Looking at that photo brings a pang of grief to my heart because it is a reminder of how vulnerable our traditional customs and language are. Our elders contain the oral history of our people. Now that the COVID-19 pandemic has put our elders at risk of dying, our culture, traditions, and language are at risk of dying with them. Some COVID-infected Natives camped in tents over the winter to prevent exposing their family members to the virus. Natives living on the reservation usually dwell in multigenerational households, so if one person is sick then everybody in the house gets sick too.

Our sense of identity and self-love come from our language, because it is such an integral part of our spirituality. Through our traditional language we understand our traditional world-view even more clearly than if it is spoken about in English. We are losing a lot of that traditional wisdom. Given the loss of language, culture, and land combined with centuries of forced assimilation, many Native Americans struggle with identity issues.

In the media we hear a lot about vulnerable populations, but we hardly ever hear any mention of the struggle of Native Americans. It feels like people don't care. Many of us cannot see beyond the limiting beliefs society passes on to us. We cannot imagine ourselves being successful because we do not believe we are capable. We don't believe we can make a difference or change things. It is not that we don't want to be successful; it's that we don't believe we can because all we ever hear is how we are less-than. All of it comes back to historical and inter-generational trauma.

Native Americans receive so many negative messages about ourselves from the time we are born. And for many of us, we go on to internalize those messages into our belief system and begin thinking we are not good enough. Then if you throw verbal, emotional, psychological, or physical abuse on top of that, we start to feel as if we deserved such treatment. This is why I hear, time and time again, my clients tell me their core belief is that they are unlovable. Many of us don't know how to challenge these negative beliefs that are thrust upon us. We never confront the negative voices in our heads to unravel what our true core beliefs about ourselves actually are. Instead, we lead lives filled with negative self-talk, self-defeating beliefs, and suicidal ideation as we are crushed by the weight of inter-generational and historical trauma.

MOVING PAST SUICIDAL IDEATION

Throughout my life, I have found that the Creator guides me to where I need to be, and one way this guidance manifests is through dreams. Seven years ago, I struggled with migraines and chronic pain due to a series of unfortunate accidents that included slipping on ice and getting whiplash from a car accident, resulting in occipital neuralgia. The headaches became so severe that I went to get myself checked out to see if it was something more serious. Because they were happening at the base of my skull, the doctors wanted to confirm it wasn't brain cancer, so they sent me off to get a CT (computerized tomography) scan. My husband was worried but I remember thinking, *I don't feel like I have cancer. I think I'm okay.*

The night before the scan, I had a vivid dream that helped me move past the suicidal thoughts I was struggling with at the time. In the dream, I was with my three children and I was helping them pack their suitcases to go somewhere. We all knew that I was going to die soon, so I was telling them, "Remember to do this, and take care of this, and do that"—teaching them how to take care of one another. As we continued walking together, I thought maybe they forgot about me, as if I wasn't going to die anymore. All of a sudden, I actually died in my dream. I felt my physical body fall away from my spirit, my spirit lifting upward and traveling to where the sky and clouds became all white. Then I was standing there and across from me was a crowd of a hundred people, who were all talking about me. I was trying to hear what they were saying, and I couldn't make out anything when, suddenly, the talking stopped. One person came forward from the crowd and asked me, "Why did you make this decision?" Then the crowd erupted in talking again. This happened four different times, where the crowd would stop and someone would ask me questions like that. After they asked me the last question, I felt my spirit fall back down to earth, where I was following my children while they were walking down the road. It felt like I was with them for a really long time, just watching them. In my dream, my spirit thought, *They are going to be okay, so I can go now*, and it began to drift away.

When I woke up, it was the day of the CT scan and I was trying to understand the meaning behind the dream. I felt it was telling me that I could die if I wanted to, and it would be my choice. So I had to choose: Did I want to live or did I want to die? I thought about that. As a sexual assault survivor, I'd struggled with suicidal ideation my whole life up to that point. I felt I could condemn myself for all of eternity and live within the prison of my own mind, but then where would my three beautiful children be? Where would my love be? The dream finally made me realize I didn't want to die. I needed to move into healing to free myself from the pain and suffering that suicidal ideation brings, and to begin to truly love myself and teach my children to do the same. Since then, every day I've chosen to honor myself and the life given to me by the Creator and my ancestors. I choose to live my life. But I needed to forgive those who hurt me and those I hurt to end the cycle of despair and self-hatred. It is important that I create beauty from my pain, and what is more beautiful than healing?

Lakȟóta Laws

*(Living cultural values through action is how
Lakȟóta people live in integrity)*

"Waúŋšila" means *to have compassion,
kindness, or mercy.*

"Wówičakȟe" means *holding honesty and truth
with yourself, your higher power, and others.*

---

7 WAYS TO HEAL FROM TRAUMA

Healing can come in many different forms: the right person
coming into your life when you need help the most; a sacred
ceremony or ritual grounding you; or a dream showing you
that you are worthy of self-love and self-forgiveness.

Negative self-talk is damaging to our mental health and
well-being. It can range from simple thoughts like *I am so stupid*
to more catastrophic thoughts like *I will never do anything right!*
Negative self-talk makes us question our abilities by limiting
our belief in ourselves and diminishing our potential. Worse,
it can prevent us from moving forward with our healing by
causing us to doubt in our ability to grow and change. Negative self-talk results in feelings of helplessness that make our
daily challenges all the more difficult to overcome. Here are
some strategies that I have found to help my clients deal with
negative self-talk.

1. **Pay attention to and challenge your inner critic.**
   - All personal change starts with awareness, so first we
     must understand what our critic is saying for us to

change the script. Thinking is an automatic process, and much of our thoughts go unscrutinized as our brains flow from one passing thought to another. By intentionally paying attention to our thoughts, we slow down our thinking, and thus the critic begins to reveal itself. Any feelings of guilt, shame, and worthlessness that accompany a thought are good indicators that these thoughts are coming from your inner critic.

- Separate the critic from yourself. Some therapists suggest giving your inner critic a name to distinguish that voice from your own. By separating yourself from the clutches of your inner critic, you can unravel where your authentic self begins.

- Challenge your inner critic. For many Native Americans, our inner critics' opinions are not our own, but a result of intergenerational and historical trauma passed down to us from the dominant culture. We think we are bad people because that is what we are told time and again. By challenging our inner critic, we begin to see where these thoughts originate from, and by questioning their validity, we can break the hold they have over us.

- Substitute your negative critic with a new voice, one who is an ally and cheers you on. This can be done by cultivating self-love and paying attention to your strengths and gifts. At first, it might feel unnatural to you, but over time it gets easier and becomes more automatic. Remember that you are essentially rewiring your brain and thought processes. The biggest antidote to years of negative self-talk is self-love. Be kind to yourself and remember that you are doing the best you can.

2. **Continue to research and understand trauma.**
   - Figure out your Adverse Childhood Experiences (ACEs) score. There can be power in understanding yourself, your family, your people, and your community.

- Learn and understand trauma responses, recognize triggers, and know the importance of safety. It is even more important today than ever with the ever-changing political and racial landscape, including the rising number of violent incidents related to domestic abuse, police brutality, racism, and multiple shootings.

3. Begin your healing work with a trusted therapist, counselor, and/or pastor with whom you feel safe. It is important to be able to trust this individual while you work on your healing.

4. Use grounding exercises to stay present, such as being near water or walking in nature.

5. Begin the forgiveness process, whether this is toward yourself or someone else, at any pace that you are able to. This can be one of the most difficult parts of healing to undertake, but is so important. It's okay to be wherever you are in your forgiveness process. Just working toward this goal is amazing and enough.

6. Seek spiritual guidance from a trusted spiritual advisor or medicine person for further assistance in healing, as needed.
   - Sing your prayer, healing, and gratitude songs, as appropriate for your spiritual beliefs.

7. Practice healing exercises such as:
   - Talking to your spirit or the spirits of those from whom you seek healing. You can do this while meditating or praying, during which we believe Tȟuŋkášila is helping us communicate spirit to spirit so this healing may occur.
   - Creating past/present/future watercolor pictures. I learned this exercise while attending healing workshops.

We would use a large paper and divide it into three sections to represent the past, present, and future. Then draw and/or paint what you envision your past, present, and future to be. Share with others as you're able to.

JOURNAL PROMPTS TO HONOR YOUR HEALING

- What or who helped you begin your healing journey? What support and guidance did you receive from them?

- What self-defeating belief has held you back from healing?

- What is the truth behind the self-defeating belief?

- What action(s) do you plan to take to eliminate the self-defeating belief?

With visible breath I am walking
across the golden prairie, down the canyon,
to the sundance tree at sunrise.

With visible breath I am dancing,
following the drum of the sandy mist on the ocean shore
to the sunset glow.

With visible breath I am climbing
up through the swirling wind at the top of the sacred mountains
to the one I love.

With visible breath I am rising,
beyond the nighttime clouds in the starry sky through the Milky Way
to the old ones.

With visible breath, I am.

—SARAH EAGLE HEART

CHAPTER 7

The Sacred

BY SARAH

WE BELIEVE THAT from the time a Lakȟóta emerges from their mother's birth canal, they are surrounded by spirits. There is never a time when we do not know Tȟuŋkášila, and we know our ancestors are guiding us every day. One of the first stories we are told is about our ancestor White Buffalo Calf Woman, the one who brought the Lakȟóta people the sacred pipe.[1] It is said that a beautiful Lakȟóta woman in white appeared on the prairie to two Lakȟóta men when the Lakȟóta people were starving. One man had bad thoughts about her and he disintegrated immediately into ashes. The other man knew she was wakȟáŋ. She told him to tell the people to prepare, as she would come to their camp. In four days, the White Buffalo Calf Woman appeared and taught us the songs and ceremonies of the čhaŋnúŋpa (pipe), inípi (sweat lodge), haŋbléčheyapi (vision quest), wiwáŋyaŋg wačhípi (sundance), huŋká (adoption), and ishnati awichalowan (preparing for adulthood). A core part of all of the ceremonies is smoking the sacred pipe and singing prayer songs. As the smoke rises, our prayers also rise to Tȟuŋkášila as we continue drumming and singing. The first song she taught us is still sung today: *With visible breath I am walking* . . . The visible breath is the smoke from the pipe. As she left, the Lakȟóta people saw her change into a black buffalo, which then changed from red to yellow to white. Then she disappeared into the sky. This is our first understanding of who we are as pté oyáte (people of the buffalo).

THE LITTLE CHURCH

My first job out of university was working for Viejas Casino and Outlet Center in San Diego, owned by the Kumeyaay tribe. My boss at the outlet center described me as a "real go-getter" because I had climbed the ladder pretty quickly there. I even created my own positions and wrote my own job descriptions. For four years I worked there and loved it, until Rich was restationed to Pensacola, Florida, requiring us to move. On my last day of work, my boss called me into his office and told me that I had a real future ahead of me, that I could really make something out of myself. I think he didn't want to see me give up a career in marketing. He wanted me to know that he saw my leadership potential.

But there I was suddenly sitting on the beach in Pensacola, enjoying the warm waters and sunshine. It would have been paradise except I could not find a job, despite my two degrees and my MBA. Instead, I was serving tables at a restaurant with peanut shells littering the floor so I could save extra money for us to afford the Christmas trip home. I wore a red ketchup-stained T-shirt and smelled like grease. To say I felt lost is an understatement.

I wasn't one of those military moms who was happy sitting at home taking care of her children. I really enjoyed working and I wanted it all. En route between our home and my sons' school, where one attended kindergarten and the other second grade, I drove past Holy Cross Episcopal Church. I thought, *I should go in there*, but I never did. I was contemplating taking my sons to church because we were far from our reservation where they could access Lakȟóta spirituality, and I figured the church could provide a spiritual foundation for them. Old Grandma was a devout Episcopalian. When we were children, she told us, "There is no difference between Christianity and traditional Lakȟóta spirituality because it is all about praying to the same God." We also heard tales of how Black Elk, a Lakȟóta holy man, would carry the pipe in one hand and the Bible in the other. This was the way we looked at things—it is the same God, just a different name—so we did not have to choose between Christian and Lakȟóta beliefs. Old Grandma made sure we were baptized and confirmed. We sang hymnals that were translated into Lakȟóta and Dakȟóta, back from the days the church was working to convert all of our people. We went to church on Christmas and Easter and prayed before dinner, but we also attended sundance ceremonies, sweat lodges, and powwows. Somehow, even through all the death and suppression of our own traditional Lakȟóta belief system, our people found a way to embrace another spirituality along with their own.

After nine months of driving past that church every day, I received a call from an employment agency that they had not just one but two job opportunities for me: a position as an administrator at that Episcopalian church or a job at the Chamber of Commerce. I thought to myself, *There is no way I'm going to work for the church. It's going to be my practice interview for the Chamber of Commerce position.*

The day of the church interview, I walked in armed with all the articles I wrote in college while interning at *Indian Country Today* and newsletters I'd designed for the casino. As the interviewers looked through them, one said, "We love your background and that you have an MBA. We are excited to see what you could bring to the church."

However, I didn't want to work there, so I told them every reason I could think of why they shouldn't hire me. I said, "I have children, two young sons, and I'm a military wife"—two things I would never say in any job interview. One of the interviewers said, "We love that. That's great. We both have two sons too. Plus, this is a military congregation, and since you already have health benefits from being a military wife, we can pay you more. And how would you like to have Friday afternoons off?" I sat there dumbfounded, but I still didn't want to work there.

Then I went to the other job interview. It turned out to be for a temporary full-time position that paid next to nothing. Plus, I'd have to commute thirty minutes each way. I always struggled with commuting at the casino because I felt like a bad mom, always running late to pick up my young sons from childcare. The message was crystal clear: at the church, I would have a stable job and be able to spend time with my sons. I thought, *Okay, Creator, if you want me to work at the church, fine, I will go.*

My first year there, I couldn't believe I was just getting coffee and making copies—nothing stimulating. I kept asking myself why I had gone from climbing the corporate ladder at an Indian casino to working at this tiny church. But I also knew, deep down, there was a reason that I was there. It was as if I were being called to learn something. I had to let go and have faith. I knew that if I could trust in the Creator, I would always be led down the right path—even if it was difficult or unclear at the time. So I stayed and continued to find my spirituality as well as began to guide the spirituality of my sons.

WINTER TALK

After a year, Father Ray saw that I wasn't stimulated and began to introduce me to different ministries within the church. Within a few months, the missioner (a.k.a., program officer) for the Office of Indigenous Ministries invited me to attend the Winter Talk, an annual event held for Native Americans within the church to gather and share ideas. At my first Winter Talk, I rarely spoke up, since Lakȟóta are taught to speak only when they need to. At the end of the event, Reverend Anna Frank gave me a white eagle feather and said, "I see leadership in you and I'm grateful that you came." I was shocked. Receiving an eagle feather is a sign of high honor among my people.

Immediately after receiving this gift, I walked by a table of bishops and priests. A bishop pulled me aside and asked, "When are you going to become ordained?" I almost had a heart attack! There was no way that I was going to become ordained, I thought then, not in a million years. After retreating to the safety of my friend circle, I said, "A bishop asked me when I'm going to be ordained."

A friend said, "You just take whatever he says and put it in your back pocket and don't pay any mind to that. They are always trying to make priests out of people who show leadership." That was a kind way to soothe my anxious heart, but it would be only a matter of time before I found myself taking on more responsibilities.

STEPPING INTO LEADERSHIP

Despite being brand-new to the church, I built up a network fast. I became involved in the women, young adult, and Native American ministries. But after four years at the small church, the slow pace became too much for me. One day a Native church friend said, "I'm going to throw your name in the hat for program officer for Indigenous ministry serving on the staff of the presiding bishop headquartered in New York." They called right away for an interview.

When I had first begun working for the little church, I would notice that whenever something important came up for me, like a conference or a job interview, life always tossed me a curveball. Leading up to this job interview was no exception. I was dating my toxic boyfriend, Dale, at the time, and he phoned me at 2 a.m. to pick a fight and yell derogatory things at me, calling me a "slut" and a "whore." I was so confused and dumbfounded about why he would treat me that way. Then the next morning, I woke up to the voice of my landlord outside. She was talking loudly about me to someone who was wondering if I was home. So I opened the door to groggily greet them, and waved hello to let her know I was home, and later she left a voicemail yelling at me for being rude to them. It felt odd to me that all these things were happening while I was trying to get mentally prepared for this interview.

That same day—a Wednesday—I called in sick to work. Normally I would never call in because that was our busiest day of the week. But I still attended a spiritual-direction appointment, after which I stopped by my boss's office and mentioned the problems I was having with my boyfriend and my landlord. Father Jeff said, "Sarah, these occurrences are not a coincidence. They are happening for a reason. I don't want to say that your boyfriend Dale is evil, but remember that evil can work through people. Remember to stay focused and continue to pray and reflect. Don't worry about anything at work, I will handle everything so you can prepare for this." Leading up to the interview, I became quiet and reflective and tuned out the chaotic distractions as I traveled to Minneapolis for the interview. When I arrived, I turned off the TV, turned off my phone, and did my tasks in silence. I wrote in my journal. I paid attention to my thoughts. By the morning of the interview, I felt poised and ready.

The interview was in front of a hiring panel of twelve Native leaders from across the United States. Half the people liked me, but the other half thought that at age thirty, I was too young and inexperienced for the role. But during the interview, I was completely at peace. I joked around and laughed with them. I knew all I could do was give it my best. In the end, it came down to me and one other candidate, a priest in his seventies. We weren't even sure if he had an email account, but he was an elder and well known. Because it was a tie, the decision was sent up to the presiding bishop, Katharine Jefferts Schori, the first woman to hold the position. My supporters said, "We think she'll pick you," and she did.

I got the phone call back in Pensacola as I sat in the administrator chair of the little church. I was completely overwhelmed with emotions. I walked over to the priest's office, where he was visiting with a church member. I stood in the doorway with tears in my eyes, unable to speak. Father Jeff looked at me and said, "You got the job. I knew you were being called." I nodded as tears streamed down my face, and he crossed the room to hug me. Suddenly, I became one of the youngest missioners working at the Episcopal Church and my salary was more than doubled. This job would change my life by moving me to a regional office on the West Coast. I was excited, but didn't expect what came next.

Before being hired into this role, I had volunteered in these communities for three years. Everybody knew me and liked me. But the minute I received that title, I was treated differently because people thought I had power. They were not privy to the more complicated power dynamics playing out behind closed doors, so they had no way of knowing that I was still bound by this crazy patriarchal system of the church and its entrenched hierarchy.

In the early days of my tenure, I sat in a meeting with the Executive Council Committee on Indigenous Ministries and it was obvious that not everyone was happy I had been hired. They went around the table saying passive-aggressively that I was too young, too inexperienced, and not a priest. When it was my turn to speak, I said, "I hear you all and I appreciate your feedback. I am here because I feel called to do this work and I am here to work with you."

Erma Vizenor, a tribal leader from the White Earth Reservation, stood up to speak after me. She put her hand on my shoulder and addressed the council: "Sarah is our leader, and we're here to support her. That is our role—to support her as our representative within the church." Her validation of my leadership made everyone else stop questioning it, and I was especially grateful for her trust. Fortunately, I also had the support of the presiding bishop Katharine Jefferts Schori. We were all aligned on Indigenous rights, and she would often attend the events I recommended or planned.

Immediately, I started working in partnership with the department of Lifelong Christian Formation, which is really just about transformation and how we understand and make sense of God and Jesus. I appreciated the educational component, I loved the rituals, and I was drawn to the transformational aspects of the teachings. Though I never became a die-hard Christian from my many years at the church, I loved learning about the different spiritualities. I always felt like this was where the Creator wanted me to be, so this was where I would go.

Within a few months of my hire, I was appointed team leader of the diversity, social justice, and environmental ministries team. I held roles as missioner for Indigenous ministries and team leader too. I stayed in the position for seven years, working alongside a diverse range of people from places all over the world, like Australia, Bolivia, Ecuador, New Zealand, Switzerland, and South Korea. Even though I was the youngest program officer, I believe the other BIPOC members supported and encouraged me because as a lay leader, I had more freedom to share my opinions than they did. And I was a pretty dynamic leader, if I do say so myself. I was grounded in our Lakȟóta values and I was a vocal advocate. I learned how to teach Lakȟóta spirituality in parallel with Christianity. I shared my stories of growing up in poverty on the reservation and I supported young leaders as they followed their callings, oftentimes to the priesthood. I also knew how to work in teams because of my Lakȟóta upbringing under collectivism.

My team was the "team of color" because of our group's diversity in comparison with the other groups. Whenever I had meetings with the other seven team leaders, I was the only BIPOC woman. Under my purview were issues that affected youth, women, Native Americans, diversity, climate justice, poverty alleviation, and intercultural ministries. Through this work my awareness around intersectional advocacy grew because I saw many racial and social groups dealing with similar struggles as Native Americans. My team supported my leadership, even though they were at least twenty years older than me. I never took their trust for granted.

I loved my job. I had meaning and the Creator in my life every day. Along the way, I had made many friends, some lifelong. One of those people was Alejandra, a Colombian priest with whom I went salsa dancing all over the country and traveled with to Rome and Barcelona. One day after several years, over dinner and drinks in New York City, I mentioned to her, "I know many people would love to be in this position their entire lives, but I just don't see myself being here long-term."

She looked at me carefully, as if she were studying me, and said, "Yes, this is a stepping stone for you. I see it." In that moment, I was grateful that somebody else saw what I could sense and was not demanding that I become a priest or a bishop instead.

MY FIRST GENERAL CONVENTION

Two months into my new role, the church held its 2009 General Convention—an annual event where the church determines policy. It is comprised of individuals who are elected or appointed by their churches or state dioceses to represent their communities at the convention, which has upward of ten thousand people in attendance. This was my first time going, and it turned out to be a historically important convention year because the Episcopal Church was deciding on a resolution to repudiate the Doctrine of Discovery.

Staffers provided their expertise on different issues, and I was there educating on Native American issues. I sat through many conversations where I had to teach others who didn't understand the history of this doctrine and the impact it has had on Native Americans. I discovered I could influence others by sharing my story. Being a young woman who comes from a poor community on a reservation is not a perspective people hear every day, especially within the Episcopal Church. My role felt important for creating change. With what other employer could my work reach and impact nearly two million members in eighteen countries around the world?

In 2009, the Episcopal Church became the first church in the world to repudiate the Doctrine of Discovery, thanks to an amazing coalition of Native priests and bishops who pushed the resolution through the convention. My role was to support them in their endeavor. Despite the resolution passing, virtually no one in the church knew the history of Manifest Destiny or the Doctrine of Discovery. I doubt the church would have passed it if they had really known and truly understood the history and significance. I think they did it because it sounded good. Meanwhile, international papers started spreading the word that we repudiated the doctrine. For a month our church didn't say much about it, but the rest of the world wouldn't stop talking.

Some church members felt apathetic. A resolution must pass before we can do anything within the church, but it's one thing to pass a resolution and another to actually fund the necessary resources and education afterward. So we knew that the church could pass a resolution and then decide not to do anything else about it and at first, that is what happened. But I took it upon myself to educate people about the importance of this issue, to say, "We need to do something. What are you going to do about this—what are the actionable items?" I also worked with church archivists to identify how many boarding schools the Episcopal Church had been involved in—we found at least twenty.

I developed a curriculum alongside my colleague Ruth-Ann, a redheaded Irish person from the Lifelong Christian Formation. Together we educated many groups throughout the church on the importance of this resolution, the history of this doctrine, and how it led to the Indian boarding schools. We knew the content had the potential to trigger resistance from the mostly white church members, so I said to Ruth-Ann, "You say 'white privilege' first and then I'll say it second and hopefully, people won't be mad by the time I say it." As predicted, some people, even priests and deacons, got triggered and left when they heard me say "white privilege."

THE DOCTRINE OF DISCOVERY
AND MANIFEST DESTINY

Reconciliation and education are difficult work because many non-Native people find it hard to accept the true history of how this nation came to be. Many still believe in the fantasy that North America was peacefully settled instead of colonized through Manifest Destiny, resulting in Native

---

In the nineteenth century, Manifest Destiny became a national rallying cry for westward colonization, essentially ratcheting up the rhetoric of the Doctrine of Discovery. The term was first used by editor John L. O'Sullivan in 1845 to promote the annexation of Texas and Oregon country to the United States. This public attention on westward expansion eventually culminated in the Oregon Trail, the Mexican-American War, and the California gold rush.

Americans being massacred and forcefully removed from our land, and stolen generations enduring colonization through Indian boarding schools. The truth is excluded from all the schoolbooks.

When the European invasion of North America started in the 1400s, the Christian Doctrine of Discovery specified that the entire world was under the jurisdiction of the pope, as God's representative on earth. Any land not under the sovereignty of a Christian ruler could be possessed on behalf of God. Western legal regimes deemed our land as "terra nullius," literally meaning *land belonging to no one*. When they combined the Doctrine of Discovery with the theory of social Darwinism, European settlers saw themselves as the superior race destined to rule all of America.

This systematic invasion forced my great-great-grandmother to give up a nomadic way of life. My people endured massacres, including the Wounded Knee Massacre on December 29, 1890, where an estimated 250 to 300 Lakȟóta people, mostly Lakȟóta women and children, were gunned down by US cavalry. Despite the shame America should've felt for this heartbreaking Christmastime event, the massacre was celebrated by awarding twenty Medals of Honor to members of the US Army. Around this time, Native parents across the United States were forced to send their children, sometimes as young as infants, to one of the over five hundred Indian boarding schools across the nation or risk jail and starvation.

The Indian boarding schools were funded by the US government, and Christian denominations divided up territories to enforce the school founder's slogan of "kill the Indian, save the man." Native children were taught that their language and culture was evil. Their hair was cut, a sign of mourning for many tribes, and traditional tribal clothing was replaced with European clothing. Military-style teaching and punishment ensued at the schools. Many children were raped, and many others did not return home. Cultural genocide ensued within these schools until the last one closed in 1973. Many tribes lost their language and the traditional practices that guided optimal development of Native American identity. The historical and colonial trauma that Native Americans experienced have left our tribal communities in ruin.

Our allies must understand the Indigenous worldview, a holistic one that espouses how we are all related, including our issues and their solutions. Being a good ally is acknowledging what you don't know, then investing the time to learn, being an advocate for us, and making sure we are included at the table. Keeping us from finding out the true history has been part of the patriarchal colonizer playbook from the beginning.

When we try to hide from the shame by erasing and denying what happened to Native Americans, the dominant culture is apt to repeat the trauma and cause more suffering. Our ignorance of this history finds echoes in the way our society overlooks the disappearances of Native girls, or the way it dismisses solvable problems that are harming and killing our youth, resulting in the highest suicide rates in the nation.

The Repudiation of the Doctrine of Discovery is a step toward healing because it means the church finally acknowledges and understands the trauma inflicted on Native Americans. Native history is everyone's history because the colonial mindset is still alive and well today. Together, we are rewriting history to include the truths of more than just the dominant group. The way to bring healing to our country is by no longer hiding our eyes and ears from the difficult realities on which this country was built.

REPUDIATION AT THE UNITED NATIONS

In 2012, the United Nations Permanent Forum on Indigenous Issues made the Doctrine of Discovery its annual theme. That year, I worked with the church to prepare a statement on the

Repudiation of the Doctrine of Discovery. The presiding bishop attended to give the statement. Many people gave testimony about what happened on their traditional lands because of the doctrine. People spoke for hours and the presiding bishop listened to everyone speak, but due to time constraints, by the end, she was unable to deliver the Oral Intervention of our statement.

While this was going on, Ruth-Ann was in the New York office putting together a video for the curriculum we were creating with our communications team. They were all talking about the statement that the presiding bishop was supposed to give. Ruth-Ann told me later, "Sarah, you should have heard them when they were talking about the presiding bishop being at the UN. They said it was such a waste of her time for her to be sitting there all day."

Annoyed by what the team said, I wrote them an email explaining how important it was for the presiding bishop to be there listening to the testimony of these people and their tribal communities. Her presence alone was an essential part of the healing process for Indigenous communities. There were no other denominational representatives present that day, though I felt that all of the denominations should've been present to hear the testimony detailing the aftermath and contemporary challenges caused by the Doctrine of Discovery.

Too often, I found myself in the center, trying to educate and translate two different cultures to each other so they might somehow meet in the middle. Sometimes I was successful and sometimes I wasn't. Over time, my advocacy and translator skills improved because I learned how to code-switch and communicate things in a passive way. However, I also experienced others trying to use me for their own gain. Usually when white men played power games with me, often their mentality was that I was either with them or against them. Support usually consisted of being a spokesperson and legitimizing the old power structures that were embedded in the church and which maintained their privilege.

Throughout my career in advocacy, I have learned that many systems are set up to reinforce individualism and personal maximization (including nonprofit sectors of Christianity and philanthropy). These hierarchical systems are a capitalistic merry-go-round. Some benefit from staying on; they have no need to get off or make changes. But I have never been content with injustice. I know we can change this structure. We can change it because we are all in the middle of it, operating it.

We all struggle with shame and most people have a hard time breaking down their shame—myself included. However, white people have been extremely privileged, and their shame isn't of the same kind. It is centered around how they benefit off white patriarchy and capitalism. Many refuse to acknowledge how they got this land or came to live in their house because that disrupts the narrative that they acquired or built it themselves through individual exceptionalism. But in order to shift narratives, the individual must do the work of breaking down that shame. Only then can we go through the process of repair, which is the greater challenge because all of the systems are built upon individual gain, not collective gain. First you must do the work on yourself, and then you can fight the system by transforming it into something that supports the collective instead of the individual.

I've learned to find allies who want and are humble enough to take a step back and say "I don't know." Many people want to pretend they know when they don't. For me, it's been about finding those allies who can mobilize resources and create possibilities. And I have met some great people that have been willing to do that, people who are spiritually grounded and focused on transformation, people who want to innovate and change the world. Through allyship I learned how to work across different dynamics, issues, and belief systems.

LAKȞÓTA SPIRITUALITY

While I was working for the Episcopal Church, I was also caring for my sons, who lived with me. The job often had me traveling one to two weeks out of the month, so I asked my younger cousins to nanny (or "manny") for me while I traveled. I figured my sons would get to connect with their relatives, while my cousins would get to leave the reservation for a bit and see California. It was a win-win.

But at age fourteen, my unlicensed eldest son, Aarron, stole my car at 3 a.m. while I was sleeping and drove it on the freeway. He had never driven on the freeway before. He drove my car into the road's median because he dozed off as the sun rose and was lucky he didn't hurt himself or others. It was like a light switch had flipped and my previously responsible son had turned into another person. It scared me.

I realized he needed a spiritual foundation. I decided the best route was to take him home to attend sweat lodge ceremonies. It was difficult to get home because the choice was either a very expensive flight to South Dakota or a twenty-four-hour drive, but I started sending him to the ceremonies whenever we were home for the holidays. He ended up pledging to sundance at age fifteen. This pledge meant he would dance annually for four years, plus would be expected to dance a fifth year as a wóphila, during which the family would hold a giveaway ceremony.

The first year, I gathered under the circular arbor shaded by a cedar branch with my three aunties and grandma. I drove from Los Angeles and another aunt came from Colorado Springs to be there. Aarron is the oldest in his generation, but his Lakȟóta father does not follow traditional Lakȟóta spirituality, so one of my younger cousins/his young uncle had to be there to help advise him during the sundance. We all pulled together to get Aarron ready, with his sundance skirts sewed by Grandma in colors of the four directions—red, yellow, black, and white. We combed our great-grandmother's land in Hisle, South Dakota, to find sage for his crown, wristlets, and anklets wrapped in red cloth that would protect him while he prayed. We helped him make tobacco ties as offerings to secure on the cottonwood tree before it was placed in the center of the arbor. Auntie Mabel, a former sundancer, guided us every step of the way. The whole family also later committed to feeding the two hundred plus attendees one night during the sundance ceremony. It was a thiwáhe affair.

During the first round, we stood under the arbor, dancing to the drumbeat together, praying with the dancers standing in a circle facing the tree. After the round ended an hour or more later, the dancers stood single file to pray with the tree before leaving the circle. As my son touched the tree, he bowed his head in prayer. Tears filled my eyes in gratitude because I was relieved to see that he knew how to pray and would be safeguarded. I looked back at my grandma and aunties and they were crying too. We didn't need to say a word. We all understood the importance of this moment where Aarron continued the Lakȟóta tradition of sacrificing for himself and for the people.

When Aarron finished his fourth year of sundancing at age eighteen, my youngest son, Brenden, also wanted to pledge to sundance at age fifteen. He had been talking about it for a while, but you must pledge at least a year in advance, and because it's a serious commitment, I waited to ensure he was ready. I remember how Brenden stood before me under the arbor, Aarron next to him and ready to continue the Lakȟóta male duty of guiding his brother through his sundance commitment. I was proud of Aarron because he did this without any prompting from me. I smiled at both of them and handed them the tobacco to take to the helper. Inwardly I wanted to walk with them and guide them through this activity, holding both of their hands like they were little boys, but I knew they needed to do this by themselves as young Lakȟóta men. They left side by side and ran into their father, who went with them to pledge. I was happy to know their father supported them during this moment and I was happy I had followed through on my duty as a Lakȟóta mother to help mend the sacred hoop, thereby ensuring that another generation knew how to pray.

PUSHED OUT BY THE OLD BOYS' CLUB

Back at the church, I was balancing my precarious career as an educator and advocate. I was close to celebrating my seventh work anniversary. I was very well liked and my work was popular, but the last six months at the church had been intense because we were electing a new presiding bishop and the top replacement candidate was Bishop Michael Curry. Bishop Curry is African American, so my white male bosses became paranoid in the lead-up to his coming on. Our employment contracts stated that we had to be "collegial" with our bosses, but how does one define "collegiality"? Well, it was up to these bosses to decide, and if we disagreed with them, that could give them reason to fire us. In essence, I believe they used this clause to silence us and stifle the advocacy work that we were doing. In my view, they wanted to keep us from telling the truth about their one-way decision-making processes, their microaggressions, and the sexist or racially insensitive things they may have said to us. I believe the bosses had ambitions to continue on as staff with Bishop Curry, and they were worried that we might say something to the potential presiding bishop about the quality of their leadership. Even though I was doing all the same things I had always done since I started in my role, it seemed like these white male bosses now took issue with everything I did. I believe I was perceived as a threat because I was a team leader for a diverse group and was known for speaking up.

In my last few months working there, I was preparing a vigil for missing and murdered Indigenous women during the United Nations Commission on the Status of Women at Trinity Cathedral in New York. I found partners in other departments. I communicated directly with the cathedral staff. I ensured updates were provided in my reports to the management. Everybody agreed we should hold the vigil, but a week before the date, my boss said, "You didn't get permission first, so you have to cancel the event. You can have the vigil at the UN Permanent Forum on Indigenous Issues in the future. You know, they were really upset that you didn't go through our office for this event."

It was obvious that this was an excuse, because we had had weekly meetings and it was in my reports that this event was supposed to happen. Plus, this was the first time I had ever been required to include him in planning an event. I said, "But it is not Indigenous people who need to know about missing and murdered Indigenous women. It's the privileged white women at the Commission on the Status of Women who need to know. We have church members who lived in North Dakota who told us they do not feel safe going outside with their kids at night because of work camps nearby. This vigil is important for them, and for starting a dialogue within the church." My bosses would not be swayed, and I suspected it had to do with the oil investments the church had. There was nothing I could do. The next month, they also banned me from attending an event I had planned and was meant to host, the Anglican Indigenous Network gathering, with attendees from Australia, Canada, and New Zealand, and that's when I knew it was time for me to move on.

A few months later, I was miserable at the General Convention, feeling muzzled by an appointment to serve a task force that met for ten days straight during the conference, when a new job opportunity came out of nowhere. I got a call from a headhunter who said I had been recommended for a job as a CEO of Native Americans in Philanthropy. It was like an answer to my prayers. I was able to leave the church on a good note, and wouldn't have to feel like I was walking on eggshells because anything I said could be misinterpreted. I knew that by leaving, I would have the power to speak up. The day after my last day, I wrote a letter to the current presiding bishop. I told her that lately there had been many instances in which working for the church felt disingenuous, and that decisions were being made without consultation or regard to how they would affect the communities we served. I asked her to be with the staff at this time because the morale was very low. This letter gave my colleagues the opportunity to be open about what they were experiencing too. After I left, there was an internal investigation on misconduct, and those white male bosses eventually got fired.

Leaving the church was a difficult decision because I knew it was a spiritual calling, and that the Creator wanted me to be there. The work I was doing felt impactful, but at the same time I was dealing with these toxic white male bosses, and going up against these colonial power structures where only one or two people carried most of the power while everyone else was subservient. We must change the culture of how we

---

"In our fight for our freedom, our collective liberation, Indigenous peoples must center our inherent ways of knowing and strive for balance in all of our relationships—within ourselves, with each other, the four-legged, winged, Mother Earth, and all other living beings. In doing so, we denounce colonizer narratives and notions of power. It is not about, nor has ever been about, building or gaining white man's power. Rather, Lakȟóta people understand the only real strength comes from a connection to our sacred way of life and this restoration of balance." —Tatewin Means, Sisseton Wahpeton Dakota, Oglála Lakȟóta, Inhanktonwan, Executive Director, Thunder Valley Community Development Corporation

---

work together by showing up for each other and uplifting and amplifying omitted narratives.

Still, my time at the Episcopal Church provided me an opportunity to pray, travel the world, study spirituality, and work with so many different cultures with so many different issue areas. The church's ability to come together to advocate for meaningful change is unparalleled and a true force in today's society. I pray the church continues to use their voice to advocate for societal change that ensures all of God's children receive the equity and justice they deserve. I am overwhelmingly grateful for the time I spent surrounded by the love of Tȟuŋkášila and the people who serve Jesus Christ.

After I stopped working for the church, I moved away from Christianity. For eleven years I had spent at least six days a week working with the Church! While there, I learned another way of prayer, ritual, and spirituality. I loved absorbing these different cultural and spiritual aspects, but I never really saw myself as the type of Christian who attends church every Sunday. The church reinforced my Lakȟóta spiritual beliefs and practices more than it supplanted them with new ones. My church equivalent today is hiking Pahá Sapá (the Black Hills), walking by the ocean, smudging, praying on summer and winter solstices, giving offerings of wasná and tobacco, and attending the annual sundance.

When it comes to spirituality, Native Americans can go deep and connect quickly to the source of life. We have a thin veil between the spirit world and this world. Spirituality is the reason we do anything and a lot of us get through our healing through spirituality. It's integral to who we are. Non-Natives don't understand how we view the world and how we look at things differently once we have that connection to spirituality. For many of us, spirituality is so strong we can feel it, and we know it exists.

Lakȟóta Laws

*(Living cultural values through action is how
Lakȟóta people live in integrity)*

"Wóčhekiye" means *prayer, spirituality,
religion,* or *belief.*

"Wówičakȟe" or "wóowotȟaŋla" means
integrity and *honesty.*

---

7 WAYS TO FOLLOW YOUR CALLING

A "calling" is defined as *a strong inner impulse toward a particular
course of action, especially when accompanied by conviction of divine
influence.*[2] As I strengthened my intuition and inner guidance
working at the church, I became aware of my calling, and this
helped me stop trying to control everything all the time. The
Creator has bigger plans for me, even if I do not necessarily
know what they are.

Everyone has a calling, but not everybody pursues it. To
follow your calling, you must be able to recognize when you
are getting called to something. If you learn how to pay attention and chase your calling, then great things can happen. The
Creator sends guiding messages so we can learn and grow.
When I receive a calling, the signs will come in different forms,
usually in sets of three. Maybe my sister mentions something
to me, and then another friend brings it up in conversation,
and then I will stumble upon it in a book—then I know that
it is a sign and I should pay attention and pursue things in
that direction.

Opportunities often arise because I surround myself with
people who are also spiritual and following their callings. When

a friend asks me, "What do you think about this project?" it is because that person sat with it themselves and thought, *This is a project Sarah is supposed to be involved in.* And then when it is offered to me, I may think, *Yeah, I feel like there's something there.* A friend of mine, Dr. David Washington, always says, "Follow the force!" or, as he also calls it, a "there, there." In other words, you feel an unexplainable energy drawing you to the project—there, there. We can learn how to cultivate that knowing inside of ourselves. Below are some tips I have included to help you become aligned with your calling.

1. Identify your sacred alignment. It's usually something that you have been interested in all along, something that makes you feel the happiest and the most at peace.

2. Prioritize creative expression in any form. Journaling has helped me through some of the most challenging times because with it I can process my feelings and make sense of what is going on around me. Since journaling is a deeply reflective process that can reveal themes and connections in your life, it has also helped me identify my calling. When I worked for the church, journaling became another outlet for me to explore my interests, my spirituality, and my relationship to the Creator.

3. Experiment: try new experiences regularly and see how you feel about them. This will assist you with identifying how and what you are called to do in this life.

4. Share your story and find allies. When I began to tell the story of my childhood, I felt empowered from seeing how my storytelling could transform hearts. When I shared my story, allies would show up, and I would pay attention to the people who got it and wanted to do the work. If you find the right people motivated by the intention to create

211

an impact, pathways open and magic happens. My work is not done in a vacuum, but is a culmination of the mentors, teachers, and healers whom I have been blessed to find along the way.

5. Identify how the Creator communicates with you by reflecting and keeping an open mind.
   - Find spiritual leaders who speak to you.
   - Turn off distractions like TV, email, or outside disturbances. I never know what the Creator is going to call me to do next, so I try to keep an attentive mind.
   - Sometimes the Creator is calling me to do things I don't want to do—working for the church was one of these. But I also knew I was called to be there despite challenging moments.
   - Stay open to the signs when they come. Sometimes it's a dream. Sometimes something unusual will happen. For example, if a crow were to show up outside my window and start loudly cawing, I may think, *That crow is not usually there. Why is it here today? Is something bad going to happen? Should I pay attention to something?*
   - When you follow the signs, where they lead you can be quite unexpected. Sometimes it's toward a lesson you need to learn. Sometimes it's toward a pathway of work you are meant to do. You can say no, but often the lesson or pathway will come again until you learn what you need to.

6. Pray for guidance from the Creator. You can manifest things in your life through prayer. I pray for things all the time, like for the Creator to bring people into my life who will help me with whatever project I am currently working on. When I don't know what to do next, I pray and wait.

The Creator will always answer. Open your eyes and stay grounded, and when you see those signs or coincidences . . . FOLLOW!

7. Love yourself enough to listen and trust your own inner guidance from the Creator.

JOURNAL PROMPTS TO HONOR YOUR HEALING

- How did you learn about the Doctrine of Discovery and how does it compare to what you know now?

- Have you ever felt drawn to a particular calling and if so, how did it impact your life?

- What guidance have you received from your elders/Creator/ Higher Power that has helped guide you in your life?

Many Native Americans suffer in silence due to historical trauma. We can move toward healing to free ourselves from pain and suffering. We can heal so our children do not have to suffer. It is not easy; it is a process to work through each aspect of healing.

—EMMA EAGLE HEART–WHITE

CHAPTER 8

Healing Women

BY EMMA

WHEN I WAS thirteen years old, I remember so clearly the image of my iná holding vigil by the kitchen door. It was the early hours before dawn, and she was watching for the abuser, who she expected to come at any moment. She was so badly beaten and so scared. I could feel her fear. I wondered why the gas stations didn't open up until 6 a.m. I saw her standing there alone, staring out over the fields to the main road and back to our driveway. As soon as dawn came, she was gone. She didn't come back to South Dakota for quite a few years afterward. I didn't understand then what I know now. I have always wanted to help people not feel alone when they are at some of their most vulnerable moments in life. I don't want them to feel alone because I know what it is like.

After my master's program, I began work in the domestic violence/sexual violence field with survivors of intimate partner violence on the Oneida Nation of Wisconsin reservation for children and family services. As a survivor of sexual assault, I prefer to use the term "survivor" versus "victim" because I do not want to think of myself as a victim anymore. I stayed in that role for five years. This line of work taught me a lot about the importance of self-care, because as advocates, we feel the need to be strong while supporting survivors. My job was to help survivors file petitions for restraining orders. There are four types of restraining orders: Domestic Abuse, Harassment, Child Abuse, and Individual At Risk. If the judge grants a temporary

Murder is the third-highest cause of death among Native girls and women ten to twenty-four years of age, and the fifth leading cause of death for Native women between twenty-five and thirty-four years of age.[1] The 2016 NIJ Research Report on Violence Against American Indian/Alaska Native Women and Men conducted a phone survey of 1,542 participants in 2010, and their results revealed that 84.3 percent of Native women have experienced violence in their lifetimes. Of those women, 56.1 percent experienced sexual violence; 55.5 percent experienced physical violence by an intimate partner, with 90 percent of those victims reporting being victimized by a non-Native perpetrator; 48.8 percent experienced stalking; 66.4 percent experienced psychological aggression by an intimate partner; and 41.3 percent have been physically injured by intimate partners.[2]

restraining order (TRO), an injunction hearing will be scheduled within fourteen days. We also handled crisis intervention and anger-management counseling, making for a very demanding and intense job.

Working as a domestic violence advocate helped me realize I had to work on my own healing in order to better assist the survivors. I felt I needed to be grounded and present, not only for myself, but for the women I worked on behalf of. I was fortunate to have amazing mentors who taught me about healing, using my voice, and practicing self-care. I loved working as a domestic violence advocate and with all of these strong women because I learned just how much I am not alone. It hurts my heart to think of the many others who have suffered as I have.

FEARS OF RETALIATION

On our reservation, fear of retaliation is a very real threat to survivors who choose to report their abusers. That was the same issue I had with my sexual assault, which is why

I ultimately didn't report it. I knew if I did, nothing would happen—except I would become a target for retaliation by my perpetrator's family. As an advocate, I saw how many survivors did not choose to report their sexual assault or domestic abuse. Often the survivor goes into hiding because of retaliation. Native American extended families are huge, and retaliation can open the survivor up to more abuse within their communities in a myriad of ways.

Within Indian boarding schools, sexual abuse was rampant alongside the many other horrific physical, emotional, and psychological abuses Natives had to endure. Multiple generations were forced to attend these schools, where they were shamed, humiliated, and punished for being Native. Our languages, cultural practices, and spirituality were banned. These schools caused a devastating loss of culture and identity. They have left a mark on our people that is still felt today, and it will take generations to heal due to intergenerational trauma being passed on from one generation to the next. Even now, for many Native survivors, the abuse can almost always be traced back in time through a line of victims who then became perpetrators, with the first act of abuse originating at a boarding school.[3] The Wellbriety Journey to Forgiveness documentary that was part of the Mending Broken Hearts curriculum details how the legacies of domestic violence, addiction, sexual abuse, internalized oppression, and suicide all come from the boarding-school era.[4] There is a lot more healing that needs to be done at a community level and within those family systems to help protect survivors. Most of the time, the perpetrator's family believes the word of their family member against the victim, thus perpetuating victim blaming.

For a survivor, safety for themselves and their families is most important. Going to court is a very difficult decision for any survivor because they know it opens them up to retaliation and they also know that a restraining order is just a piece of paper. We have to explain to them, "We are building your case with documentation so we have a paper trail."

A survivor stays with an abusive partner for many complex reasons. Survivors struggle to leave because of the emotional, exploiting privileged status, medical neglect, deprivation and isolation, economic control, monitoring and stalking, spiritual conflict, legal harassment, psychological torment, sexual coercion and force, physical assault, and grooming and luring they endure and the many threats their abusers have used to trap them. Threats of "I will kill you if you leave" or "I know so-and-so on the police force and I will call them if something happens and they will believe me over you" are too common. As advocates, we do our best to not hold judgment if the survivor decides to go back. Instead, we let them know that we are there no matter what happens. We have always strived to be kind, compassionate, and gentle in this work. We know healing is a process.

"Leaving is not easy. On average, it takes a victim seven times to leave before staying away for good. Exiting the relationship is the most unsafe time for a victim. As the abuser senses that they're losing power, they will often act in dangerous ways to regain control over their victim."[5]

I always would tell survivors, "You are the only one who knows what it is like to be in your abusive relationship." This means they are the expert in their particular cycle of abuse as well as when it is safest for them to leave, and this knowledge helps when we are creating their safety plan. I also would tell them that it's difficult to see the abuse when they are in it. The plans detailed when they could escape, who to ask for help, where in their home was safe, and what important documents they needed. We also assisted with finding them temporary housing when our program was awarded grant funds for this kind of support.

Native women know that nine times out of ten, nothing will happen when they file a police report, so often they will choose not to report it, because doing so can make the abuse ten times worse and still leaves them to deal with their trauma on their own. This is why so many Native women are vulnerable to abuse. Many times, a survivor will say that a restraining order is "just a piece of paper," and they are not wrong. If Native survivors saw more being done to ensure justice in their cases, I think more women would come forward and could then be connected to the resources they need to recover and heal. During my time working in behavioral health, I had abuse survivors come in who were struggling with systemic trauma because they were victimized by the systems that were meant to help them but which instead caused more harm and failed them. Anytime those survivors or one of their family members had to deal with that type of system again—whether police, courts, child protective services, or shelter services— the survivor would become triggered, as the experience would bring them back to the same anxiety and hopelessness they had first felt when no one believed or helped them. With survivors, we see the impacts of broken trust. Most survivors neither trust the police to actually follow through, nor do they trust that domestic violence advocates are unbiased. For example, a survivor will not want to go to a shelter if one of the people working there is related to the abuser's family.

Pine Ridge Reservation is 2.1 million acres, making it the among the largest reservations in the country based on land size.[6] That is a lot of land to cover to make sure people feel safe and have access to adequate services. Time and time again, I have seen tribal police head out on a call for a domestic disturbance and by the time they arrive, the perpetrator has already fled. There are just not enough tribal police and resources going into these areas to help everyone. Some reservations do not have any law enforcement at all. Plus, many inhabitants don't have access to cars, resulting in another obstacle.

Survivors can also face policy barriers to accessing mental

health resources. The health clinic I work for now deals only with Native Americans, and even they still sometimes overlook the impact that certain policies can have on clients. I know everyone working there has a good heart and wants to help, but sometimes, due to their lack of knowledge about our perspective and history, they don't understand how difficult maintaining trust can be for our communities. I am one of the few on our team who can give a Native perspective, and I will speak up when I feel I must.

> As of 2016, there were 5,712 reports of missing Indigenous women and girls in the United States. Only 116 have been registered in the Department of Justice database. In addition, the Urban Indian Health Institute reported in 2018 another 506 unique cases of missing and murdered urban-living Indigenous women and girls across 71 selected cities.[7]

SAFETY FOR ADVOCATES

While I worked in domestic violence, I often did not feel safe. This is one of the downsides of living and working in the community you serve. There were numerous incidents that occurred while I was a DV advocate where perpetrators intentionally attempted to intimidate me. I was often on high alert when I wasn't working and just going about my day-to-day life. I had to pay attention to where I parked my car and who was around me. To whether I was in a public location. Are there cameras to record anything that may happen? Do I feel safe?

As advocates, we did not keep records or documents in order to protect our clients. We didn't want our records to be used against the clients in case the records were ever subpoenaed. We were either trained as lay advocates to represent clients or as expert witnesses in court hearings, as needed. Assessing safety was an essential aspect of our work. I believe there needs to be more funding set aside specifically for security updates to protect advocates and others who work in the field.

Going to court was intense, not only because the advocate's safety was on the line, but also because the abuser and his whole family would glare at us and our clients. Part of my role was trying to shield and protect the client from the abuser and their family. Often I would physically place myself in between the two. Sometimes this also involved getting the judge to acknowledge when an abuser and their family were intimidating the victim; I have seen judges direct the abuser and his family not to even look at the survivor.

In another instance, the abuser knew I was the advocate for his ex-partner and knew my work schedule. He figured out that I left work at five, after everyone else left around 4:30 p.m. I felt my whole body tense up when I saw him sitting out behind the building at the picnic tables, waiting for me to come out. Fortunately, nothing happened, but the message was clear and the fear I experienced was real. I began to park in the front of the building after this. He later attempted to intimidate another work colleague as well. When she went grocery shopping, he parked his car in the parking lot of the store and sat there with his headlights on, waiting and watching for her. He wanted to let us know he could get to us if he wanted.

There is also the spiritual abuse that perpetrators inflict. Many survivors do not speak of it, and rightly so. It is taboo. But it is real and it does happen. People often call it "bad medicine." When I first began working in the domestic/sexual violence field, I was forewarned that this would take place. Many abusers use it to instill fear in their victims, telling them they know how to use bad medicine against the survivors. It can be so devastating to these individuals and their loved ones. We helped survivors navigate the protocols and connected them with spiritual advisors or medicine people.

Many went to ceremonies for healing of this spiritual abuse. I am so thankful for our medicine people and our healing ceremonies. I can't express my gratitude in words, because it is so immense.

The secondhand trauma experienced by advocates is real, and this is why self-care is so important. Advocacy can be triggering to our own traumas. Burnout in this line of work is normal. The fear and worry for yourself and your family can become too much after a while. After five years, I was feeling burned out and like we didn't have enough support.

Per the National Institute of Justice, Native women are 1.5 times more likely to be injured by an intimate partner and are more likely to lack access to critical services than white women.[8]

INTERGENERATIONAL TRAUMA LEADS TO A LEGACY OF ABUSE

Domestic violence and sexual assault often go hand in hand for survivors. This means that many are not experiencing just one, but multiple incidents of trauma. When you include intergenerational and historical trauma, you can understand how trauma for Native American people can become so complex and intertwined. For many of the victims, we ask an array of questions: What was their upbringing like? Were there attachment issues? Were there abandonment issues? Were they raised in a home where abuse was normal? All of these factors play a big part in why a victim might choose to stay in an abusive relationship. As for Native abusers, often they have been abused themselves, thus they are continuing the cycle of abuse.

I first heard about the Mending Broken Hearts program when I started working for the Oneida Domestic Violence program. There were three different instances of people coming to me because they wanted my help to launch Mending Broken

Hearts in our community. The first time I was asked, I said, "I'm overwhelmed in my new position and surely there's someone else who's been here longer who can help you." The second time another person mentioned it to me, I said, "Okay, what the heck? Why isn't someone doing this yet?" Then the third time I was asked directly by Kateri, who is the daughter of Don Cohyis, the founder of White Bison. She messaged me on social media and asked if I could help bring this healing program to Oneida. I realized I was the one supposed to help with this. I had to laugh at myself because Tȟuŋkášila had been trying to tell me and I didn't understand at first. It wasn't difficult and just involved connecting community programs to bring Mending Broken Hearts to the Oneida Nation of Wisconsin, where it still continues today. White Bison taught us how to be facilitators for this program and it was amazing. They offer healing programs on quite a few reservations now. Currently, they have numerous community programs throughout Wisconsin, and the completion rate for that program is 99 percent.

The program is rooted in Native American beliefs and spirituality, and it emphasizes our connection to our culture and traditions as the medicine we need to heal our communities. I saw changes in those who went through the program. It really did help them move through some things, grieve, and heal in whichever ways they were able and ready to. It changed how they were able to handle different situations. They understood that they needed to work through the intergenerational and historical parts of their complex traumas to be able to cope better with the other stressors and traumas in their lives. The program also deals directly with the negative self-talk and beliefs many Natives struggle with, as well as many sexual abuse survivors.

The first time I went through the program, I was trained to become a facilitator. After that, we held the training with the survivors and support staff at the White Buffalo Calf Women's

Society shelter. The women at the shelter are from the Pine Ridge and Rosebud areas. They have fled their partners and are living at the shelter as they transition and find a place to live. Most have harassment and restraining orders against their abusers and they come to the shelter to get away and stay safe. We shared with them how survivors tend to wear different masks to hide their pain and grief, as well as how to look at their belief systems to understand how it shaped who they are today. They also worked on their trauma timelines, an exercise where we put on a timeline all the different traumas we experienced over the course of our lives and draw a line for each one, the length of which indicates how deep each hurt was. After, we made tobacco ties and brought them up to a butte, a local sacred site near the shelter, to set them out. It was beautiful to witness. A wiping the tears ceremony was also taking place the same day at Pe'Sla in the Black Hills, which is another sacred site.

Working in domestic violence helped me with personal healing too. A colleague named Vange, who had worked in domestic violence for roughly fifteen years, became my mentor and older sister. She had so much experience and was so positive. She taught me about self-care and being kind and gentle to myself. She helped me to trust myself and my own intuition again. Since many survivors struggle with negative self-talk, we often second-guess ourselves and become unsure of our decisions. I remember worrying about what others thought about me and she said, "Emma, they don't KNOW you." This helped to take the power away from my anxiety. We both followed traditional ways. Vange filled the Oneida Long House ways as an OnΛyote?a·ká (People of the Standing Stone). I really felt there was a purpose for my being in that field of work at that time. I felt that Tȟuŋkášila was guiding me to where I needed to be to heal and, through this, I was also helping others to heal. Working there made me strong within myself, so I could be strong for the women I was supporting. A lot of survivors don't feel like they are strong, but they are. I remember how I always struggled with just trying to survive daily, and it helped me to acknowledge my healing and to honor myself and how far I have come in my healing process. Working with other survivors showed me that I have been through a lot and still made it this far. There is a reason for why I am still here.

It is extremely difficult to change things within the Native community when there's still so much healing that needs to be done. Help and resources are available, but it's still not enough compared to the level of need. The history of boarding schools and cultural genocide that Natives have endured means we start our healing journeys with multiple layers of trauma. I always tell my clients that there can be many aspects to our healing. We think we are done with it, only to discover another aspect of the hurt hidden underneath. Healing is complex and interwoven, and we don't always know why we feel the way that we feel. Without sufficient resources available, it is hard for Natives to process all the layers of complex trauma. In addition to injustice from all directions, we also face lateral oppression within our communities. It is really challenging. I think that we are increasingly moving toward healing, but it has taken a long way to get where we are and there is so much more help that our communities need.

There needs to be more emphasis on incorporating cultural healing techniques within the behavioral health model. Often non-Native counterparts do not understand our cultural traditions, protocols, spirituality, or worldview. This is why I found White Bison's programs to be so impactful. Native spirituality is at the core of healing work. It takes a community approach to healing, which is aligned with the collectivist worldview of Indigenous cultures. We thrive best together when we strengthen our traditional ways. Many are still reclaiming their cultural identities. *Journey to Forgiveness* uses a healing-forest analogy to describe the healing work we are doing together as a community. Each one of us represents a tree within our community, and the nutrients we thrive on are our connections to culture, spirituality, ceremonies, language, and elders' teachings. Traditionally, we knew how to care for our children and one another, so by rediscovering our traditional ways, we can begin to heal and thrive again as a community, or a "forest."

> **Native women are murdered at more than ten times the national average on some reservations.**[9]

MURDERED AND MISSING INDIGENOUS WOMEN AND GIRLS

Growing up, Sarah and I heard many stories about women and girls who would go missing. We heard stories about women being dragged through the fields by pickup trucks and dying. Or about other women going missing out in the Badlands, never to be seen or heard from again. We heard so many stories like these that over time, we became numb. We began to expect these kinds of things.

Still, when I first learned that over 6,000 Native women and girls have gone missing since 2016,[10] I found it hard to comprehend. I was shocked by the number, and it made me realize how long the crisis has remained hidden. It is mentioned in protests here and there, but is it on the mainstream media? No. Not really. Sarah is trying to change that and is creating a docuseries. In the sizzle reel she was prepping, one clip shows all the missing and murdered Indigenous women's and girls' faces at the same

> **In South Dakota, a state database for 2021 shows that out of the 102 missing people reported, 68 are Native American—despite the fact that Native Americans only make up 9 percent of the state's population.**[11] **Pine Ridge Reservation is also in the top five reservations with missing incidents reported to the National Center for Missing & Exploited Children.**[12]

time. Seeing their faces all on one screen was overwhelming because I could finally comprehend just how extensive the loss is to our communities.

As shocking as the above statistics are, these figures are considered an undercount due to the incompleteness of the data involved. It is not uncommon for police officers to misclassify the ethnicity of Native victims, and in some police databases, if race is left unfilled then it defaults to "white," thus erasing our existence in the data.[13] Further, police officers can be dismissive of family members' worries because they do not give the same time and attention to missing Native women and girls. Officers will also often mislabel the cause of death as "accidental." These data gaps impact how officers handle and follow up with these cases and as a result, many of them slip through the cracks.[14] The Justice Department has failed to collect data, and no national database has been established on missing and murdered Indigenous women and girls, making it impossible for us to know the true scope of this epidemic.

According to the US Department of Justice, 67 percent of sexual assaults experienced by Native women are perpetrated by non-Natives, 80 percent of sex offenses on reservations are perpetrated by non-Natives, and 86 percent of all reported sex offenses against Native women are perpetrated by non-Natives.[15]

Clearly, we have a major epidemic of non-Natives coming onto tribal land to commit violent crimes against our women and girls. Incidents of these crimes rises when "man camps," which house transient male workers in extractive industries like logging, mining, and oil, are located near tribal lands.[16] Native Americans are 2.5 times more likely to experience violent crimes and 2 times more likely to experience rape or sexual assault compared to all other races.[17]

Tribal nations are sovereign nations, and we have the right to protect our women and children; however, violent crimes fall under federal jurisdiction, rendering us powerless to enact our sovereignty. Instead, we must navigate a federal legal system that seems intentionally blind to the epidemic of violence we face. Federal law enforcement often fails to consult with tribal nations while investigating, which further shreds any remaining trust that Natives have in the legal system.

The problem of murdered and missing Native women and girls is a continuation of colonialism and genocide. It is important for everyone to learn Native American history and how we continue to persist in the face of all these interlocking crises. When these issues are hidden from plain view, progress is stymied and people suffer. Ignoring history makes it easy for the government and people to overlook when our women and girls go missing. We have been here since the beginning despite thousands of attempts to end our way of life. We are still here, and we are at a pivotal point in America because we can no longer be complicit in the system. For so long, we have been hidden and invisible, but we have a voice and we will be heard. The success of our next chapter will come when mainstream society truly understands the issues and the history of our people.

Without the tireless and persistent efforts of many of our Indigenous sisters, there is a good chance that this crisis would have never seen the light of day, and would have instead stayed relegated to hushed whispers in women's circles on the reservations. Traditionally, Indigenous women held high positions of power and respect within our communities. Many North American tribes were matrilineal and matriarchal before colonization came in and disrupted our traditional systems by imposing patriarchy and hierarchy and trying to erase our cultural connections through cultural genocide by way of boarding schools. Indigenous women, and all women of color, understand the harms of a colonial legacy that perpetuates and normalizes racism. Harmful stereotypes often reduce us to subhuman caricatures. However, as Indigenous women we are rising to say, "Enough is enough!"

Sheila North Wilson, a Canadian journalist and former Grand Chief of Manitoba Keewatinowi Okimakanak Inc., noticed that even within her traditional community, only the women were talking among themselves about murdered and missing Indigenous women and girls. She started the hashtag #MMIW in 2012 to garner interest for this epidemic. This hashtag started a grassroots movement led by Indigenous women that captured the attention of law enforcement, legislators, and the public, resulting in the Canadian government initiating a national inquiry in December 2015.[18] Further, this movement has garnered attention internationally and propelled Native American leaders and organizers in the United States to advocate on social media, build and maintain their own community databases, start youth initiatives, and hold red-dress exhibitions, marches, and vigils.

In 1994, the US federal government took its first swing at trying to address the rampant violence on tribal lands with the passing of the Violence Against Women Act (VAWA). The act was the first to allocate resources to states and tribes to help prevent and improve responses to domestic violence, dating violence, sexual assault, and stalking. It was reauthorized in 2000, 2005, 2013, and as of 2021, it is waiting in the Senate for a reauthorization vote after lapsing in 2019. Before 2013, tribes were not permitted to prosecute non-Natives for domestic and dating violence; however, with the reauthorization of VAWA in 2013, a provision was added to allow tribal courts to claim jurisdiction over non-Native suspects who commit violent crimes against Native women living on tribal lands. Prior to that change, when a non-Native committed a crime on a reservation, the only thing a tribal officer could do was escort the perpetrator off of tribal lands.

Unfortunately, the provision did not go far enough, because gaps remain in the law. For example, as of 2021, it excludes the 229 federally recognized Indian tribes in Alaska. Further, the law only recognizes tribal jurisdiction for a limited set of crimes, thus doing nothing to close the gaps for non-Natives who commit sexual assault, stalking, trafficking, or child abuse crimes on tribal lands. The federal government classifies these as major crimes that fall under their jurisdiction.[19] The latest version of VAWA, awaiting reauthorization, has been strengthened by permitting tribal courts to prosecute perpetrators of sexual violence, stalking, and sex trafficking. It also includes crimes against children and tribal officers—neither of which were covered in any of the previous versions of VAWA.[20] Further, the latest reauthorization also requires the attorney general and the secretary of the interior to compile annual reporting and statistics on missing and murdered Indigenous women and girls.[21]

On March 18, 2021, Deb Haaland made history by becoming the first Native American woman to serve in a presidential cabinet as secretary of the interior. She understands the urgency around this crisis and wore a traditional ribbon skirt at her swearing in as secretary (ribbon skirts have become a symbol honoring our missing and murdered Indigenous women). Only two weeks into her new role, Haaland announced the creation of the Missing and Murdered Unit within the Bureau of Indian Affairs. The unit will focus on analyzing and solving missing and murdered cases involving Native Americans. It will work alongside tribal governments to solve these cases as well as to coordinate resources, allocate funding for training and equipment, and provide tribal governments with access to federal criminal databases.[22] Hopefully, a newly strengthened VAWA alongside a dedicated Missing and Murdered Unit will go a long way to ensure accurate data collection and provide the much-needed support to tackle this crisis.

Our communities know that the solutions to this crisis go beyond the legal and penal codes. We need a real commitment of resources to help survivors heal. Too often I have seen survivors who are ready and want to go to a shelter discover instead that there are no available beds. Having more shelters would go a long way toward protecting our communities. Increased grants for culturally informed healing programs alongside mental health services are another need. The Mending Broken Hearts program has helped the Oneida community as well as a lot of other surrounding Native communities, but there need to be a lot more healing programs, as well as more education on the different dynamics of domestic abuse. Physical well-being is an important aspect of healing as well. When I worked as a DV advocate and survivors were starting out on their own and trying to heal, we would try to get them access to high-quality nutritious food, aromatherapy, sage, and other self-care stuff they could use at home.

Many reservations do not have an AMBER Alert system to caution the community when a child goes missing. In missing-persons cases, the first seventy-two hours are the most critical for following up on leads and ensuring safety of the victim. Improving broadband and communications systems will assist emergency responders during that sensitive time period and could help solve missing-persons reports before they become murder investigations.

There also needs to be more training for police officers who work with Native populations because I had an incident with the police that impacted me and an advocate colleague for a long time. The incident involved my reporting child abuse. The police officer that got the report went directly to the abuser's house and told them my name, where I worked, and that I reported the incident. I think the officer was new and didn't know the repercussions we would face. My name is out there once a case goes to court and the person is prosecuted, but before that happens, my information should remain private, as it makes me a target within the community again. This oversight from the officer caused me pain for years.

If the police officer had known how to handle the situation, it could have helped me avoid the aftermath of his revealing my identity to the abuser. After that incident, now I make sure to put "Do not disclose the name of the person reporting" into every report I prepare. It's happened to many of my colleagues as well. I share this information with many other providers too. We are healers invested in seeing our communities heal, but we are also community members within small, tight-knit communities and we still must face and interact with many of our clients outside of work settings. Police officers need to be sensitive to this fact before revealing any information that can identify us and make our jobs all the more difficult by forcing us to deal with retaliation and fallout.

Many Native Americans want to work in jobs that will help their people, but working in the community can feel like a double-edged sword because people know you. As a community member, I am invested in seeing my community do well and heal, but sometimes that puts me in the awkward position of having to report abuses that are impacting community members. There is no separation for Native healers who work within their communities. At times, my expertise can be called into question because I am seen as just another community member.

Even worse was when I had to liaison with someone within the community who was related to a survivor I was representing. While doing my job as an advocate, most times people were friendly and helpful, but occasionally I called somewhere and got someone who had some major attitude toward me. I would ask my coworker, "Is this person related to any of the abusers?" and she would reply, "Oh, yeah. They are related to so-and-so." I had to be mindful of how community members could retaliate through work too. There are all these little ways that I could be retaliated against and not even know it.

Since local, state, and federal levels of government have all done a horrendous job of collecting and reporting the data on missing and murdered Indigenous women and girls, the concept of Indigenous data sovereignty was adopted by the National Congress of American Indians in 2018. What that means is that as sovereign nations, we have the right to govern the collection, ownership, and application of our own data, including the data collected on our people. Urban Indian Health Institute, which conducted the study on missing and murdered urban-dwelling Natives, has been leading the way in data collection. The tagline on their website reads, "Decolonizing data, for Indigenous people, by Indigenous people." It was through their study that they were able to identify 506 unique cases of missing and murdered Indigenous women and girls across 71 US cities.[23] Data sovereignty will ensure that we can accurately report on this crisis. Data should reside in the communities that are impacted by the statistics because we are the most invested in seeing these crises resolved.

We also need to increase opportunities for Native women and girls through employment opportunities, business loans, and free postsecondary education. People often assume that we get free education already, but we do not. Sarah and I both have student loans. Native women have always had to fight for survival and to be respected, so we can live safe and care-free lives. Providing opportunities to our women gives them the tools to become resilient and self-sufficient, thus making them safer too. And since many of our tribes are matriarchal, taking care of our women goes a long way to strengthen the support and connections within the rest of our communities. Plus, many of us want to be involved in helping our communities to heal. Getting access to education and support would help us unleash our great capacity to be healers.

When talking to my iná, I told her one of my main motivations to write the book was to share about my rape as a teenager. She said, "I've been raped too." She proceeded to tell us how she had been at a friend's house in Colorado when a friend of a friend raped her. But somehow, after all she had been through with her head trauma, she found the courage to go through with the rape kit. It must have been her previous training as a tribal police officer.

She said she received a phone call a few years later from officers in Colorado telling her they had found a match for the DNA in her sample. They asked her to testify because they had found he had raped more than one woman and was in prison. She asked for a week to work with her memory and was given that time to share her experience. He was convicted and received additional prison time. My mother received justice. I told her I was so proud of her. I know how hard it is to go through with the police proceedings.

Somehow, someway, my mother found healing and justice … despite all odds.

Lakȟóta Laws

*(Living cultural values through action is how
Lakȟóta people live in integrity)*

"Wóčhekiye" means *prayer, spirituality,
religion,* or *belief.*

"Wówičakȟe" or "wóowothaŋla" means
integrity and *honesty.*

---

7 WAYS TO HONOR YOUR SACREDNESS

1. Honor your experience. Do not minimize your trauma.

2. Seek forgiveness of yourself and others, as you are able to.

3. Be still, listen, and pray. Set your intention. Express gratitude to Tȟuŋkášila for your healing.

4. Seek spiritual guidance from elders or medicine people so you can learn rituals and traditional teachings as they relate to your sacredness.

5. Begin a new legacy of honoring sacredness within your family, relatives, people, and community.

6. Use breathwork to breathe through your pain in order to release it. You may use the 7-4-7-4 breathwork exercise or another breathwork exercise you like.

7. Try the child-spirit meditation: First smudge with sacred medicines, such as sage or cedar. Sit or lie down in a comfortable position. Pray to Tȟuŋkášila and/or set your intention. Then imagine your child self from your earliest memory where you felt safe and loved. Cradle yourself and go to your child. Tell them all the things that will happen. Anything you want them to know about how their life will be. Hold them and be still. Love this child, your child self. Let them know it is time to go and when you are ready, you may set them down where you picked them up. Tell them you love them. You may return as many times as you need.

JOURNAL PROMPTS TO HONOR YOUR HEALING

- What beliefs did you hold prior to beginning your healing? If you are just now starting your journey, what beliefs do you currently hold?

- What are the traditions that the women in your family continue? How do you honor these traditions?

- Who helped you understand your trauma?

- What actions can you take to honor your traumatic experience?

She rises
to paint her sister's warrior face in red.

She stands
serenely in the center of the circle of thousands.

She prepares
the altar of four directions upon the concrete earth.

She kneels
as sage smoke circles from the abalone to the sky.

She smudges
herself confidently as though she is home in this stone city.

She nods
to her sister holding the drum to sing the prayer song.

She circles
clockwise to purify the people with cedar smoke.

She prays
and the energy is electric as we all hold hands.

She smiles
in joy with all of the people gathered.

She dances
a round dance of celebration with the people, as if we already won the fight.

She knows
we won the battle
because
we are still here, we are still here, we are still here.

—SARAH EAGLE HEART

CHAPTER 9

Rising

BY SARAH

IN 2018, I was invited to attend a retreat in Montana with thirty diverse women who work in climate justice. We were seated in a circle while nearby, dragonflies flitted over the small lake reflecting the sky and the sun set over the mountains. The amazing community of biologists, scientists, nonprofit executives, media strategists, and entrepreneurs began to introduce themselves and share why they were there. Each woman who spoke had a clear hourglass filled with sand placed in front her and every time the minute was up, the facilitator would yell "NEXT!" regardless of whether or not the speaker was finished. (A few years later, when this group was struggling to stay together, I jokingly told friends I didn't have many expectations from the group because that first circle had told me everything I needed to know.)

The blatant disrespect was communicated with every jolt of "NEXT!" and it angered me, and believe me, I said something that day when it was my turn to speak. I was the only Native American in this circle and given my upbringing around collective sharing, this behavior went against everything I knew about listening in talking circles with humility and respect. To tell you the truth, this is the problem with Western society these days. No one wants to listen to one another. No one wants to work through conflict. No one has patience. I fight to have patience, too, especially when Mother Earth is screaming for everyone to listen while she burns and tribal communities carry the brunt of the violence in their bodies.

Ever since my high school protest, my destiny and career have been intertwined with my sisters in our many fights to save the world. I have organized, allied, worked, and prayed with women since the very beginning. However, women's movements have a long way to go in achieving the type of success we all dream of. I've seen the same disruptive scenarios play out over and over again: cultural values are pitted against the rules of the nonprofit industrial complex; inciting cultural clashes; being unwilling to truly listen or learn; reinforcing hierarchy, competitiveness, scarcity thinking; and wielding power negatively. In order to move forward, we need to learn how to address harm in a good way so we don't keep replicating unhealthy patterns. Healing requires truth-telling.

THE MOVEMENT OF MOVEMENTS

In 2016, I first heard the phrase "movement of movements" from Dr. David Washington, a former consultant. This term is intended to build unity by acknowledging that social, economic, racial, and environmental justice are intertwined. Across the country, we are seeing groups collaborating in powerful ways to push cultural, narrative, and policy changes toward increased equity and inclusion for all. I believe that the formation and sustainability of a "movement of movements" will be critical to advancing social justice and equity conversations, and that Native Americans need to be deeply embedded in all aspects of this movement.

On January 21, 2017, just one day after President Trump's inauguration, we saw a clear resurgence of this unified movement of movements when an estimated 5 million women and their allies held marches around the world to advocate for their rights. This was the Women's March on Washington, and it would go down as the largest one-day protest the world has ever seen. A total of 3.3 million people marched in the United States across 653 locations, with 1.2 million people marching in Washington, DC—three times the number of attendants at Trump's inauguration.[1]

I started to hear rumblings about a women's march shortly after Trump's election win in November 2016. I began calling some of my Indigenous contacts and asked, "Is anybody going? Are Indigenous women going?" Everyone said no. The organizers were in the process of naming who would be on the "Conveners' Table," which had been created to ensure the authenticity and inclusivity of the Women's March. So far, there was no Native representation at the table, and I felt that this event was too important not to have Native women participating. I began to send emails.

Indigenous voices offer a unique and authentic perspective that challenges this country's civic and moral foundations. Many communities of color share the same issues and the same narratives, both harmful and helpful. It's vital that we unpack these societally imposed narratives and make clear the collective impacts they have so we can work on changing them. Through this movement of movements, we can create a shared space for truth by truly acknowledging one another's truths and having one another's backs in the struggle.

The organizers for the march aimed to create a platform based on "intersectional feminism," a term coined by Dr. Kimberlé Crenshaw that acknowledges that women do not all face the same amount of prejudice and oppression, not when we take racism, ableism, classism, and LGBTQIA+ issues into account. Having an intersectional identity means that the amount of discrimination you face is magnified. Whenever I think about intersectional feminism, it is impossible for me not to be reminded of truth and healing. Our common bond is that all of us have experienced what it's like to have our truths denied, misrepresented, or rendered completely invisible. If we want our truths to be recognized, then it is our responsibility to also recognize the truths of other marginalized groups. Through reciprocal acknowledgment of each other's identities, stories, and traumas, we can begin to heal.

A couple weeks after those initial rumblings, Carmen Perez, one of the four co-chairs for the Women's March, reached out to my friend and colleague Chrissie Castro and asked, "Will you be on the women's table, the Conveners' Table?" Chrissie told her, "I'm not going to do it by myself. If I'm going to do it, I want to bring my sisters with me." Carmen agreed, and Chrissie called me first to invite me to join her. Together we handpicked our team: Deborah Parker, Rosalee Gonzales, and Anathea Chino. Each leader held specific knowledge on Indigenous women's rights, had advocacy expertise or policy-development experience, and/or had worked directly with grassroots communities. Kandi Mossett was also organizing a group to march and we merged our groups. Bethany Yellowtail would later decide to join the collective too. We all became the cofounders of Indigenous Women Rise Collective (IWR). Our main mission was to raise awareness for our missing and murdered Indigenous women at the march, as well as to stand:

- united on behalf of Indigenous women and peoples;
- for the rights to attain health and to live free from all forms of violence and bodily harm;
- for protection of our land, air, water, and sacred sites;
- for the United States' implementation of the UN Declaration on the Rights of Indigenous Peoples, and for its honoring of existing treaty rights and promises made with regard to health, education, and land rights;

- for reclaiming our historical, cultural, and social inheritance, and eliminating the structural barriers between our Indigenous youth and their opportunities to succeed;
- for investment in Indigenous peoples' development of healthy and sustainable communities; and
- in solidarity with all marginalized groups for the protection of our collective rights, safety, health, and families.

BETHANY'S THOUSAND BANDANAS

Artists have long played a role in social movements by creating branding and iconography that have become the symbols for many historical change-making campaigns. I was in talks with my social-impact consultants about gifts we could give out at the march. We wanted something visual, impactful, and artistic to raise awareness for Indigenous women's issues—similar to the famous "Hope" poster that became emblematic of Barack Obama's 2008 presidential campaign. My consultant, Dr. David Washington of Partnerships for Purpose, said, "It's going to be cold in January. Perhaps it could be something you wear."

During the Standing Rock protests, I went there to help educate tribal staff on philanthropy and connect them with funders. I remember seeing the frontline protesters wearing bandanas to cover their faces from being teargassed by the police. That was the moment I said, "I think it's a bandana."

We needed an artist to do the design, and I immediately thought of my friend Bethany Yellowtail. Her designs are both stunning and contemporary, and are inspired by her Crow and Northern Cheyenne heritage. Bethany returned my phone call on Christmas Eve while she was driving home for the holidays. I told her, "I have this idea for the Women's March, and I think having your art there would be amazing. I'm picturing the woman warrior on a bandana."

Bethany had created this beautiful ledger silk scarf from artist John Isaiah Pepion's artwork of four Native women adorned in warbonnets and dancing the Shoshone Warbonnet Dance. It is a dance performed to honor the young leaders of our Indigenous nations. Participating in the dance is the highest honor for Crow women and is also the only time a Crow woman wears the sacred warbonnet. Given the political climate and the coming together of these diverse women to march, I couldn't think of a more appropriate image. Bethany said yes and we adapted her original design of the women onto a turquoise cotton bandana with the women depicted in a circle.[2]

THE DAY OF THE MARCH

In New York City, in front of the National Museum of the American Indian, one thousand Indigenous women gathered in a circle. Our chorus of voices cut through the air, calling out to our sisters both present and past, and to our future sisters whom we haven't met yet. Meanwhile, the madness and swell of the crowds swirled on; I was stunned by the sheer number of diverse people who came to march. An elder medicine woman prepared a simple altar on a blanket, a seashell filled with burning sage and an eagle feather to fan the smoke. Each one of my sisters proudly wore the turquoise bandanas we had created for them. Despite the steady stream of people moving around us, it felt as if time stood still, and I could feel the Creator working through us all. I clasped hands with the two women on either side of me, and then we bowed our heads, closed our eyes, and began to pray.

After our prayer, we broke the circle and descended, single file, into the crowd while singing the "Women's Warrior Song," which is "a song that does not belong to one family or nation but was gifted by Martina Pierre of the Líl'wat Nation to bring strength to all those fighting for justice."[3] We sang it to highlight the issue of our missing and murdered Indigenous women. The crowd parted at the sound of our song and we moved to the beat of our drums like a river flowing calmly through the storm of people. I looked out at the sea of faces, many framed by pink pussy hats. Native women are raised to value modesty so we would never wear pussy hats, but I appreciated the unity, their support for us. Together, we were a multitude of diverse and beautiful women. Their smiling, teary-eyed faces are etched into my memory as a reminder of our collective strength.

I believe Indigenous peoples will never be conquered because my sisters will never give up. Their spirits have continued to hold on to our culture despite the pain intentionally inflicted on them and their aunties, their mothers, and their grandmothers. Their hearts have guided them to protect what is most sacred, our wakȟáŋheža, our *children*.

> Cheyenne proverb: "A nation is not conquered until the hearts of its women are on the ground. Then it is finished, no matter how brave its warriors, or how strong their weapons."[4]

I remember how Deborah Parker yelled into the megaphone: "When your communities are under attack, what do you do?"

The women shouted, "Stand up! Fight back!"

That day, we succeeded in creating visibility for our murdered and missing Indigenous women. Bethany's bandana was front and center as the symbol. Beyond this, several founders of Indigenous Women Rise served on the Conveners' Table, advocating for inclusion on the Women's March Unity Principles. They addressed the diversity of participants and spoke to how women are impacted by a multitude of intersecting social justice and human rights issues. This march felt like a huge victory for Indigenous women, and I am so incredibly proud of the hard work we did as a collective to pull it off.

MTV VIDEO MUSIC AWARDS

In 2017, Jimmy "Taboo" Gomez (from the hip-hop group Black Eyed Peas) was nominated for a VMA in the newly created category of "Best Fight Against the System" anthem. He wrote and recorded a song with the "Magnificent Seven" Native artists from different tribes—Zack "Doc" Battiest, Spencer Battiest, Emcee One, Drezus, PJ Vegas, Supaman, Natalia Pitti, a.k.a. MyVerse—entitled "Stand Up / Stand N Rock #NoDAPL," which was written to show solidarity with the Standing Rock protesters. Taboo is of Shoshone and Mexican heritage, and has quickly established himself as a social justice activist. He asked Bethany and I if we would like to join him on the blue carpet for the 2017 MTV Video Music Awards (VMAs) so we could raise visibility for murdered and missing Indigenous women. I immediately said yes, because it is critical to showcase Indigenous issues on large and far-reaching platforms. In the spirit of inclusion, I extended the invite to the rest of the IWR cofounders.

At this point, Taboo and I had already worked together for over a year. He was venturing into philanthropy and wanted to leverage my expertise. We have been fortunate to work with incredible people like Taboo who can share their powerful platforms and help us advocate for change to a larger, more mainstream audience than we could speak to on our own.

The day of the VMAs, Bethany and I got ready together with some help from the professional beauty team that she usually hires for her fashion shows. I wore a skirt designed by Bethany with the warrior-women print, a beaded belt that belonged to my great-grandma, and these beautiful diamond earrings loaned to me by Lakȟóta designer, dear friend, and entrepreneur Twila True of Twila True Fine Jewelry. I felt the strength of my community in these clothes, which had nods to both my historical ancestors and my contemporary Indigenous sisters.

248

Taboo asked Bethany and me to stand on either side of him for the press junket and photos. He asked us if we could speak to the cameras about Indigenous issues but reminded us that it was an MTV audience, so the questions would be pop culture–related. I am no stranger to public speaking, but rarely had I spoken at anything as off-the-cuff as this event would be. Both Bethany and I were very nervous. The other cofounders were supposed to meet us at the studios so we could go over the plans before heading to the VMAs, but they all were flying in that day and still hadn't arrived. I didn't end up seeing them until we were leaving for the VMAs.

Taboo worked hard to gather four tickets, but there were fifteen people in our entire group, including IWR cofounders and the Magnificent Seven, so we were eleven tickets short. We devised a plan to rush the carpet while singing the Women's Warrior Song. We thought security wouldn't stop us and ask for all our tickets and luckily enough, it worked! We looked beautiful. We sang the song reverently to the sound of the hand drum as we walked slowly toward the entrance and were welcomed inside. It was a big victory to have the issue of Missing Murdered Indigenous Women and Girls amplified at MTV.

On the blue carpet, I could feel the energy from the crowds all around; it was electrifying. The audience was cheering and there were cameras everywhere. As soon as we walked in, Taboo yelled, "Everybody stay together!" However, inside a star-studded affair full of musical icons, this was easier said than done. Some of our party broke off to talk to other musicians and take selfies, but Bethany and I were all business—we had taken to heart the opportunity Taboo had gifted, so we stayed next to him the entire time.

We had to wait to enter the main blue carpet where all the photographers for the major publications were. The MTV staff kept attempting to usher our group around the main photo opportunity, but we held firm and we were one the last groups to get the iconic photographs with the MTV logo backdrop. There were at least a hundred different photographers taking pictures. The cameramen kept trying to get our attention, telling us where to look and snapping photos. There were tons of big celebrities on the carpet, but I was too anxious psyching myself up for the interviews to even pay attention to them. I kept thinking, *What are they going to ask? What should I say? What's going to happen?* Let's just say that for me, it wasn't a fun experience, despite how glamorous and high profile it all was.

The layout of the blue VMA carpet is in an oval, with the audience in the middle and all the cameras on the outside, pointing in. The first ten cameras are for the major networks, and the others are for local and international networks. Taboo's manager was running ahead to see who wanted to interview us, then returning to tell us which networks to stop and talk to.

In each interview, I spoke on the issues of missing and murdered Indigenous women, violence against women, violence against the earth, and access to health care and education for women. I stuck to these talking points while somehow relating them to pop culture, as Taboo had requested. Taylor Swift had just been in the news for the sexual assault case involving the Denver-based DJ who grabbed her butt, so we fielded lots of questions regarding the incident. The film *Wind River* had just come out, too, which told a powerful story set on a Wyoming reservation about a young Native woman who is sexually assaulted and murdered. The film was controversial in Native communities because the Native female lead is not an enrolled tribal member. Many of the interviewers made comparisons between our messaging and the film's premise. Thankfully, despite my nerves, I made it through the press junket without any embarrassing blunders.

After the media blitz, we received tickets for our seats to watch the awards show, but none of us were sitting together. Taboo didn't like that, so he suggested we leave early and grab

dinner instead. So we went to a Mexican restaurant to celebrate. Some family and friends came with us, and we took over
the restaurant's patio. During dinner, somebody looked at their
phone and saw that Taboo and the Magnificent Seven had all
won a VMA. MTV had awarded a Moon Person to all nomi-
nees in the "Best Fight Against the System" category. The band
had been skeptical of their chances of winning, so the news
came as a big surprise. That night, Natives from all over the
country won a VMA Moon Person. Immediately we all started
hooting and hollering, and quite a few of us became teary-
eyed—including me.

It was a privilege to share the message of IWR with a large
mainstream audience and an honor to share the carpet with
Taboo and the Magnificent Seven. This was a real victory for
Native visibility and for issues that impact us—something I
have been fighting for all my life. I felt excited about where
our activism would take us. When we started IWR, we thought
it would only last for the Women's March; I had no idea we
would find ourselves at the VMAs with Taboo. I was so proud
of this collective of beautiful Indigenous women sharing their
talents for the betterment of all Indigenous women. It was the
first time Indigenous women had collectively stepped into the
spotlight, not only at the VMAs but also on social media, calling
all of our Indigenous sisters to use the hashtag #Indigenous-
WomenRise. This whole process was beautiful and wonderful.
But it was startling how quickly solidarity among the IWR
cofounders fell apart after that.

CONFLICT AFTER THE VMAS

A few weeks after the VMAs, I was on a work conference call
with Elder Sandy White Hawk. We both were on the call early,
waiting for the others to join, when she said, "Sarah, I have

to tell you, I'm so proud of you. I saw that you were on the VMAs. It was incredible to see all these Indigenous women—strong women—at the VMAs ... and that's when I began to pray for you."

I was surprised, and asked, "Why?"

"I know what it's like. You start doing this great work, you get more visibility, and then you open yourself up to negativity. But I know how hard you work. I know there is a lot of after-hours time that you have committed. People don't understand that you're opening doors, and that it takes a lot of work behind the scenes to make this happen. But I want you to know that I see you. I'm watching you and I'm cheering you on—and I'm praying for you."

I replied, "It's funny you say that because, yeah, I've experienced that."

"Well, you just have to continue. We need you to continue doing this work," she said.

For me, it was really important to hear an elder remind me of my commitment to my community and that this commitment is bigger than my individual feelings of hurt, anger, and betrayal—all of which had come up since the amazing high of being at the VMAs.

The night of the VMAs, I thought everything went great. We were all able to get in despite not having enough tickets. Taboo and the Magnificent Seven won the award. We made a powerful statement. We had incredible photo opportunities and a chance to raise awareness by speaking to the media. The very next morning, the plan was that all of the IWR cofounders would gather to discuss an upcoming podcast and the future of IWR. I showed up to the meeting at the scheduled time. Chrissie was distracted by fielding calls for Los Angeles's Indigenous Peoples' Day. The other cofounders arrived an hour and a half late for the meeting. We had a lot to do, so we sat down and started the meeting immediately, without the usual prayer for grounding. Big mistake. I could sense tension in the air, and soon, two of the cofounders started to make passive-aggressive comments directed at me. I was confused about where this tension was coming from, but I tried to push forward with the agreed-upon agenda, partly because we also had volunteers waiting to help us with the podcast. Two hours later, there was still no answers, no podcast progress, and no decisions. Most of the conversation had revolved around things that had nothing to do with our agenda. I had to go because I had a flight to catch, which I had shared prior to our gathering, so I got up to hug everyone before I left, but two of the cofounders started to criticize me. They began attacking what I'd said at the VMAs, and I knew this was an attempt to escalate or provoke a conflict. Unfortunately, I have been a part of many unhealthy group discussions and I knew this pattern of behavior. I knew there would be no winning and I didn't have time to address the comments without missing my flight. I was very hurt and disappointed. I said, "I've got to go," and I turned around and left.

In the weeks that passed, the passive-aggressiveness continued over email. No one would tell me what had happened after I left. Because of lack of consensus, we missed opportunities for additional funding and to contribute to the Women's March book *Together We Rise*. I was still confused about the behavior, but we all agreed to gather for a retreat to address the conflict, and I was confident we would get back on track then.

Several months after the falling-out, the retreat hadn't transpired and there seemed to be no interest in making it a priority. I met with one of the cofounders whom I considered a close friend. I was still really hurt by the behavior of some women I had considered friends for over a decade. I told her, "I had to let it go. I kept obsessing about what I did wrong. But I did my best. I shared everything I knew about the VMAs. I kept reaching out for clarification and I apologized for any miscommunications. I kept asking about the retreat dates. No response. I had to let it go. There was nothing else I could do." Having spent the last several months recounting every instance where I may have gone wrong, I was finally making peace with the whole scenario. It was at this moment that she decided to confess what had happened after I left that meeting: The other cofounders stayed to have a three-hour session where they attacked my character. They said I pushed one of them to get in front of the cameras. They also ganged up on Chrissie, too, because they felt like she and I had taken over. However, Chrissie and I felt some fiscal responsibility to the work because our organizations paid for all the flights and hotel rooms so that everyone could attend the Women's March and other related events. For me, going to the VMAs was not fun and games—it was work.

Before that conversation, no one told me exactly how pissed off they were, or why. Instead I encountered nothing but passive-aggressive behavior from a couple of them without explanation—and any of my advances to discuss and resolve the tension were ignored. My suspicions that everything was not okay were confirmed when I ran into one of the other cofounders at a conference. I went up to say hello, and she turned around and flat out ignored me. I was confused and thought, *What the heck is up?* I was hurt but I didn't push for an explanation because we were in a large crowd.

So I was shocked when I found out that all the gossip, personal attacks, and cold shoulders I received were because one of the cofounders had said that I pushed her. I also felt betrayed that my good friends hadn't told me for five months. That entire time, there were whispers and speculations about the integrity of my character. This whole ordeal could affect my career, I thought.

After the initial shock, I asked this close friend, "Why didn't you tell me sooner? You're supposed to be my friend. We're not just work colleagues."

She said, "I'm so sorry. I didn't mean to drop this on you suddenly."

I said, "Yeah, but for five months you couldn't say anything? I can't believe that this is what it was about. If this had happened to you, as a friend and colleague, I would've told you so that you could address it." Shortly after that night, I reached out to the cofounder who had the biggest issue with me.

I tried to call her but she didn't pick up, so I texted her, "Hey, I heard you think I pushed you at the MTV VMAs. That's not true. Taboo asked Bethany and I to stand next to him. You may not know this about me, but I'm actually pretty introverted and this was a work event for me. That carpet was really crowded. I could see myself maybe pushing through the crowd to get to where I needed to be, but there is a big difference between pushing you on purpose and trying to get past you."

"Well, it did happen," she texted back, "but I don't think it was intentional. Time moves on, and I wish you well."

As far as I was concerned, the issue was settled. It took fifteen minutes to resolve a six-month conflict. We didn't need to agree on what happened that night. My own integrity was intact, and I had approached the conflict directly with the person who was upset. I also knew I was up-front about how little I had known about what would happen at the VMAs. Leading up to the event, we'd had phone meetings to discuss the plan, but the two cofounders who would later have an issue with me never showed up for the calls. Their lack of participation left the decision-making to the remaining members. I thought we were all operating from a place of trust, and I continued giving them any information I had as I learned it, but they didn't understand.

Slowly, members left one by one. I later stepped away from

the group, too, when I learned funding had been spent without my knowledge or consent. (In the beginning, we had agreed that any funding raised would be spent according to collective agreement.) When I asked questions about said funding, I was ignored. After sending more emails and waiting a few weeks for a response, I decided I could no longer participate. Their avoidance behavior also went against my Lakȟóta values of honesty and respect.

What I later came to realize was that there were power dynamics at play that I had been unaware of. In the beginning, my organization was the original fiscal sponsor for the collective—part of my job was to handle funding that would go toward various opportunities for the group. I was also a relatively new CEO of a national nonprofit and had a communications team I shared to support the collective with mainstream media representation. Early in my tenure as a CEO, my communications consultant asked me, "Are you the face of this organization or not?" So I had a communications team ready to amplify our organization . . . and me. In Lakȟóta culture, we are taught that there should not be just one leader. However, in Western culture, it's the norm to identify a cause by an individual leader. I wasn't very experienced with this kind of role, but I pushed myself out of my comfort zone because I knew that for the success of my work, I needed to be visible even when I felt uncomfortable. And so, the other cofounders perceived that I was in a more powerful position because of my public visibility and my ability to make decisions about our media representation. They may have seen me as a gatekeeper rather than a bridge builder, despite extending my network and resources to the entire group without hesitation.

The Five Agreements, as taken from the eponymous book by Don Miguel Ruiz: (1) be impeccable with your word; (2) don't take anything personally; (3) don't make assumptions, (4) always do your best; and (5) be skeptical and learn to listen.

LATERAL VIOLENCE AND LEADERSHIP

As a Native American, I straddle two worlds—one being the sovereign Lakȟóta nation I was born into, which is collectivist in nature and steeped in our history, traditions, and protocols. The second is that of the larger dominant American culture, which is Eurocentric, individualistic, and achievement-based. This is a unique form of intersectionality Indigenous people face. I often find myself torn between upholding the value systems of my people and trying to do good social justice work for the benefit of all Native Americans. Leadership is inherently a double-edged sword because those of us who find ourselves in such roles are expected to dare greatly and tread carefully in order to not upset the delicate balance of egos and personalities working alongside us. It's a high-wire act of death-defying proportions, and a tumble off the wire can lead to real, long-lasting consequences for one's career. Making matters worse, finding pleasure in watching leaders fail has become a national pastime in some countries. Take the tall-poppy syndrome, for example, which describes an Australian cultural phenomenon in which people cut down, criticize, and attack accomplished leaders and experts (tall poppies) to the glee and delight of the general public. In North America, the phenomenon has been called the "crabs-in-the-bucket mentality" and describes the behavior of someone who tries to pull down those who are outperforming them. The metaphor is based on crabs' behavior in a fisherman's bucket. Once one crab starts to climb out, the others will pull that crab back down to remain trapped with the rest, thus preventing any of them from escaping.

In more recent years, this phenomenon has garnered the attention of academia and social justice communities because crabs-in-the-bucket mentality is seen frequently among oppressed groups. It is now referred to as "lateral violence," a term used to describe the way oppressed people direct their dissatisfaction inward—toward one another, themselves, and those less powerful than themselves—instead of confronting the system that is oppressing them.[5] It happens worldwide among minorities and it is particularly systemic in Indigenous communities. Lateral violence is a form of bullying that includes gossip, shaming and blaming others, backstabbing, tokenism, manipulation, and ignoring others. Talking about blood quantum (like calling someone a "half-blood") is also a form of lateral violence.

Native American lateral violence is a result of centuries of colonialism, intergenerational trauma, and racism and discrimination. Colonization disconnected Natives from their lands, separated families, and forced assimilation upon us. Native children were taught to reject their culture, give up their languages, and adopt European names. These were done to make us feel ashamed of who we are. Worse, Native Americans were groomed to become our own oppressors during the boarding-school era. Within these schools, children were assigned rank over each other. Those of higher rank were forced to dole out punishments to lower-ranking students, thereby ensuring the adoption of internalized oppression among our people.[6] We were literally taught how to be our own oppressors! And all of this under the guise of the "kill the Indian to save the man" philosophy. Don Coyhis and his colleagues created the excellent and heart-wrenching documentary *The Wellbriety Journey to Forgiveness* to educate on the horrors of the boarding-school era. The narrator, Kateri Vergez, says, "The ultimate evil inflicted on Indian people was teaching us to hate ourselves so deeply as a people that we began killing ourselves and killing each other. This was the legacy of the boarding schools." Before reading our book, you may have been under the misconception that these schools were there to teach us how to assimilate and fit in among our new neighbors. But make no mistake, these schools were child prisons where we were forced to learn how to become our own judge, jury, and executioner.

This horror continues to haunt us today through the transmission of historical trauma from one generation to the next. I see lateral violence as a spillover effect from the trauma we cannot contain. Lateral violence directed inward leads to feelings of learned helplessness, depression, post-traumatic stress, and even suicide. And with so many of our communities in crisis mode and reeling from the effects of complex and collective trauma, being kind to ourselves is a Herculean feat, let alone extending that kindness to others. Consequently, we come into social justice movement spaces as oppressed peoples with a legacy of trauma stored in our hearts and bodies. It is our rage, our dissatisfaction, our unworthiness that cause us to act out at the closest target. We may feel a slight relief at this fleeting moment of power; however, lateral violence is a victory for our oppressors because we end up doing the dirty work for them. Further, the infighting keeps us from organizing and becoming a real political force in this country.

Success is a rarity where I come from, and at times, it can seem like having success off the reservation is at odds with what Lakȟóta tradition determines as good leadership. Natives who find success in traditionally non-Native spaces are at increased risk of becoming targets of lateral violence because they are often seen as "apples"—a derogatory term for a Native who is considered red on the outside but white on the inside. Natives who operate in white spaces start to have the authenticity of their "Nativeness" questioned. Consequently, they can become critiqued, disqualified, and excommunicated through lateral violence. For those of us who are working to advocate for Native rights, we can have our work undermined by the very people we are working to support and lift up. It's often those who aren't working toward anything that will criticize those who are. All of this has real consequences for the victims of lateral violence, too, including feelings of worthlessness, depression, anxiety, and post-traumatic stress.

Native issues almost never receive the level of visibility that we were able to bring to them on the VMA carpet that night. Too many in America are unfamiliar with the history of genocide and oppression against Natives. Lack of visibility literally translates into missing and murdered Indigenous women, because ignoring history makes it easy for the government and the public to continue to ignore the severity of the issue as well. Through this work, we are making visible the formerly invisible and shifting narratives in this country. Together, we are rewriting history to be more accurate by including the truths of more than just the dominant social group. Once the story changes, we will use this power of narrative and our collective power of advocacy to facilitate the revision of policies to increase racial and gender equity. Attending an event like the VMAs was new ground for all of us. For one night we were surrounded by people who hold more power and status than anything we could ever imagine—it's not hard to see how you might measure your own worth in such circumstances and find that it comes up woefully short. Added to all of this, we were all operating within the nonprofit industrial complex. These systems force us to compete for funding by jumping through seemingly arbitrary loopholes created

---

"We want to look for an enemy to name, but often harm is committed by those who look most like us. This behavior is in direct opposition to our ancestral teachings of love, trust, compassion, and healing. What this behavior truly reflects is unaware self-hatred, which has been taught to us by this white supremacist system." —Carmen Perez, Xicana, National Co-Chair of the 2017 Women's March and President and CEO of the Gathering for Justice

---

by many powerful individuals and organizations who benefit from never actually seeing these problems solved. We end up throwing one another under the bus for a buck, which is absolutely counterintuitive to Lakȟóta cultural values of respect and humility.

I know that a couple of the women may have been unconsciously trying to get back at me for a perceived slight and felt that their behavior toward me was justified. But I know, too, that it was more than that because the criticisms and attacks made were personal and not constructive. They bordered on character assassination. The gossiping, questioning of my character, ignoring me at events, and not trying to resolve things or attempt conflict management in a healthy manner were all signs of this violence and a misuse of power. By acting out laterally toward me, they undermined my leadership, our opportunities, and the whole mission of our collective. They allowed their personal feelings to take precedence at the expense of the good work we were trying to do.

This is not the first time I have encountered this type of situation from within my community either. Ever since my first time in the public eye, back when I was protesting the homecoming ceremony in high school, I have been a convenient target for people to point to and say, "Who does she think she is and who gives her the right?" I have also been called an "apple" too many times to count. Lateral violence is another symptom of the healing work we need to do within our communities. If we fail to address it, we may never get out of this system of oppression.

Many of the systems in place are colonial and patriarchal systems, even within our tribal councils. Indigenous women's needs, issues, and concerns almost always get left out. Within our networks we are very diverse culturally, academically, and spiritually. We have to create space to gather and to speak philosophically, to dream big, and to redefine our vision of

261

sovereignty. Indigenous women almost never get the luxury of just being with one another to bond.

In my experience, and in my conversations with other Indigenous female leaders, conflict often arises over representation and funding. There is never enough funding to bring everyone to the critical gathering. Many also may feel there is not enough of a spotlight, so why should you be the star? We cannot allow ourselves to feel threatened by one another's successes or revert to tearing one another down when feeling slighted. I'm sure many feel justified with each angry outburst, while others encourage the bad behavior with silence. We must not allow ourselves to revert to microaggressions, and we must unlearn these colonial behaviors because there are not enough of us in influential places.

But if we all stepped back and remembered that each person is working on behalf of their people, coming from varying beloved cultures that we need to celebrate and honor, we would stop and listen instead of engaging in destructive behaviors. I want to see a world in which we trust each person's perspective and that the work they are doing is coming from a good place, as well as create spaces to share our challenges and celebrate our successes.

We must live in abundance, rather than scarcity, and celebrate each success. Like the elders we revere do. In my community, it is the relatives and the friends who celebrate the success of the individual. This is a traditional protocol of my people practiced in contemporary times so that person does not need to brag (which is looked down upon). Their loved ones uplift them and honor the sacrifices they have made through giveaways. They understand when work is being done in humility to help the people. Someone has to open the door for new opportunities, and we can't forget many of our tribal nations also traditionally recognized, respected, and valued leadership.

In the words of Dr. Rosalee Gonzalez, of Xicana and Kickapoo heritage, "Almost all Indigenous women groups I have worked with have endured some degree of internal conflict within their movements. Among other issues, who participates and speaks for the movement truly matters. We have learned to ensure the broad inclusion and rotation of new representatives who can speak for our movements. Putting this into practice not only affirms a broad united front but also deters us from being threatened by a singular leader and diminishes micro-aggressions that can tear us down. For this reason, we must learn to practice broad representation and resist individualized or idolatrous representations."

THE ANTIDOTE TO LATERAL VIOLENCE IS KINDNESS

Conflict is an unavoidable circumstance of life, and in the Indigenous worldview, conflict and struggle are the cornerstones of growth and change for everything in the universe. Without them, there would be no growth; therefore our teachings say, "When the struggle starts, get happy."[7] Conflict also acts as a guidance system; it is a signal to ourselves that we are out of harmony and that we have to struggle to find our way back to center. However, lateral violence is a manifestation of inner conflict, not outer. When we have feelings such as unworthiness, jealousy, anger, and rage, we push away from those who are our biggest allies and who face the same oppressive system as us. If we don't have the courageous conversation that addresses feelings and properly identifies where they originate, then we risk misattributing their origin as being caused by those who don't deserve it. This is neither healthy conflict nor the kind of conflict that helps us grow. This conflict discourages growth and limits the possibilities for all of us. By sabotaging an opportunity for one of us, we take away an opportunity from all, because we rob our communities from seeing Natives succeed in spaces we have been shut out from for too long.

Throughout this experience as a leader, I have tried to rise above the infighting and do the right thing. I took numerous measures to cocreate IWR from a place of solidarity and mutual respect by inviting my sisters to both share and shape this platform. But I still found myself at the receiving end of lateral violence—even from "woke" Native Americans who have done outstanding and commendable work for our community. It just goes to show how none of us are immune to engaging in lateral violence. Clearly, we have more healing and education work to do in Indian Country.

When all was said and done, not all of my sisters and colleagues conducted themselves in a healthy manner. Some jumped to assumptions and were willing to believe the worst in me, while others didn't know how to handle conflict and avoided the conversation we all needed to have to regain trust with each other. They didn't know how to approach the situation in a good, open, and healthy way by taking a step back to ask, *What's really going on here? Why am I hurting right now? Why am I so upset?*

My own inner healing journey has helped me sense when others are still struggling in theirs. In those moments, I could see how emotionally raw one of my sisters was because she'd just lost a loved one. That particular pain can make us act out in strange ways. With another, I could see glimpses of her identity issues and worries of community acceptance pointed in my direction with snarky comments.

I saw these women whom I have come to admire over the years, and instead of reacting to their hurtful words, I moved beyond them and saw their humanity. I began to see that they were not perfect, and even though I was taking the brunt of their anger and sadness in those moments, I could look at them and say, "You are neither in the right place nor in a good frame of mind." I could've decided to respond in kind; instead I pitied my sisters like I was taught to do under the Lakȟóta teachings of being unšíča. We never truly know what the other person is going through, and taking a step back to acknowledge their pain is critical. But I also had to draw my own boundaries to protect my spirit.

Interpersonal conflict challenges us to decide what kind of person we want to be. Because my sister and I were raised on the reservation by our two grandmas, we both have a strong sense of identity and we never question that. From our traditional upbringing, we've learned there is a certain way of handling things and certain protocols to follow. We witnessed these model behaviors in our grandmothers and with our elders, so whenever someone says something hurtful toward us, we behave the way our grandmas taught us. I decided long ago that I didn't want to be perceived as a bitter and angry woman; I wanted to be the respectful and compassionate woman that my grandma raised me to be.

She taught me that if somebody is mistreating me or is saying something horrible against me, I should never respond in kind. She taught me that respect is one of our highest values, and that we never disrespect another person just because that person is being disrespectful themselves. I practice this by remaining solution-focused and by not responding to personal attacks. I try to listen to what the person is really saying and to see if there is anything positive or constructive there that we can build on. I refuse to take any negative attacks directed at me

"All of these little micro-aggressions, belittling and tearing people down, come from woundedness. It's not the natural state for humans to be mean, abusive, or hurtful. It is really important for us to have space to talk about identity and explore what it means in our lives, so we can heal and be compassionate to one another." —Sharyl WhiteHawk, Lac Courte Oreilles Ojibwe, Addictions Counselor and Former Adoptee

265

personally—this approach keeps me focused on the bigger picture while maintaining my values around respect.

As a leader, you are going to take the brunt of many people's unresolved issues, and let me tell you, yes, it will hurt every time. But as leaders, it is our job to courageously heal ourselves and our duty to rise above the damaging personal attacks, the gossip, and the unresolved trauma that get hurled our way. More importantly, as leaders, it is our job to lead by example, of what is and what is not acceptable behavior. The only way to do this is to not take personally what is so often directed at us as personal because oftentimes, they don't truly know us. We must be patient with people, respectfully speak to one another, and really listen. We must meet lateral violence with kindness, compassion, and respect. If we do not, then we risk becoming perpetrators of lateral violence ourselves. And if we cannot model healthy behavior and conflict resolution, then there is no way we will make effective leaders.

If you ever get the chance to watch elders speak, you will see that they are patient and they listen to everyone's side of the story. That's my model of behavior—where I take the time to listen and share in a good, respectful way with everybody. Taking my ego out of the equation helps guide my actions because in our community, we are taught that it's not just about you or about any single person. It's about the family, or the extended family, or the clan, or the tribe. They are always present.

The value of "help your people" has been ingrained in my brain since I was a baby. Take our Lakȟóta amen, mitákuye oyás'iŋ, for example. Every time I heard myself or someone else say those words, it reinforced for me the value that we have to help our people, that we're connected to everybody. There is so much packed into those two words, and I think people sometimes blunt their meaning by not accepting their full weight into their hearts and souls. Some call mitákuye

266

oyás'iŋ an "ancient Indian saying," which entirely negates our contemporary existence and demonstrates a lack of cultural connection. Mitákuye oyás'iŋ reminds me constantly that I am tied to things bigger than myself.

Many of us in Indian Country are tired of the deficiencies-based approach to development, which lists all the problems that plague our communities, so we have shifted toward a strengths-based approach. We feel that our communities and our original teachings already contain the knowledge, stories, and tools we need to combat lateral violence and to uplift and heal ourselves. One way I already see this self-healing taking form is through the promotion of lateral kindness within Indian Country. Lateral kindness is the opposite of lateral violence, so instead of oppressing one another, we lift one another up and honor the gifts that each of us brings to the table.[8] Acts of lateral kindness include promoting and building healthy relationships, listening with respect, communicating openly, sharing information and resources, offering opportunities, avoiding judging and criticizing others, and celebrating each other's successes.[9] Embedded within lateral kindness are the same values passed down through our original teachings, the same ones my grandmas raised me to uphold, such as respect, interdependence, generosity, and patience.

In Lakȟóta culture, poverty means more than just a lack of material wealth. As previously mentioned, we use the word "unšíča" for a person who lacks kinship bonds, and who is deprived of belonging and home.[11] A person without their thióšpaye is a person worth pitying, for without connection and kinship bonds, that person has nothing. Currently, Native Americans only make up

Choctaw academic Dr. Karina Walters reminds us that the bucket is not the crabs' natural habitat.[10] In the ocean, the crabs help each other. This Western world is not our natural environment. We are meant to help each other climb to the highest points and to support our relatives with oceans of sacredness and love.

roughly 2 percent of the total national population, yet we are overrepresented in all the negative statistics that continue to impact our communities. I cannot help but think that lateral violence has overlaid another form of poverty because it has weakened our collective kinship bonds. Given the huge disadvantages we face, I don't think we can afford to be fighting one another and not lifting one another up. The positive aspects of our community have been rendered invisible in the dominant narrative, and now it is up to us whether or not we remain invisible, and whether or not we allow our lack of support for one another to be our downfall. Lateral kindness means returning to our collectivist roots by promoting generosity with our words and actions toward our Native brothers and sisters. Plus, being kind to others comes with its own rewards, like improved mood and physical health;[12] thus, kindness is the path to individual healing as well as collective.

Dr. Bessel van der Kolk writes about the importance of restoring relationships for dealing with trauma: "Our capacity to destroy one another is matched by our capacity to heal one another. Restoring relationships and community is central to restoring well-being."[13] He is talking about healing from individual trauma here, but the same is true for healing from collective trauma. Our individual healing is entwined with the healing of the rest of our people, especially since our collective trauma manifests in lateral violence. We depend upon healthy relations to support us in our times of need, but it is also vital that we continue to support one another when one of us soars. Our relationships are the backbone to healing and restoring well-being for the whole community. We can become amplifiers of lateral kindness in our communities by remembering how our actions and words carry the power of the intention behind them. In Indian Country, we have a related saying: "Hurt people, hurt people. Healed people, heal people."

I also love the idea of being a "wounded healer." I first

learned about this term (created by Carl Jung) while working at the Episcopal Church. It is the idea that some desire to heal others because they themselves are wounded. The healers are aware of their own personal wounds and continue to work on their own healing while sharing their knowledge with others. Understanding that I am a wounded healer brings comfort to me because I acknowledge I am not perfect. Sometimes it takes a lifetime to heal, and for Native people who carry compounded trauma, applying this term to ourselves gives us space to heal on our own timeline.

ABOUT A YEAR after the conflict and subsequent falling apart of Indigenous Women Rise, I recommended one of the leaders to speak at a philanthropic conference. Despite the conflict, I didn't want to withhold opportunities from her. She and I had been friends for over a decade; we had spent many hours organizing together and then salsa dancing the nights away in New York City. I was the most surprised by her behavior because I knew she came from deep tribal traditions of ceremony and had worked with many international Indigenous communities. I hadn't spoken to her in person since the breakdown of the collective, despite my many attempts to gather for a group phone call or a retreat. We met for breakfast in Tempe, Arizona, and kept our conversation to small talk and the upcoming conference. As we finished up, she said, "I'm sorry about what happened with Indigenous Women Rise. I don't know why we behaved that way." She began to cry, and with tears in my eyes, too, I said, "Thank you for apologizing. It really hurt." The conflict was addressed respectfully; she apologized and I accepted. We hugged and we moved forward in rebuilding our friendship.

Later I talked to another sister over the phone (we hadn't spoken in years), and I immediately asked if we could discuss our issues because it was important for me to address our conflict before engaging in work together again. She said brightly, "I knew this day would come!" I said, "I was never mad because I knew you were going through a lot in losing a loved one recently. Indigenous Women Rise did lose a lot of opportunities though." She said, "Yes, I'm sorry. It was a tough year for me. I had to take time off." I said, "I understand. We just thought we knew everything back then!" She said, "And we didn't know shit!" We both busted out in laughter. We later would talk about how we hadn't been ready to face the conflict because so many of us were so busy. Time, perspective, and honesty are healing.

I wish I could say these were the only times I've seen conflicts in women's circles, but they're not. I see these same patterns over and over again at the intersection of nonprofits, philanthropy, and movements. I often see a refusal to listen to criticism with humility and instead react with an immediate defense position. I've noticed this even with the Women's March, where I now serve on the national board. I am often invited to speak for a few minutes at the national march every year (a huge opportunity), and yet I often feel tokenized. I still witness very few deep discussions or engagement focused on learning BIWOC grassroots values that leaders don't agree with or understand. It's often all about the nonprofit mission and funding. It's about what the right is doing, how it might scare away funders, and how we are attempting to stay out of the fray. Oftentimes, the privileged media and philanthropic sectors are allowed to lead movement ideals. Samia Assed, my Muslim sister on the Women's March board, and I often discuss how we have to be there because of the visibility and access for the communities we serve. We often feel we are fighting an uphill battle with groups who refuse to understand the complexities of our movements and our cultures.

The fact is that philanthropy is still a majorly white- and male-led industry, and a very privileged space. There is a huge gap of lived experience between most nonprofit staff and the people they are supposed to serve, and therefore our approaches to understanding and funding grassroot solutions have a masculine colonial energy that co-opts and/or corrupts.

It's heartbreaking to have to make decisions based, not on humanity, but on the whims of an unwoke or busy funder, but our jobs as board members or philanthropic staff mean we have a responsibility to ensure funding for the organization. Other conflicts often revolve around who is in front of the camera and who isn't; cultural and movement-organizing values versus the Western values of white women; or reinforcement of the nonprofit industrial complex versus innovation.

Sometimes fear and insecurity make us doubt our brothers and sisters in the movement, but it doesn't have to be that way. Most of the time, we all want the same change. Rather than running from a conflict or being the loudest one yelling, how about we take the time to truly listen to one another with respect? It's an act of empathy and compassion to learn someone else's truth, and you still might not agree, but you can deescalate by seeing one another's humanity.

If you don't deal with your trauma, you are destined to become the judge or the gatekeeper. We are human and we make mistakes. I know many harmful actions are not taken with the intention to cause pain and are often a way to justify the mission and/or avoid our own individual pain; yet these acts are still unconsciously violent. We have to be willing to apologize to one another when we inflict harm, intentionally or not. We can't just walk away. We need one another because our fight is not over and our futures are intertwined.

Finally, it's important to recognize that we do have many spiritual leaders in our movements. We make decisions based upon our faith and understanding of the unknown. I often see those who are not spiritual unnecessarily threatened by those who are. Most of the spiritual movement leaders I know want nothing to do with the limelight but also know they must be the conduits for their community. Their actions and words are intentionally misconstrued when they are only attempting to make change for the better. It is in this place of vulnerability that they are often targeted, even by their own people, for their ability to influence others. This is why we must always take a step back and think with a humble heart and an open mind. If we continue to be threatened by innovation and change, we will *never* win.

Lakȟóta Laws

(Living cultural values through action is how Lakȟóta people live in integrity)

"Wóčhekiye" means *prayer, spirituality, religion,* or *belief.*

"Wówičakȟe" or "wóowotȟaŋla" means *integrity* and *honesty.*

---

7 WAYS TO FACE CONFLICT

It's fascinating to me how much we have internalized violence in social justice organizing. I get it, we have to fight the power … but do we have to fight one another? I come from the Oglála Lakȟóta people, known for their courageousness and leadership, as well as their ability (historical and contemporary) to fight on the battlefield. But we also believe in balance. We believe in prayer and compassion, integrity and honesty… To me that equals vulnerability. The ability to admit when we are wrong and the ability to address harm in a healthy manner. Mia Mingus from the Bay Area Transformative Justice Collective says:

> I think a lot of harm that happens is like death by a little thousand cuts, and we often don't pay attention until there's so many little cuts that we're bleeding out and then we rush to the crisis and we drop everything, but what if we started dropping and rushing to everything when there are maybe just four or five little cuts instead of when we're bleeding out?

Western values of capitalism, hierarchy, individualism, and colonization have harmed humanity. America has been lost, but it's not too late to turn the tide with a Lakȟóta worldview that utilizes healing and transformative-justice tools.

1. Embrace transformative justice, a political framework and approach for responding to violence, harm, and abuse by engaging in harm reduction to lessen and avoid creating more violence.

2. Decide to have the courageous conversation by addressing the conflict in a healthy and compassionate manner.
   - Be vulnerable. Tell others how you feel.
   - Ask questions rather than making assumptions and judgments.
   - Understand how your unconscious habits and trauma reactions influence how you respond to or avoid conflict.
   - Be open to new perspectives and constructive criticism. Try to think from the other's point of view.
   - Be willing to have the difficult conversations so your work or friendship can move forward.

3. Face your trauma. I used to obsess about why people treated me badly. My mind raced with questions about what I had done wrong. Often, I did nothing wrong but someone else was triggered by an action. It's important to learn how trauma affects your behavior and the behavior of others. A few years ago when I was obsessing, a friend and colleague of mine, Taj James, blurted out, "Because trauma. Because trauma. Because trauma. Because trauma." This simple answer stopped my spiral in its tracks and reminded me to have empathy.
   - Invest in your mental health and learn how to face your trauma (individual and collective, historical and experienced), because this affects all of our relationships (family, friends, romantic, and work).

- Take responsibility for your actions and apologize if you need to.
- Understand how trauma can affect our feelings of belonging and our ability to collaborate with others.
- Don't take it personally. I know, it's harder than it sounds. But I always tell myself that a person doesn't really know me or my life experiences or values if they are making judgments about me. It also doesn't matter if they do or don't understand; their behavior reflects on them and their community.

4. When confronted with trauma or conflict, reconnect with your spirit by utilizing healing practices. Always begin with prayer and smudging to reset and purify everyone's spirits and the place you are in.

5. Take time to learn about one another to build trust. Take into account how we are all coming together with different values and experiences.

6. Take joy in seeing the success of others. There is no scarcity, only abundance. Your time will come too. We are all meant for something. It may look differently than you planned.

7. Be kind and respectful even when others treat you badly. I learned this from my grandma, who taught us to prioritize humility and respect for others.

JOURNAL PROMPTS TO HONOR YOUR HEALING

- How have you learned to address harm growing up? Is it different from what you know now?

- Did you learn cultural or traditional methods of addressing wrongs?

- Has trust been a difficult issue you struggled with during your lifetime? If so, how have you healed this hurt?

We are all connected every day
by the first swirling smoke of sage at our emerging,
by the moon energy pulling us high,
water crashing down on us.
Our hearts rise,
but we are tethered to the ground
by the umbilical cords of Iná Makȟá,
mapping our underground pathways to the deep.
The smiling rock, the oldest one,
amused to be telling us our futures, skips off to the creek.
The red dragonfly, assertively circling our girl's head in the ceremony,
tells us who she will be,
in the hands raised high to the sun,
and in the heads bowed at the sundance tree.
We connect every day to the ones unseen.
We are the everyday sacred.
Open your eyes and you will see.

—SARAH EAGLE HEART

CHAPTER 10

The Original Caretakers

BY SARAH

PAHÁ SAPÁ (the Black Hills) is also called the "Heart of Every-thing That Is" by the Lakȟóta people. In our creation stories, it is the birthplace where we emerged from the earth as buffalo people. Unfortunately, in 1874, settlers found gold in these same hills and violated treaty agreements with the tribes of the Očhéthi Šakowiŋ (Seven Council Fires of the Lakȟóta, Nakȟóta, Dakȟóta). Year after year, the lands were desecrated. The faces of presidents who blatantly celebrated the genocide of our people were carved over natural granite formations that Lakȟóta referred to as the Six Grandfathers (based on a vision that the Lakȟóta medicine man Nicholas Black Elk had there). My people never ceded these lands. In 2012, we cele-brated as the tribes of the Očhéthi Šakowiŋ fought to purchase back 2,022 acres of our own land, Pȟeslá, a sacred site that is a high-mountain prairie nested in the Black Hills. It really was a fight, because the price increased from the initial $6 million, but the tribes successfully raised $9 million for the center of the Heart of Everything That Is. The Black Hills or Pahá Sapá is considered a place of peace, and our people have been pray-ing there for generations. Prior to the purchase, it was being used for cattle ranching. Since the land has returned to tribal hands, the local tribes are working on restoring it to its tradi-tional ecology, with the reintroduction of native species like the buffalo.

One day shortly before the COVID-19 crisis, I lay blissfully in bed in my Los Angeles Koreatown apartment as the sun rose. I started that day by putting on a guided meditation video on YouTube. The narrator said, "Picture yourself where you find peace." Instantly, I was transported to standing in the middle of Pȟešlá, with the sun shining down on me and the dark pine woods lining the edge of the prairie. I knew immediately I was supposed to go home to the Heart of Everything That Is, and I ended up moving just as the news of COVID-19 began to cause panic throughout the United States. I thought, *Wow, Tȟuŋkášila is guiding my life again.* Seeing Pȟešlá was special and I had to follow my heart to that place, where I would often pray at annual solstice pipe ceremonies. Usually when I return to the traditional spiritual spaces of my people, I'm filled with peace, but this time was different. This time, I felt panic.

I knew Native Americans would be among the most vulnerable to COVID-19[1] due to our chronic health conditions and underfunded health care systems. Our elders, who are the heart of our culture and carry our vanishing languages, were the most at risk, and since elders are often the holders of Native wisdom, a loss of Native elders is a loss of land-based knowledge for our people, and really, for all global citizens.

My life's path has focused on bridge-building and advocating with and for tribal communities. Since 2020, I have been co-CEO of the Return to the Heart Foundation, an organization that focuses on resourcing innovative Indigenous women–led initiatives. We knew Indigenous women would be organizing in the hearts of their communities to save their people and especially their elders, and we identified six regional tribal women leading the response to the virus. We facilitated in-kind donations and, within weeks, raised over $1 million to connect them to personal protective equipment, rapid testing, and traditional medicines. We have also funded traditional helpers and healers to support recovery from the COVID-19 pandemic.

Unfortunately, despite my best efforts, I contracted the virus in November from my son. He came home to do laundry at my place and had sinus and allergy symptoms, which is an ongoing struggle for my family so we didn't really think twice. But a couple days later, my son called and was still congested, and I suggested he go get tested. He was positive. I had symptoms but didn't test positive until nearly a week after my symptoms started. Luckily, I had prepared for this possibility and had already stocked up on traditional Indigenous medicines often found in sacred places like Pahá Sapá.

I always valued traditional Indigenous medicines, but now I know these medicines saved me. On day six, my worst day, when I could barely breathe, I worried I might have to go to the hospital if I got worse. At bedtime, I exhaustedly plugged in two humidifiers in the bedroom and sucked on a small piece of bear root (osha root) as I fell asleep. I also used elderberry, nettles (an herb utilized by the northwestern coastal tribes), echinacea, čheyáka (wild mint, used by the Lakȟóta), and Oneida #6 (wild bergamot, used by the Oneida). When I emerged two weeks later after an intense fatigue, I was grateful for the organizing heart of my community, Indigenous women, and the herbal remedies located in our sacred sites.

WHY DO NATIVES ALWAYS TAKE A STAND?

Shortly after my recovery from COVID, the A&E channel did a one-minute feature on me for their *Voices Magnified* series. They asked me a few questions about the climate, specifically, "Why do Native Americans always stand up? Why are they the ones who step up and who have been fighting for so long?"

As Lakȟóta people, from the time we are born, we hear these oral stories passed down to us about our connection to the land and the ecology. In our prayers, we acknowledge that we are related to all the animals—the two-legged, the four-legged, the winged. So imagine growing up with these teachings that tell you animals are your relatives, and then seeing your relatives begin to disappear. Of course you are going to speak up and say something, because who wouldn't speak up on behalf of their relatives?

Historically, Indigenous people have experienced and suffered from certain challenges before they emerge in other communities. For example, environmental issues have often affected us first. As a result, Indigenous people are usually the first ones out there trying to solve our water crises, protect our remaining old-growth forests, restore natural ecosystems, and so on. Issues that seem far-off or limited to remote areas might be closer than you think once you start paying attention. The stakes are incredibly high; whether problems like lack of access to health care, healthy food, and healthy ecology are addressed or not can mean the difference between life and death for many in our community.

Indigenous people, and especially Indigenous women, can think holistically, collectively, and in a solution-oriented way. We hold the knowledge for safeguarding and growing traditional medicines, as well as for repairing and restoring the lands. I feel like our knowledge is needed now more than ever. The constant echoes of people telling us that Native American voices are not important, or that it's too hard to learn the truth of our history, can be so frustrating to hear at times. Our government was a mastermind at developing propaganda to take our land and our resources. Even now it feels as if we are still being colonized, because though we hold a wealth of wisdom for how to care for Mother Earth, only white men can choose whether to amplify that wisdom and only white-led organizations can be funded to do climate justice work. Right now we are at a tipping point, and if mainstream society doesn't listen to us, it is only to our collective detriment—to the detriment of Mother Earth and all life on this planet.

CROW: THE LEGEND

Narrative and storytelling are both foundational to the work I do toward making change. Before I started my own organization, Return to the Heart Foundation, I was working as the CEO of Native Americans in Philanthropy, a national nonprofit that focuses on investment in Native American communities. Before that, my advocacy work at the Episcopal Church taught me transformational storytelling. My work has allowed me to partner with many celebrities, religious leaders, and grassroots allies to create narrative change on a national scale. I have also had the opportunity to work on some notable projects with the specific aim of sharing the Indigenous worldview through storytelling.

One such project is an interactive virtual reality experience and traditional animated short titled *Crow: The Legend*, created by Baobab Studios. The animated version is available on YouTube,[2] and the VR version is available on Oculus Rift. The story of Crow is inspired by a Native American myth about how the crow became black, and it is told by many tribes around the world. It is a general retelling, so this version cannot be attributed to any one specific tribe. *Crow* was directed by Eric Darnell, narrated by Randy Edmonds, and stars a diverse cast, including John Legend, Oprah Winfrey, Constance Wu, Diego Luna, Liza Koshy, Tye Sheridan, and me.

In *Crow*, you're in this world with a cast of animals—a turtle, a skunk, a moth, an owl, and, of course, a crow. The audience plays the role of the Spirit of the Seasons. The animals are telling their story and, at first, they are carefree and imagine that spring will last forever. However, winter soon arrives, and the animals realize they are in danger. You get to be a part of the story and it is amazing. You're in this VR world, and all the animals are there talking to one another about how it's really cold outside, and they are discussing who should go to the One

Who Creates Everything by Thinking to ask if she can help. The other animals convince the crow to go, and you go with him so that you're in the middle of the sky with the stars, moon, and sun all around you. And then you get up to the One Who Creates Everything by Thinking, and she lives in a huge castle made out of yellow energy, and you find out that the One Who Creates Everything by Thinking is an ant.

Crow tells a story reflecting Indigenous values of diversity, inclusion, sacrifice, community, and self-acceptance. It showcases the Indigenous worldview because we hear the story from the perspective of the animals. In one scene, you are in a forest with all of the animals and they're dancing and singing. That was a very inspiring moment for me, because it was so fun and playful to connect with the Indigenous worldview that way. So many of us need to remember how to play; it's another kind of medicine.

The first time I experienced *Crow*, it made me really emotional. A lot of our stories are about how animals are our relatives. When you are in the VR animation for *Crow*, you are dancing with your relatives and figuring out how to save the world together. Our stories and creation myths have largely been left out of the narrative of America even though they come from its soil and have been around for thousands of years, but my advocacy work has been focused on changing the narrative and creating a cultural shift that honors the Indigenous worldview. We are emotionally, physically, and spiritually connected to these stories that teach us right from wrong. These are the untold stories that need to be told now.

I became involved with *Crow* after a mutual friend introduced me to John Legend's manager, Ty Stiklorius, whom I got to know and share my perspective with. A few months later, they were inviting me to take a look at the project. When I first saw *Crow*, it was already in progress and originally, they only wanted me to give some feedback. During that process, they stepped forward and said, "We need to make sure Sarah's a part of this in every way possible." They even asked me to voice the character of Luna, the moon, and I said yes, because I thought, *Who says no to being haŋwí [the moon]?* The moon represents a feminine force within the Lakȟóta worldview, and it was an honor for me to voice that character. I met everybody who was working on the project. I thought to myself, *There is something about this project. I don't know what it is, but I'm going to follow it. Even though I don't know anything about VR.*

It was challenging but it was fun to see the process. I really shined during the studio visits. We did screenings for all the major studios in Hollywood. Many of them held panels, and I was on a number of them with Liza Koshy and Tye Sheridan and even Oprah. I met Oprah at a dinner event where I was speaking.

This project also uncovered a lack of Native artists in the VR industry, not due to lack of interest but lack of opportunities. These projects need to include more Native Americans as key members of their teams, particularly in designer and animator positions. Native Americans are essentially artists. A lot of tribes excel in artistry, but Lakȟóta people especially are creative. We need to build more creative pathways that provide opportunities for Natives to shine. Baobab Studios was willing to go all in on that. Another barrier for Native Americans in many industries is dealing with non-Native gatekeepers who perpetuate the dominant narratives by locking out Native Americans from accessing those platforms. I have personally encountered gatekeepers in Hollywood, academia, and philanthropy. Gatekeepers are notorious for not doing the appropriate tribal-community research and will often prop up people who pretend to be Indigenous to give their projects legitimacy instead of doing the real work around narrative change. This makes it almost impossible for grassroots voices to be heard and our stories to be shared. The ones who are given opportunities to share their stories usually hold a very urban, Western, or linear perspective. Narrative change is impossible unless we give grassroots people a voice.

IDENTITY AND PRETENDIANS

One day during my philanthropy work, an elder Native program officer named Martin asked my Native colleague in front of me, "So, what level of decolonization are you at?" I laughed at his directness since this was their first meeting. He followed up, "I don't want you to think I'm quizzing you for nothing. Some individuals think they are decolonized but do not come from a community lens or understand that community dynamic. Usually, they are the worst offenders to our own people."

Fortunately, I grew up rooted in the cultural practices, protocols, and nuances of the Lakȟóta value system. I danced at powwows, attended sundances, and butchered buffalos with our grandma to make pápa waháŋpi (dried buffalo meat soup) and wasná (dried buffalo and chokecherries) for ceremonies. As I grew up and traveled, I realized this life was rare. My upbringing within the Indigenous worldview of collectivity is unusual inside a patriarchal American society.

Many Native Americans never experience their culture and community. There are many reasons why this might occur; being raised by a non-Native parent in an urban setting could be one. Regardless of the reason, some of the most difficult challenges within Native communities arise from identity. One such challenge is encountering individuals who pretend to be from a tribe. Native Americans call them "pretendians." Pretendians may have Native American ancestry that can be traced back through genealogy, but without an upbringing grounded in our communities and traditions, we will never claim them

286

as our own unless they are officially adopted in a huŋká. But even then, they are expected to be honest about their relationship to the tribe. Being huŋká doesn't give you a free pass to claim our identity.

Some Native parents who raise their children in urban settings still return with them to the reservation to ensure they learn the traditional ways. My kids are urban Indians, but I took them back every summer and they stayed with our extended family. They got to know their uncles and aunties, whom they became deeply connected to over the years. They also got to experience the spirituality alongside some of the hardship and humility of living on the reservation.

From actors like Johnny Depp to Senator Elizabeth Warren to pop star Justin Bieber, claiming Native American ancestry seems to be a growing trend. In 2020, Michelle Latimer, a notable Canadian film director, was outed for falsely claiming she was Indigenous for over twenty years.[3] Throughout her career, she benefited from this false identity by receiving opportunities, awards, and grants reserved for Indigenous filmmakers. Latimer claimed to be of Algonquin descent from Kitigan Zibi Anishinabeg, Quebec, based on oral history that had been shared by her grandfather. However, the community questioned the authenticity of her claims when they could not connect her to a single tribal member. Upon further investigation, her claims turned out to be false. A genealogist determined that Latimer's ancestors were mostly French, Scottish, and Irish, except for two Indigenous ancestors dating back to the seventeenth century. In other words, she is white.

Too often, I have seen white communities find one Indian and turn them into a spokesperson for a community without verifying if that person is a good representative. For the white community, uplifting a pretendian may not matter, because they only want to legitimize their project. We each have a role to play in ensuring that the projects we are involved with have cultural integrity. I am someone who comes from a culturally grounded community that follows and understands these types of protocols because this is important when sharing an Indigenous worldview. The community often knows when someone is misrepresenting themselves. Normally, Native people can name who their families are. Often the first question someone from within the community will ask is "So, what family are you from?" It is a vetting process. If you can name your family and your larger thiwáhe, people can usually place you based on that information. When someone lacks that type of connection, it is obvious.

Ancestry and identity are not the same, and just because one has ancestry does not give that person the right to claim Native American identity. We are not a race, but a people, and we have the right to self-determine who belongs to our communities. Pretending to be from a community without being validated by them violates the value systems intrinsically woven into our collective culture.

I have deep empathy for those who have been disconnected from their tribal communities and the lands on which they practice ceremonies. But being grounded in one's identity is about learning those cultural practices and spending time in the community with one's people—a significant amount of time, not just passing through, not just once a year. To know the Indigenous worldview, a person must understand what that means in practice. Native Americans are experiential teachers; thus to learn our ways, a person must spend time in the community. They cannot learn our worldview by reading articles on Google alone because the information will be devoid of cultural nuances. I can neither separate Native spirituality from my identity nor Lakȟóta culture from Lakȟóta spirituality, because it's embedded in the language and everything we do.

Ten years ago, the founder of White Bison Inc., Don Coyhis, was talking with my sister and me about how we grew up to become successful women who are focused on our healing while also trying to help others. He asked us, "Considering all of the trauma and everything that has happened in your life, why do you think that you are the way that you are, and doing the work that you're doing?"

For me, it comes down to understanding my values and how I live them. People can say they know Lakȟóta, or the values of humility or generosity and so on, but if they don't walk the walk, then they don't really know. My sister and I are strong in our identities because we were raised with these values, so they are part of who we are. I grew up in Pine Ridge, the poorest place in America, with an absentee father, a mentally impaired alcoholic mother, and more, but coming out of those kinds of circumstances has pushed my resiliency and challenged me to strive to be better. My resilience is deeply rooted in my connection with our culture and spirituality. I was taught that helping my people is the most important accomplishment, and I believe the Creator has guided me in my journey to do this work however I can. Every day I ask the Creator: What can I do to help my people?

If you have Native American ancestry and wish to find out more about the community attached to that ancestry, many tribes will welcome you freely, but you cannot pretend to be what you are not. It's okay to admit you are still learning—in fact, you'll gain more respect by being honest. Find out who you are by investing in relationships and engaging with those communities. Take the time to learn the traditional ways by connecting with others who are already grounded in them. It may take time to gain trust, even from your own people. Be brave, but humble and always respectful. Last, find out what issues that community is facing so that you can approach the problems together.

THE POWER OF ALLYSHIP

Part of my work in narrative change has been figuring out how to step around the gatekeepers to share my perspective and uplift my community, but working with Baobab Studios was one of the first times I didn't have to do that. Baobab sent me little updates as we went along. They would tell me, "Tye Sheridan signed on. Constance Wu said yes. Liza Koshy is in. Diego Luna joined the project. We are trying for another person, but we don't know who it's going to be yet. It could be Michelle Obama or somebody as big." I was talking to them on the phone one day while I was at a San Francisco airport, and I was very business-like talking about marketing and advertising. Then they said, "Oh yeah, did we tell you who we just booked?"

"No."

"We just got Oprah to sign on to voice the One Who Creates Everything by Thinking."

I totally lost my cool and screeched out loud in the middle of the airport. Then we all burst out laughing. Once I calmed a bit, I said, "Oprah? Really? That's amazing!"

When I was in high school, still dealing with all the racism from our peers, I would come home after school, and Grandma would have *The Oprah Winfrey Show* on. She and I always watched it together. It was my favorite show because Oprah shared so many different perspectives on healing, as well as her own healing experiences with racism as a Black woman. Seeing those stories portrayed on the Oprah show helped me begin to piece together some of the issues I was seeing and experiencing in my own community at the time. In a way, I learned about the power of narrative change, storytelling, and healing from Oprah; however, I never really saw Natives represented on the show either. But having Oprah come and get involved with *Crow: The Legend* was really special for me because it felt like this full-circle moment. And at the point of this writing, I'm excited that more of our stories are being told from our own perspectives and celebrated on bigger platforms.

Throughout my career, I have built relationships and have committed to bridge-building that I think is critical for making impacts. For me, it's important to see an impact in my community on the ground—quickly. I started working with influencers and artists, whether they are actors or musicians, because I want to see change now. Having all of these different stars play these voices on *Crow* helped to amplify the project and allowed us to reach a much larger audience.

I have been surprised by the real, genuine connection that so many artists have to Spirit—whether they are in Hollywood or from the reservation. I can tell that they are committed to building a better world and are in it for the long haul. It's not just a one-off PR opportunity for them. They actually care about these issues and believe that Native Americans can speak for ourselves while also having the ideas and implementing them. I have so much gratitude for the allies who have stepped forward, lent their voices and their platforms, visited the communities, gotten on Zoom calls, and shared their music and artistry. It's a genuine spirit of giving that is not unlike our Native American concept of giving your time and your talent.

The Indigenous worldview is inclusive, not exclusive. We are trying to build a better world and a better community for our children so they can also walk through those doors of opportunity. It's not about power-building for one person, one entity, at all—it's about working together for the greater good and utilizing the Creator to do that work.

UNBOXING THE EMMY

Crow won four Daytime Emmy Awards in 2019, receiving the most awards of any animated program or series, traditional or interactive. Baobab Studios fought for me to have a credit and get an Emmy. When they won the Emmy, this feisty little studio said, "Sarah deserves to get a statue, too, and we want her to get credit for the project." Throughout the process, they wanted to do right by me and honor what I had contributed.

To my knowledge, I'm one of the very few Native people to have received an Emmy—and probably the first Lakȟóta woman to win an Emmy. I get a lot of excitement from elders and young Native Americans who are happy to see this type of representation on such a massive scale. I never expected to win an Emmy. It wasn't something that I was chasing after, and I hadn't known it was a possibility. I just felt that *Crow* was a cool project that would allow us to create narrative change. So I know a lot of the success I'm having right now is because people are attracted to the way that I tell stories.

When *Crow* was released, Baobab Studios was relatively new on the scene, and they had the attitude of going after every opportunity they could. They wanted me to appear at every major studio screening to talk about my experience. I was willing to go to whatever event they wanted me to go to. The number of screenings was part of the submission eligibility process. If they needed me to go somewhere to speak or do something, I did. I was willing to go to whatever studio they wanted me to go to, which is part of the process for a project to be nominated.

While I was still living in California, my Emmy was mailed to me, but I decided not to unbox it until I could take it home to South Dakota and unbox it with Grandma. I wanted to share the experience with her. My boys, Aarron and Brenden, were there, and Sivan Alyra Rose was videotaping. She was the first Native American lead of a TV series for Netflix called *Chambers*, and I consider her part of my family because she and my son have been dating for years.

We were all gathered in Grandma's HUD house, which I grew up in, when I opened the box and held up my Emmy for the first time. My children were excited by it and one of my sons said, "Yo, an Emmy! Mom, what does it say?"

"It says, '2018/2019 Daytime Emmy Awards, outstanding interactive media for a daytime program, *Crow: The Legend*, Baobab Studios, Sarah Eagle Heart, consulting producer.'" I looked over at Grandma and asked, "Grandma, what do you think?"

"I'm crying," she replied. It was a really emotional experience. We both cried and it was such a special moment to share with her. She was so excited and proud. It's funny, because these types of high-profile awards are really not even a part of our daily lived reality on the reservation. I would have never in a million years imagined that I would win an Emmy with John Legend. That's just ridiculous! I don't look at it as a prize; instead I see it as a gift from Tȟuŋkášila to help me continue my work. I look at it as a gift because I didn't ask for it; I didn't expect it. Now I get to be a producer on other projects, working on things I never could have imagined for myself, such as developing documentaries and stories that reflect my Lakȟóta worldview. This is one way we can bring the Indigenous worldview to a larger audience, and I doubt I would be working in this space if it wasn't for my time on *Crow*.

While we were back in South Dakota for the unboxing, I said to Sivan, "Let's host an event as a way of giving back to the community." We paid to host an event in Rapid City, South Dakota, at a place called the Racing Magpie. We had posters of Sivan made that she signed; I shared the story about *Crow: The Legend*, and she talked about her experience working on *Chambers*. We planned the event super last-minute, but we just wanted to share it with the community. To the surprise of both of us, we had a good turnout. Some of the elders who came were taking pictures of me and expressed just how happy and proud they were. People tell me they are so appreciative of seeing me out there and being the first to do a lot of these projects. They are inspired by some of the doors I'm opening and bringing other people through. For me, it comes down to being brave enough to say yes. If everyone else can do it ... why not you too? I knew nothing about VR before this project, but I had faith in my relationship with Tȟuŋkášila, which gave me the courage to say yes. Now I just executive produced *Lakota Nation vs. The United States* with Mark Ruffalo and Marisa Tomei, which premiered at the 2022 Tribeca Film Festival. And I just started the company Zuyá Entertainment with Oglála Lakȟóta entrepreneur Twila True.

NARRATIVE CHANGE AND HOW INDIGENOUS AND WESTERN WORLDVIEWS DIFFER

Ever since Trump incited an attempted coup on the nation's capital in January 2020, everyone has been asking, "Who are we right now?" Many Americans are beginning to re-envision America, and I hear people within the various movements talking about how we need to develop a shared narrative where we all have one another's backs. However, if we are really rethinking our shared narrative and who we are, that new narrative should include Native Americans—our history, perspective, and worldview. There is an urgent need for mainstream America to understand our perspective and how history has brought us to this point of many intersecting crises. Storytelling is inherent to Indigenous cultures and is utilized to share wisdom, create role models, and provide examples of what not to do. Our stories have been ignored, especially our stewardship of the earth. We need the Indigenous worldview now more than ever to help address the climate and ecological crisis we face today. My life is committed to storytelling that can create change. And if I can support the healing process as well as social justice, that's where I know I'm supposed to be.

Indigenous wisdom implies a duty of care to our environment and to one another, thus emphasizing values of cooperation, sharing, and reciprocity. As a result, Native

Americans see their responsibility as living in harmonious and balanced relation with all creation—including other tribes and racial-ethnic communities. The Indigenous worldview is centered on the land and our place within it. Our concept of connectedness manifests in our developing an intimate and spiritual connection to nature and all living beings. Further, Indigenous wisdom is predicated on collectiveness, meaning we consider knowledge not to be owned by any one individual. We hold it collectively in our people through our shared experiences, which are the summation of our collective wisdom.

In contrast, Westerners understand the world and the meaning of life in terms of history, and tend to orient their lives toward the future, goals, destiny, and final purpose. This worldview reflects temporal concepts of progress, development, and colonization. Western cultures emphasize autonomy and independence, which has resulted in society becoming disconnected from the greater natural world as well as from one another. What we end up with is an individualistic culture that stresses the needs of the individual over those of the collective whole.

When European settlers first came to Turtle Island, the Indigenous worldview was seen as inferior to the Western worldview. Our perspective was considered an obstacle and threat to Western expansionism, which continually wanted to carve up our lands for exploitation and extraction. Yet exploitation was only part of the picture; within the United States we must ground our political analysis on settler colonialism. The settler society benefited from the loss of land by its Indigenous inhabitants, then worked to erase the original peoples from the settler history. This explains why hardly anyone is familiar with Native American history, despite it being the history of all Americans.

> Settler colonialism has come to develop a distinct identity that perpetuates through the replacement of Indigenous populations with an invasive settler society.

Many of us understand that this country was built around the narrative of the "other." Native Americans had the distinction of being the first "others" because of our collectivist cultures and connection to the land. Before we can change this harmful narrative, we must come to terms with how pervasive it is in America and reconcile how our own beliefs have been affected by these shared narratives. Narratives work in our subconscious all the time, and most are not even consciously aware of them. However, through storytelling and lifting up grassroots voices, we can shift the harmful narratives that have been baked into the legacy of this country. We can begin to effect a corresponding cultural shift as well.

Too many of America's current issues are the result of a drastic values crisis. For example, less than 1 percent of our society hoards so much wealth that we experience deep suffering on the other end of the continuum. The Western perspective promotes individualism and consumerism while subverting the natural world for personal gain. In contrast, the Indigenous worldview is built on collectivist principles that nest our identities back within the collective ecology, and this is a huge strength of our people. Projects like *Crow* can share this vision with a wider audience; it is important for others to know that it is not only possible to think and live this way, but that it is accessible.

When we as Native Americans are allowed to reclaim our culture, we as a human species become more resilient globally because it expands the frameworks we can operate within by validating alternative knowledge systems. Decolonization through culture not only rejects Eurocentric ways of doing things, but also offers settlers the chance to familiarize themselves with and embrace Indigenous knowledge systems around spirituality, history, cultural practices, social interactions, language, and healing. A rejuvenation of Indigenous traditions and customs could become the foundation that guides policy, development, and sustainable land management throughout the next century.

CLIMATE CRISIS EXPERIENCED AS TRAUMA

From Extinction Rebellion to Greta Thunberg's #FridaysFor-Future to Conference of the Parties 26 (COP26) in Glasgow in 2021, the climate and ecological crisis has captured the public's attention in the last few years. Nations came together in 2015 to agree to limits on carbon emissions with the adoption of the Paris Climate Accord, but so far global emissions continue to grow year-over-year. The World Wildlife Fund's 2020 *Living Planet Report* also shows an average 68 percent fall in monitored vertebrate species between 1970 and 2016, and that we are overusing Earth's biocapacity by at least 56 percent.[4] Industrial agriculture is leading to degraded forests, rivers, and oceans, and the further we entrench upon the natural world, the greater the risk of zoonotic diseases like COVID-19. American author and journalist Elizabeth Kolbert wrote a book arguing that we are in the midst of the sixth mass extinction event on Earth, and some are calling this the mark of the Anthropocene. It is hard to exaggerate the severity of the threats we collectively face.

The climate and ecological crisis takes a toll on our mental health as well. The consequences vary from minimal stress to clinical disorders like anxiety, depression, PTSD, and suicidal thoughts.[5] Research suggests higher temperatures increase suicide rates in the United States and around the world, as well as increase aggressive and violent behavior.[6] Worse, climate risk is described as a "threat multiplier," meaning it magnifies trauma impacts due to poverty and racism.[7] The most vulnerable groups include the elderly, children, women, immigrants, and Native Americans. According to a study conducted by

Ashlee Cunsolo Willox in which she worked with Inuit populations in Canada, climate change has had a huge impact on their mental health because their way of life is tied to their identity as people of the sea ice.[8] Ice that is now melting rapidly. The climate in the Circumpolar North is warming over twice the global average rate and is one of the fastest-changing places on the planet.[9] Rising temperatures result in thawing permafrost and ice-level changes that threaten their ability to live off their land and utilize traditional knowledge. This impacts their cultural identity as well as increases family stress, drug and alcohol abuse, and suicidal ideation.

"Going out on the land is everything to us—it's our heart and our soul. That's real. A lot of people think of spirituality as just a church thing and it's not, that's just one portion of spirituality. For us, going out on the land is a form of spirituality and if you can't get there, then you almost feel like your spirit is dying and then when you get out again, then you feel so much better when you come back." —Inuit woman[10]

Further, awareness of the climate crisis can cause secondary trauma all on its own. "Ecological grief" is used to describe the profound sadness people feel in response to the loss of species, ecosystems, and landscapes. Eco-anxiety can also be triggered by the looming threat of climate change. The crisis can feel so overwhelming that it invokes feelings of helplessness, hopelessness, and uncertainty.[11] One aspect of ecological grief is "solastalgia," a term coined by Australian philosopher Glenn Albrecht to describe a type of homesickness one gets while still at home due to a rapidly changing landscape.[12] This area of research is nascent and, so far, most of the research consists of qualitative interviews, usually from those who have witnessed ecological degradation firsthand.

Despite the proliferation of terms used to describe ecological grief, none of them capture the vulnerabilities Native Americans face because of our unique relationship and connection to the land. Indigenous wisdom is land-based and this is codified in our language, customs, and traditions. Not being able to utilize our land-based knowledge due to a rapidly changing environment makes our knowledge vulnerable to disappearing altogether.

The climate crisis is a collective trauma, and now the settlers are facing the same loss of home and displacement that Indigenous people have faced for generations. Many, if not most, have no clue what to do in the face of climate change. There are no solutions lying around in the capitalist toolbox that seem sufficient to address a crisis of this magnitude. There are no ways of thought or being in the settler-colonialist mentality that can conceptualize an answer to this problem. No magical invention, no technological solution, and no amount of greenwashing will solve it. Western culture, built upon individualism, has disempowered Western society by obliterating our capacity for collectivism. But Native Americans know there is power in collectivism. We know the power of belonging as much as we know the violence of disconnection. Everything Emma and I have written about in this book has touched on the power of community and collective healing through the restoration of Indigenous knowledge systems. Individualism will not solve a collective crisis. Only through collective power can we address the scale of the problem. This is why we cannot recycle or purchase our way to a greener future. These actions focus on the individual, but this crisis demand large-scale systemic change involving many areas of our society.

When we treat the climate problem as one that requires a response from the individual, the individual feels powerless. We feel like there is nothing we can do alone to change the collision course with climate collapse. However, when we start to think collectively and come together to use our "we" power, then it becomes possible to radically reimagine our systems and institutions so that they respond to and abide by the physical limitations of our ecosystems.

299

Science is presented as facts with no moral imperative to have a culture shift. Taking our societies to carbon-negative will require a complete overhaul of all these historical systems. The longer they continue, the more collective trauma they will cause to the planet. Native wisdom traditions are earth-based, cyclical, and expansive. They reach their tendrils out to touch everything in the web of life. A respect for Indigenous cultures could go a long way to creating a wider cultural shift toward carbon-negative lifestyles and toward the restoration of our ecology. By accepting our Native cultures, the wider culture can also learn and be challenged by an alternative system—it can maybe even be compelled to adopt some of the wisdoms contained in our traditional knowledge.

NATIVE AMERICANS ARE A KEYSTONE SPECIES

In 2016 American biologist and author Sean B. Carroll published a book titled *The Serengeti Rules: The Quest to Discover How Life Works and Why It Matters*. He argues that nature follows rules of regulation—whether at the microscopic level within human cells, or within the larger ecology and food webs.[13] Ecosystems contain food chains made up of different species, and food chains can be broken down into different levels, called "trophic levels," based on what food each level consumes. Decomposers that eat organic debris are at the bottom trophic level, followed by the producers or plants, then herbivores who eat the plants, followed by predators who hunt the herbivores. Some species within a food web are more critical than others to the diversity of the ecosystem, and their removal can cause what are called "trophic cascades." Elimination of certain "keystone species," like the gray wolf from Yellowstone National Park, can have far-reaching consequences throughout an entire ecosystem.

When wolves were reintroduced to Yellowstone National Park, the formation of the river was changed because the wolves cut the elk population in half, who were overgrazing willow plants—a necessary building source for beavers. Reintroduction of the wolves stopped the elk from overgrazing, which allowed the beaver populations to grow, who then changed the hydrology when they dammed up streams and rivers to form wetlands.[14] Wolves also act as food distributers because many scavenger species, including ravens, eagles, magpies, and bears, will scavenge food from prey that wolves have killed. Because of the outsized importance wolves play in the greater ecology of that ecosystem, they are considered a keystone species by biologists.

Biology has shown that rules regulate ecosystems much in the way that Indigenous peoples recognized long ago. Our original teachings, orally passed down through the generations using origin stories, provide instructions on how to be a good human being by living in a reciprocal relationship with all our relatives. These original instructions celebrate our interdependence and our interconnection with the diversity of life. Our stories have always cast the crow, the buffalo, the wolf, the trickster coyote, Mother Earth, and so on as characters in the story, because how could they not be when we see them as our brethren? We even name ourselves after the animals because that is how sacred they are to our cultures. Native Americans already saw the environment as an integrated system—in which animals play pivotal roles and plants act as medicines—well before trophic cascades were discovered by Western biologists.

Because of our unique relationship to and understanding of the natural world, Indigenous people act as keystone species. We manage the lands we occupy better than government lands held in conservation. Satellite images of South America show lands managed by Indigenous people experience

301

lower deforestation rates.[15] We already protect the majority of the remaining global biodiversity, with 80 percent under Indigenous stewardship.[16] Plus, in some ecologies, stewardship requires a human touch to properly manage. Traditional Indigenous techniques of cultural burning helped save some owners' properties during the 2019 Australian fires, for example.[17]

Indigenous people have maintained a vital relationship to the earth despite centuries of cultural genocide. We continue to act as caretakers even when it could cost us our lives—and it does. Global Witness put together an annual report tallying the deaths of environmental defenders, and in 2019, 212 were killed, with 40 percent of those people being Indigenous despite our people only making up 5 percent of the global population.[18] The Indigenous worldview distinguishes us as caretakers, not consumers, of the land. Perhaps this perspective is a medicine that we can bring to the rest of the world. Westerners have the capacity to act as a keystone species, too, but currently do not because they view the natural world as something to be owned and conquered, as opposed to worked in relation with.

Because we see the land not as a resource, but as alive, Indigenous people are at the forefront of the growing Rights of Nature movement, which argues that nature should have the same rights as humans. In the summer of 2019, for example, the Yurok tribe declared rights of personhood for the Klamath River.[19] Drought is impacting both the health of the river and the salmon populations, plus it's exacerbating tensions over water usage by farmers. Salmon are important both culturally and economically for the Yurok, which makes protecting the river a necessity for them to continue their traditions.[20] The year prior, the White Earth Reservation of Ojibwe adopted the rights of Manoomin to protect wild rice and its freshwater sources in Minnesota, including the right to pure-water and freshwater habitat, to a healthy climate, and to a natural environment free from human-caused climate change.[21] Recognizing nature as worthy of rights codifies Indigenous knowledge into our legal systems, even if it is only within tribal law. This would be an excellent forward-thinking strategy to protect our ecosystems in other jurisdictions as well.

Since Indigenous people already act as a keystone species through our land stewardship, giving as much land back to Indigenous people as possible should be a top climate priority. We should want to invest in the original people of this land because they have a track record of caring for it for over eight thousand years. It would be a direct way to support a better world immediately—it would provide economic help to our poverty-stricken First Nations, supporting us as we help heal the earth.

Creating land trusts and giving lands back to Native American tribes through inheritance are a couple avenues for returning land to Natives. Recently, First Light, a collection of organizations that serves as a bridge between conservation groups and communities, helped the Passamaquoddy tribe in Maine buy back Pine Island by connecting them with the Nature Conservancy. The conservancy gave the Passamaquoddy a grant to cover the costs of the repurchase of the island.[22] The island has cultural significance to the Passamaquoddy, who never ceded the land. For years, the island has been used mainly for timber harvesting, but the Passamaquoddy plan to use it for fishing, camping, and ceremonies.

The United Nations recognizes the importance of Indigenous knowledge, practices, and values in contributing to conservation efforts. They conclude that providing legal and political rights for Indigenous people to continue caring for their lands would go a long way toward supporting global sustainability efforts.[23] Climate justice must include recognizing Indigenous and local communities' legal rights to their lands. Indigenous sovereignty means recognizing our rights to manage the land according to our traditions—including our right to reject extractive developments and industrial agricultural practices imposed on us without consent.

Currently, almost all donor funding in climate change philanthropy goes to environmental organizations run by white people.[24] We must change this. The environmental movement has been dominated by white middle-class and upper-middle-class Americans who have a real vested interest in controlling the money. They think it makes sense to invest the money into white-led organizations because white people have more power.

My organization, Return to the Heart Foundation, is part of a network called Donors of Color, which has been telling philanthropic organizations to get serious on climate justice for years. Donors of Color asks these organizations to take the Climate Justice Funders Pledge, which is a commitment to giving at least 30 percent of their funding to organizations led by people of color within the climate justice space. Our organizations are "chronically underfunded," with less than 2 percent of philanthropic giving going to groups dedicated to environmental justice.[25] For too long we have been underrepresented in decision-making surrounding this issue, even though our communities are the most vulnerable to climate change. By changing the flow of money, we can unlock our community-specific climate solutions for the benefit of everyone.

ECO-FASCISM

Environmental issues are really nonpartisan, despite the right's best efforts to make them a partisan issue. Although young conservatives are more accepting of the realities of climate change than their older counterparts, the alt-right has been shifting its message to recruit these young conservatives into eco-fascist ideologies.[26] Eco-fascists blame people of color and immigrants for over-production and resource utilization, even though wealthy people produce the majority of greenhouse gas emissions.[27] They desire an authoritarian regime that demands sacrifices from minority groups to protect the environment while disregarding human rights. With the rise of the extremist alt-right movement, there have been attempts to co-opt the environmental movement and make it about population control, anti-immigration policies, and forced sterilizations of marginalized groups. Instead of uplifting everyone together to take care of the planet, white supremacy still makes it all about power and control by blaming the "other."

> "The climate crisis has never just been about things getting hotter and wetter. It's about the intersection of that extreme weather with the barbarism of white supremacy and supremacist ideologies of all kinds." —Naomi Klein[28]

As a result, we are seeing a rise in mass shootings motivated by eco-fascism around the world. The Australian neo-Nazi who killed fifty-one people in Christchurch, New Zealand, is a self-described "Ethno-nationalist Eco-fascist" who wrote about his views in the following terms: "Ethnic autonomy for all peoples with a focus on the preservation of nature, and the natural order."[29] He wrote that non-whites from the Global South are "invading" Europe and America, and that in order "to save the environment," the invaders must be killed.[30] Five months later, a shooter from El Paso, Texas, shot and killed twenty-three people in a Walmart. The shooter said he targeted "invaders" as a way to depopulate the planet and make "our way of life . . . more sustainable."[31] These shooters not only accept that climate change is real, but they want it to happen because they see it as an opportunity to purify the human race. It makes no difference to them if Black, Latino, and Indigenous communities die from climate disasters.

Experts warn that climate change has a greater impact on the global poor, who are facing a climate-driven apartheid due to inaction. This century, millions of people around the world will face food insecurity, forced migration, disease, and death.[32] Already the death rate from natural disasters is seven times higher in poor countries versus rich countries.[33] Evidence of climate apartheid exists within America too. For example, as forest fires burn hotter and longer in California (thanks to climate change), the rich are hiring privately contracted firefighters to protect their properties.[34]

AT THE BEGINNING of this chapter, I shared how A&E asked me, "Why do Native Americans always take a stand?" Another answer is that we have to if we want to continue our way of life. We are constantly having to defend not only our culture and traditions but also the lands that are inextricably linked to our worldview. With the rise of eco-fascism and its infiltration of the environmental movement, we are forced to stand up yet again. Far-right eco-fascists are obsessed with Indigenous culture because they see themselves as their own version of indigenous. But their version of indigenous is extractive. Their version is all about the individual and only saving themselves. It is not about the collective or living in harmony with the land.

The climate crisis is a threat multiplier that has the power to worsen all of the individual and collective traumas we have suffered. Without the natural world, we would not exist. Nature has the power to heal us and bring peace when we are feeling overwhelmed and stressed; however, if we don't do our best to live in right relation to Mother Earth, then even her healing powers will abandon us. Given the complexity of the crises we face, we need everyone to help mitigate the risks. We need the

"The beauty and brilliance of Native women is a gift to the world that is only just beginning to be discovered. Indigenous solutions and ways to heal our Earth run deep through our DNA." —Gina Jackson (Western Shoshone and Oglála Lakȟóta), Co-Founder & Co-CEO, Return to the Heart Foundation

instigators and the radicals, but we also need the good cops and the healers who will come in and translate knowledge both ways. We need all of us. And we must shift our thinking from a scarcity mindset to one of abundance, because the only way we are going to overcome this is if we all lift one another up at the same time. Such transformation is what we are trying to seed with all this narrative change, but transformation has never happened at this level before. We are just at the beginning, which is really exciting.

Lakȟóta Laws

*(Living cultural values through action is how
Lakȟóta people live in integrity)*

"Wóksape" means *wisdom comes
with practicing knowledge.*

"Wówičakȟe" means *holding honesty and truth
with yourself, your higher power, and others.*

---

7 WAYS TO RECONNECT

Since time immemorial, Lakȟóta people have been connected to everything around them, including the two-legged, the four-legged, the winged, the skyworld, and Mother Earth. Our buffalo-people creation stories describe us emerging from sacred sites like Wind Cave. We hear other stories, like of the animals painting themselves to race around Pahá Sapá, that teach us about equality between the animals and humans. Through these narratives, we grow up seeing the animals and nature around us as guides: an eagle flying overhead lets us know we are on the right path; lightning signifies that the wakíŋyaŋs have returned; the oldest ancestor in the form of a smiling rock answers our questions; a baby red dragonfly buzzing around my niece's head during her naming ceremony alludes to her new name, Thuswéčha Lúta Wíŋyaŋ (Red Dragonfly Woman). The everyday sacred is all around you; all you have to do is look.

1. Learn about your regional tribal history and the contemporary issues that local tribes are facing.
   - Find the tribes at www.native-land.ca.
   - Intentionally watch films and TV shows created by Native people or starring Native people, and rate them highly! These ratings determine what is funded and created.
   - Learn from Indigenous writers and scholars by identifying trusted community leaders or credible news outlets. Pay them for their time!
   - Follow trusted tribal community leaders on social media and share their knowledge with your network.
   - Advocate for the Indigenous worldview, Indigenous rights, and Indigenous equity at the community, local, state, national, and international levels.
   - When seeking spiritual expertise, remember to triple-check with the community for trusted spiritual leaders.

2. Dance it out and move your body. Movement is another great way to activate your intuition by tapping into the five senses and body awareness. Our digestive systems contain the enteric nervous system (ENS), which is two thin layers of nerve cells that are able to receive and relay messages to the brain. Because it serves as a communication system between the gut and the brain, the ENS has become a hot topic in medical research. Many researchers even refer to the ENS as a "second brain."[35] Yoga, stretching, going for walks, jogging, and dancing are all fantastic ways to connect with your body and potentially help you activate your second brain, thereby unlocking your intuition.

3. Talk to a friend, family member, or mentor or advisor. Form your own interest and support circles. Create retreats for those who share the same passions.

4. Learn creation stories from the local tribes of your community. Understand how those creation stories are tied to sacred sites and why it's important to advocate for their safeguarding.

5. Practice breathwork, mindfulness, meditation, grounding exercises. Everyday activities like cooking or walking can be opportunities to practice mindfulness if you turn off distractions. You can ground yourself to Mother Earth by walking barefoot. Even prayer is mindfulness.

6. The everyday sacred refers to the ceremony in the "little" things we do every day.
    - We often think that a ceremony means a big event with a lot of people, but it can be as simple as saying a prayer while placing wasná and tobacco outside for the spirits.
    - Smudging with sage or cedar is a common Lakȟóta practice. I often woke up to cedar burning as a little girl.
    - Prayer songs are also a powerful way to connect to Tȟuŋkášila. Some prayer songs are shared online and in person at ceremonies. Learning how to sing or drum or simply listen is important in developing your spiritual practice.

7. Invest in credible Native American/Indigenous helpers and healers in your area. The Return to the Heart Foundation focuses on funding traditional helpers and healers to ensure traditional healing knowledge is not lost.

JOURNAL PROMPTS TO HONOR YOUR HEALING

- How has the COVID-19 virus impacted your life both positively and negatively?

- How do you stand up in your life for issues you believe in?

- Why is it important to stand up for climate change issues?

- How has the climate crisis impacted your life both directly and indirectly?

Conclusion

NOW YOU KNOW some of the chapters in our life story that have made us who we are. We dug deep in writing this love letter to our younger selves, our sweet innocent selves, and to the women we are today. We went deep into our vulnerability and shame to get to joy. Many of these experiences we wouldn't wish on anyone. We were very sheltered as children growing up on the reservation but still knew about death, rape, and violence. We were safe because our family kept us safe, but we still saw pain. We didn't know how to heal ourselves from our trauma. We didn't understand our iná's or our grandmother's traumas. We learned it is okay to talk about our trauma to professionals and our family. In talking to our thiwáhe about their experiences, we learned to open our hearts, even if it was painful. We learned that pain can be transformed into acceptance, love, and joy.

It's critical to find professionals who understand your experiences and culture. It's important to gather those who have worked on their own healing processes for over a decade. Often, those who are new to healing don't understand the depth and humility it takes to get to a space of deep healing. Currently, more privileged individuals with less experience are co-opting healing spaces. Find someone who fits your needs.

And remember, these days Indigenous women don't get to make mistakes and live. Indigenous women are preyed upon. It is so easy to fall into the wrong crowd, looking for love because we feel unloved. There are too many Indigenous women who fall for the person who says things without acting on them. Learn from our experiences and take our stories to heart. Sometimes we don't have anyone to protect us, so we must protect ourselves. You deserve unconditional love. Love yourself enough to walk away from any person who doesn't honor and respect you as the prize. Love yourself and live, my girl.

Finally, we have found that when Tȟuŋkášila strikes, or calls to you or shows you the truth or moves you from a bad situation or toward a new experience, it's best to listen and follow with naïve faith, trusting in the everyday sacred. If you don't learn the lesson the first time, rest assured the lesson will find you again. When you are ready, the joy of cocreating with Tȟuŋkášila will come. In the meantime, show everyone kindness.

Wóphila Tȟuŋkášila for guiding all of us to healing. This is just the beginning of your joy to come.

Wóphila by Sarah and Emma

WE GIVE GRATITUDE to every person who has come into our lives. Everyone has a spiritual pathway to follow in order to learn the lessons needed for their life. Our journey has included many individuals and groups who contributed to our understanding of spirituality. Some people come for a season and some people come for a lifetime. Wóphila to each person that has been a part of our journey and demonstrated their support through love and action.

Wóphila to our uŋčí Emma Brave Hawk, who role-modeled a love for spirituality to us by reading her *Book of Common Prayer* daily, circling the prayers for the family, and carrying the family čhaŋnúŋpa in to the wiwáŋyaŋg wačhípi. Wóphila to our fierce uŋčí Grandma Rose, who gave us unconditional love and a permanent home when she picked our iná up from where she was sitting outside the trailer house, holding two small six-month-old babies and all of her belongings. Wóphila to Tȟuŋwíŋ Jan and the late Tȟuŋwíŋ Mabel, who sat at the table with us as young ones, sharing stories of spirituality and the spirit world, then drove us to sundances and powwows. Thank you to Tȟuŋwíŋ Deb, who showed us that the world was bigger than the rez when she invited us to see the ocean in California in eighth grade. Our tȟuŋwíŋs may not have always understood our world, but they always told us to go for it and, with their support, gave us courage to go into the unknown. Thank you to our lekší Ike and the late Lekší Howard, who stepped in as our atés and were always willing to help cook soup for the sundance meals. Wóphila to our Knife Chief relatives and Two Dogs Wiwáŋyaŋg Wačhípi. Wóphila to the Around Him family and Around Him Wiwáŋyaŋg Wačhípi.

We also want to acknowledge our extended family, especially our tȟuŋwíŋ Mable Eagle Heart and lekší Howard Red Bear, who passed in 2021. They showed us unconditional love. Auntie Mable taught us everything that we needed to know to be good Lakȟóta women. Uncle Howard taught us to laugh but also was present as a fatherly/older brother figure. We knew we were and are loved because of their love. We are eternally grateful to have known their love.

Shout-out to Iyanla Vanzant, Brené Brown, and Oprah Winfrey for being our inspirations to dig deep in writing this book and in life. Wóphila to Cathy Wasserman for coaching us through our original outline for the book. Wóphila to our 2017 Storia Summit friends and Ariane Conrad for connecting us to Geoffrey Szuszkiewicz, who made this book come to life. We couldn't have done this without you, Geoffrey! Wóphila to Hedgebrook, Ghost Ranch, and the Flounders for creating space to create. Wóphila to those who donated to support us in developing our book, including the Reis Foundation, Accelerate Impact Fund (a sponsored program of the Social Impact Fund), Cynthia Reddrick, Christa Orth, Emy Syrop, Janine Kovac, Kerrien Suarez, Claire Lavagnino, Gene Takagi, and Nora Ranney. Wóphila to Jamia Wilson and Lauren Rosemary Hook at Feminist Press for believing in us and letting us tell our story in all of its holistic, collective Lakȟóta grassroots worldview and hybrid splendor.

Wóphila by Sarah

WÓPHILA TO MY SONS, Aarron and Brenden, who grew up with me as a young iná, moved all over the country for my career without complaining, and always keep me laughing with their hilarious insights. Elephant Shoes.

Wóphila to my čhantéskúya and main thought partner, Oglála Sioux Tribal Chairman Kevin Killer, who has taught me love and spirituality beyond anything I ever dreamed of. Wóphila for loving me unconditionally. Wóphila for supporting my dreams, even if they take me far away to the ocean and all over the world.

My early journey of healing included Episcopal priests who lovingly held space for a young woman searching and set me on the path of my calling: Rev. Ray Waldon, Rev. Jeff Jencks, and Rev. Dennis Gibbs. I was also blessed to be a sister to those who followed their callings and gave me their friendship, shared their ability to see the stars, and served as reflective travel companions. Wóphila to Rev. Cornelia Eaton for gifting me protection in the form of stones representing the sacred mountains of the Diné and to Rev. Alejandra Trillos for being my CS. Wóphila to my diversity, social justice, and environmental justice team of Rev. Angela Ifill, Rev. Fred Vergara, Rev. Anthony Guillén, Michael Schut, Angie Cabanban, and Rev. Christopher Johnson at the Episcopal Church, who trusted my leadership and supported my understanding of how to utilize calling in work. Wóphila to Ruth-Ann Collins and Bronwyn

Clark Skov from Lifelong Christian Formation, who helped me understand transformation from a Christian perspective. Wóphila to Presiding Bishop Katharine Jefferts Schori for believing in my leadership and giving her time to Indigenous issues.

Wóphila to tribal leaders who also supported my leadership in so many ways, former White Earth Ojibwe Chair Erma Vizenor and Poarch Band of Creek Indians Vice Chairman Robbie McGhee. Wóphila to National Indian Gaming Chairman Ernie Stevens Jr. for always supporting my leadership. Wóphila to Rev. Marlene Helgemo, Sandy White Hawk, and Vance Blackfox for their enduring friendship, spiritual conversations, and laughter. Wóphila to our Oglála Lakȟóta elders for sharing their wisdom and role modeling: Tȟuŋwíŋ Ethlene Two Dogs, Tȟuŋwíŋ Emily Koenen, Cecilia Fire Thunder, Shirley Murphy, Arlana Bettelyoun.

Wóphila to Gina Jackson and Red Dawn Foster for allowing me to take time away from our work at Return to the Heart Foundation to write this book. Wóphila to Taj James at Full Spectrum Labs for showing me anything is possible. Wóphila to Dr. David Washington for following the force with me. Wóphila to dear social justice friends, always in the fight together: Julia Walsh, Mónica Ramírez, Nathalie Molina Niño, Shirley Murphy, Lori Pourier, Cheryl Crazybull, and Arlana Bettelyoun. Wóphila to my dear friend Twila True for inspiring me always!

Wóphila to social justice allies in the entertainment industry who I've been blessed to work with: John Legend, Mark Ruffalo, Marisa Tomei, Anne Hathaway, and Portugal. The Man.

Wóphila to my friends who kept it real with me. Big shout-out to the 29ers Club (Joannie, Vance, and Farzana), who kept me laughing during the pandemic and inspired me to get healthy! Wóphila to cousins Shawn and Angie for the beloved Oglála candor and laughter. Wóphila to my friend Eddie in

San Diego, who taught me courage when he directed me at twenty-one years old to take my résumé to the VP in person. Wóphila to my friend Randy in New York City, who listened to my worries as a new manager in my early thirties and advised patience.

Wóphila to Auntie Erin for allowing my boys to crash at her home every summer. Wóphila to my younger sisters/cousins and brothers/cousins Chris, Dave, Alyssa, and Maryssa, who came to whatever city I was living in to nanny (or "manny") for my sons while I traveled for work. Their willingness to help me ensured my sons had a connection to home and their relatives. Wóphila to Rachel, Ede, and Charlotte in Pensacola, Jamie in San Diego, Nancy and Yecenia in Los Angeles, Sarah and Shilo in Spearfish, for being there for my sons when I need you all. I would've never made it to where I am today without the support of your friendship and love for my sons.

A special wóphila to my dog daughter, Zuzu, who reminds me to play and is always seated next to me while I write.

Wóphila by Emma

WÓPHILA TO MAHÁSAŊNI, Sid White (Oneida Nation of Wisconsin/Kickapoo Nation/Cheyenne and Arapaho Nation), my best friend and mahásaŋni of nineteen years. He is a continual source of support, strength, encouragement, safety, and unconditional love in my life. His unwavering and unconditional love has allowed me the strength to continue my healing. To my wakȟáŋheža (Gavin, Elise, and Josalyn), whose spirits chose me and my hásaŋni to be their parents. For giving me strength to heal and for saving my life. My sources of unconditional love, support, and healing. I would not be where I am today without them. Wóphila to the Skenadore family of the Oneida Nation of Wisconsin and especially to my uŋčíši (mother-in-law), Sandra Skenadore, for her unwavering support, kindness, and love. Wóphila to the late Warren and Josepha Skenadore, who will be forever missed and loved. Wóphila to my father-in-law, Jerry Hill (Oneida Nation of Wisconsin), and family for his guidance, support, love, and Oneida language teachings to our family. Wóphila to the White family of Albuquerque, New Mexico, for welcoming me into their family, for their love and support. Wóphila especially to my late father-in-law, John White (Kickapoo Nation/Southern Cheyenne and Arapaho Nation), and late sister-in-law, Henrietta "Hattie" White. Their gentle love and support are so missed. We will forever miss and love you—until we see you both again. Wóphila to the members of the Oneida Nation of Wisconsin for accepting me and sharing their love of the community, Longhouse, "Good Mind," culture, ceremonies, and traditions. Oneida has been an amazing and beautiful source of love, belonging, and healing for myself and my family.

Wóphila to Vange (Oneida Nation of Wisconsin), my big sister, dear friend, and mentor while we worked together for five years as DV advocates. I was so fortunate to have been able to work alongside her. With her twenty-three years of DV knowledge, she helped me move through many stages of healing. She reminded me to trust myself and my intuition in such a loving way. I really cannot thank her enough. Interestingly enough, four or five years prior to my working with her, I chose to recognize her at a community recognition event at the Norbert Hill Center. Everyone was encouraged to nominate someone from the community and I decided to nominate her even though I didn't know her. I knew intuitively that she helped so many in the community and was not recognized for her amazing work. Little did I know how much of an impact she would have on my own healing process.

Wóphila to Julia McLester (Oneida Nation of Wisconsin), whom I met when I began working in the domestic violence/sexual abuse field. We connected as survivors of sexual violence. She holds twenty-six years of experience in domestic abuse and sexual violence. She has always been a very kind, wonderful, supportive, dear friend and colleague. She encouraged me to join the American Indians Against Abuse (AIAI) board, where she held a seat for many years, and I learned so much from these beautiful and strong women. When I told her I wanted to write a book, she was so supportive and connected me with a publisher friend of hers. Then she would send me emails about writing workshops every so often to remind me to keep pushing forward to reach this dream. I credit her for keeping me on this path of becoming a writer.

Wóphila to Leo Chinana and family for being my source of

Lakȟóta/Dakȟóta traditional spirituality, teachings, and healing ceremonies so far away from home. Wóphila to Debbie Murphy-Chinana for teaching me about Reiki, healing, and energy work.

Wóphila to Don Coyhis (Stockbridge-Munsee Band of Mohican Indians), Kateri Coyhis (Stockbridge-Munsee Band of Mohican Indians), and the late Marlin Farley (White Earth Nation). Marlin trained me in the first Mending Broken Hearts program in Oneida, Wisconsin. He saw in me that which I couldn't see. He told me I was a healer. His kindness and gentleness during this sacred healing program meant more to me than words can express. I know he is missed by so many.

Wóphila to Diane DuBray (Oglála Lakȟóta/Wakpá Wašté Lakȟóta), my best friend since middle school on the Pine Ridge Reservation. I love how time never skips a beat with our friendship.

Wóphila to the late Judy Torres and family (Oneida Nation of Wisconsin). Judy was my first friend in Wisconsin and welcomed me to my new home. She encouraged me to become Treasurer of the Native American Student Movement at the Milwaukee Area Technical College. This led to my becoming President of the American Indian Student Association at the University of Wisconsin-Milwaukee. She helped babysit our newborn son. I love and miss you so much. I know you would be so proud of me.

Wóphila to my colleagues Mary Beth King (Oneida Nation of Wisconsin) and Lisa Shaw (Menominee Nation), who introduced me to brainspotting therapy. I have learned so much from the both of you in this healing work. I am truly grateful.

Wóphila to Paulette Leschig, Oneida, and Cari Chapman, Lac Du Flambeau, and Jenny (Hinkfuss) Powless, my respective second, third, and fourth dear friends in Wisconsin.

Wóphila to all my amazingly wonderful colleagues: JoAnn Ninham (Oneida Nation of Wisconsin), George Skenandore

(Oneida Nation of Wisconsin), Mari Kriescher, Kate Sayers, Dr. Michael Sayers, Dr. Christine Garstka, and Rob Haen for all your unwavering support, encouragement, and guidance. It has meant the world to me.

A special wóphila to my igmú (cat) son, Haŋhépi (night), a.k.a, Honey. He has been a wonderful emotional support animal to me during this writing process. He keeps me grounded and reminds me to stay present.

Notes

Chapter 1. The Original Warrior Princesses

1. "Pine Ridge Reservation, ASD-NE, 2015–2019 American Community Survey 5-Year Estimates," United States Census Bureau, accessed June 6, 2021, https://www.census.gov/tribal/?aianihh=2810.

2. "About the Pine Ridge Reservation," Re-Member, accessed June 6, 2021, https://www.re-member.org/pine-ridge-reservation.

3. "About the Pine Ridge Reservation," Re-Member.

4. Patrick Strickland, "Life on the Pine Ridge Native American Reservation," *Aljazeera*, November 2, 2016, https://www.aljazeera.com/indepth/features/2016/10/life-pine-ridge-native-american-reservation-161031113119935.html.

5. "About the Pine Ridge Reservation," Re-Member.

6. Rob Harris, "Animals That Circle to Protect Their Young," Pets on mom.me, retrieved June 6, 2021, http://animals.mom.me/animals-circle-protect-young-8287.html.

7. Maria Yellow Horse Brave Heart, "The *Return to the Sacred Path*: Reflections on the Development of Historical Trauma Healing," presentation, retrieved June 6, 2021, https://www.ihs.gov/sites/telebehavioral/themes/responsive2017/display_objects/documents/slides/historicaltrauma/htreturnsacredpath0513.pdf.

8. Erin Blakemore, "The Little-Known History of the Forced Sterilization of Native American Women," JSTOR Daily, August 25, 2016, https://daily.jstor.org/the-little-known-history-of-the-forced-sterilization-of-native-american-women/.

9. Don L. Coyhis, *Understanding Native American Culture: Insights for Recovery Professionals and Other Wellness Practitioners*, ed. Richard Simonelli, 2nd ed. (Aurora, CO: Coyhis Publishing & Consulting Inc., 2009), loc. 208 of 1740, Kindle.

10. Dominic Strinati, *An Introduction to Theories of Popular Culture* (London: Routledge, 1995), quoted in Debra Merskin, "Sending Up Signals: A Survey of Native American Media Use and Representation in the Mass Media," *Howard Journal of Communications* 9, no. 1 (1998): 333–45, doi: 10.1080/106461798246943.

11. Merskin, "Sending Up Signals," 333–45.

12. Peter A. Leavitt, Rebecca Covarrubias, Yvonne A. Perez, and Stephanie A. Fryberg, "'Frozen in Time': The Impact of Native American Media Representations on Identity and Self-Understanding," *Journal of Social Issues* 71, no. 1 (March 2015): 39–53, doi: 10.1111/josi.12095.

13. United Nations Department of Public Information, "State of the World's Indigenous Peoples," press release, January 14, 2010, http://www.un.org/esa/socdev/unpfii/documents/SOWIP/press%20package/sowip-press-package-en.pdf.

14. "Indigenous Peoples," The World Bank, last modified March 19, 2021, https://www.worldbank.org/en/topic/indigenouspeoples.

15. "The Issues," Cultural Survival, retrieved June 6, 2021, https://www.culturalsurvival.org/issues.

16. John Vidal, "The Tribes Paying the Brutal Price of Conservation," *The Guardian*, August 28, 2016, https://www.theguardian.com/global-

development/2016/aug/28/exiles-human-cost-of-conservation-indigenous-peoples-eco-tourism.

17. "American Indian Suicide Rate Increases," National Indian Council on Aging Inc., September 9, 2019, https://www.nicoa.org/national-american-indian-and-alaska-native-hope-for-life-day/.

18. Erik Stegman and Victoria Phillips, "Missing the Point: the Real Impact of Native Mascots and Team Names on American Indian and Alaska Native Youth," *Center for American Progress*, July 22, 2014, https://www.americanprogress.org/issues/race/reports/2014/07/22/94214/missing-the-point/.

19. "APA Resolution Recommending the Immediate Retirement of American Indian Mascots, Symbols, Images, and Personalities by Schools, Colleges, Universities, Athletic Teams, and Organizations," *American Psychological Association*, retrieved June 6, 2021, http://www.apa.org/about/policy/mascots.pdf.

20. Jamil Smith, "The Revolutionary Power of Black Panther," *Time*, retrieved June 6, 2021, http://time.com/black-panther/.

Chapter 2. Happy New Year

1. "The Indigenous Lifecourse: Strengthing the Health and Well-Being of Native Youth," Native Americans in Philanthropy, 2016, https://www.nativephilanthropy.org/wp-content/uploads/2015/11/Indigenous-Lifecourse-NAP-Report.pdf, 13.

2. Maria Yellow Horse Brave Heart, "The *Return to the Sacred Path*: Reflections on the Development of Historical Trauma Healing," presentation, retrieved June 6, 2021, https://www.ihs.gov/sites/telebehavioral/themes/responsive2017/display_objects/documents/slides/historicaltrauma/htreturnsacredpath0513.pdf.

Chapter 3. Wašíču Išnála or *White Man Stands Alone*

1. Vincent J. Felitti, "The Relation Between Adverse Childhood Experiences and Adult Health: *Turning Gold into Lead*," *The Permanente Journal* 6, no. 1 (2002): 44–47.

2. Nadine Burke Harris, *The Deepest Well: Healing the Long-Term Effects of Childhood Adversity* (New York: Houghton Mifflin Harcourt, 2018), 48–61.

3. "Toxic Stress," Center on the Developing Child at Harvard University (2015), https://developingchild.harvard.edu/science/key-concepts/toxic-stress/.

4. "Pine Ridge Info," Sew for Kids, accessed June 6, 2021, https://sewforkids.wordpress.com/about-pine-ridge/pine-ridge-info/.

5. Courtney E. Ackerman, "What Is Attachment Theory? Bowlby's 4 Stages Explained," April 27, 2018, https://positivepsychology.com/attachment-theory/.

Chapter 4. Reclaiming Spirit

1. Francine Russo, "Sexual Assault May Trigger Involuntary Paralysis," *Scientific American*, August 4, 2017, https://www.scientificamerican.com/article/sexual-assault-may-trigger-involuntary-paralysis/.

2. Grace Galliano, Linda M. Noble, et al., "Victim Reactions During Rape/Sexual Assault: A Preliminary Study of the Immobility Response and Its Correlates," *Journal of Interpersonal Violence* 8, no. 1 (March 1, 1993): 109–14, doi: 10.1177/088626093008001008.

3. David Lisak and Paul M. Miller, "Repeat Rape and Multiple Offending Among Undetected Rapists," *Violence and Victims* 17, no. 1 (2022), https://time.com/wp-content/uploads/2014/09/repeat_rape.pdf.

4. André B. Rosay, "Violence Against American Indian and Alaska Native Women and Men," National Institute of Justice, last modified June 1, 2016, https://nij.ojp.gov/topics/articles/violence-against-american-indian-and-alaska-native-women-and-men.

5. Anna Möller, Hans Peter Söndergaard, and Lotti Helström, "Tonic Immobility during Sexual Assault: A Common Reaction Predicting Post-Traumatic Stress Disorder and Severe Depression," *Acta Obstetricia et Gynecologica Scandinavica* 96, no. 8 (June 2017): 932–38, https://doi.org/10.1111/aogs.13174.

6. Juliana Kalaf, et al., "Sexual Trauma Is More Strongly Associated with Tonic Immobility Than Other Types of Trauma: A Population Based Study," *Journal of Affective Disorders* 215 (June 2017): 71–76, https://doi.org/10.1016/j.jad.2017.03.009.

7. Bessel van der Kolk, *The Body Keeps the Score: Brain, Mind, and Body in the Healing of Trauma* (New York: Viking, 2014), 77.

8. Möller, et al., "Tonic Immobility," 935–36.

9. Catrina Brown, "Women's Narratives of Trauma: (Re)storying Uncertainty, Minimization and Self-Blame," *Narrative Works: Issues, Investigations & Interventions* 3, no. 1 (August 2013): 1–30, https://journals.lib.unb.ca/index.php/NW/article/view/21063/24305.

10. "Maze of Injustice," Amnesty International, August 8, 2011, accessed June 6, 2021, https://www.amnestyusa.org/reports/maze-of-injustice/.

11. Joe Flood, "What's Lurking Behind the Suicides?," *New York Times*, May 17, 2015, https://www.nytimes.com/2015/05/17/opinion/sunday/whats-lurking-behind-the-suicides.html; Joe Flood, "Sherman Alexie and the Sexual Assault Legacy of Federal Native American Boarding Schools," Medium, March, 6, 2018, https://medium.com/athena-talks/sherman-alexie-and-the-sexual-assault-legacy-of-federal-native-american-boarding-schools-f460e796e241.

12. "Victims of Sexual Violence: Statistics," Rape, Abuse and Incest National Network, accessed June 6, 2021, https://www.rainn.org/statistics/victims-sexual-violence.

13. Flood, "What's Lurking Behind the Suicides?"

14. "Mending Broken Hearts: Healing from Unresolved Grief and Intergenerational Trauma," White Bison Inc., accessed June 6, 2021, https://www.whitebison.org/wp-content/uploads/2021/05/MBH.pdf.

15. "Study Links Sexual Assault to Legacy of Indian Residential Schools and Childhood Abuse," First Nations House of Learning, University of British Columbia, Vancouver, April, 10, 2015, http://aboriginal.ubc.ca/2015/04/10/study-links-sexual-assault-to-legacy-of-indian-residential-schools-and-childhood-abuse/.

16. Rupert Ross, *Indigenous Healing: Exploring Traditional Paths* (Toronto: Penguin Canada, 2014), loc. 3346 of 4906, Kindle.

17. Peter A. Levine, *In an Unspoken Voice: How the Body Releases Trauma and Restores Goodness* (Berkeley, California: North Atlantic Books, 2010), 355.

18. Lee Irwin, "Freedom, Law and Prophecy: A Brief History of Native American Religious Resistance," *American Indian Quarterly* 21, no. 1 (1997): 35, doi: 10.2307/1185587.

19. Qtd. in Doyle Arbogast, *Wounded Warriors: A Time for Healing* (Omaha: Little Turtle Publications, 1995), 319.

20. "'Mitakuye Oyasin,'" Sitting Owl, Earth People Productions, last

modified May, 26, 2015, accessed June 5, 2021, http://sittingowl.com/mitakuye_oyasin.htm.

21. The National Center for PTSD, US Department of Veterans Affairs, "DSM-5 Criteria for PTSD," Brainline, WETA, last modified March 28, 2019, https://www.brainline.org/article/dsm-5-criteria-ptsd.

22. Rianne A. Kleine, Muriel A. Hagenaars, and Agnes van Minnen, "Tonic Immobility During Re-experiencing the Traumatic Event in Posttraumatic Stress Disorder," *Psychiatry Research* 270 (June 2018), 1105–9, https://doi.org/10.1016/j.psychres.2018.06.051.

Chapter 5. Standing in the Center

1. Brianne Theobald, "A 1970 Law Led to the Mass Sterilization of Native American Women. That History Still Matters," *Time*, November 27, 2019, https://time.com/5737080/native-american-sterilization-history/.

2. David Melmer, "Cecilia Fire Thunder: A Year of Confusion Draws to an End for Former Oglala Sioux Leader," *Indian Country Today*, September 12, 2018, https://indiancountrytoday.com/archive/cecelia-fire-thunder-a-year-of-confusion-draws-to-an-end-for-former-oglala-sioux-leader.

3. Chloe Atkins, "Report Details Wave of State Legislative Attempts to Restrict Abortion in 2021," NBC News, March 26, 2021, https://www.nbcnews.com/politics/politics-news/report-details-wave-state-legislative-attempts-restrict-abortion-2021-n1262070.

4. Feifei Sun, "Are You in a Codependent Relationship?" WebMD, August 7, 2014, https://www.webmd.com/sex-relationships/features/signs-of-a-codependent-relationship.

5. Christina G. Mello, "Gender and Empowerment: Contemporary Lakota Women of Rosebud," *McNair Scholars Journal* 8, no. 1 (2004): 35–51. https://scholarworks.gvsu.edu/cgi/viewcontent.cgi?article=1037&context=mcnair&httpsredir=1&referer=.

6. This is a great article for those who want to work toward self-improvement in these areas: Sherry Gaba, "A Primer on Codependency," Psychology Today, June 11, 2019, https://www.psychologytoday.com/us/blog/addiction-and-recovery/201906/primer-codependency.

Chapter 6. Life and Death

1. "What is Brainspotting?" Brainspotting Trainings LLC, accessed June 6, 2021, https://brainspotting.com/about-bsp/.

2. "About," White Bison, accessed June 6, 2021, https://whitebison.org/about.

3. Don Coyhis, *The Wellbriety Journey to Forgiveness*, White Bison, March 1, 2011, accessed June 6, 2021, https://www.youtube.com/watch?v=vZwF9NnQbWM&t=1197s.

Chapter 7. The Sacred

1. Joseph Epes Brown, *The Sacred Pipe: Black Elk's Account of the Seven Rites of the Ogala Sioux* (Norman: University of Oklahoma Press, 1953).

2. *Merriam-Webster's Collegiate Dictionary*, 11th ed. (Springfield, MA: Merriam-Webster, 2003), "calling," https://www.merriam-webster.com/dictionary/calling (retrieved March, 28, 2021).

Chapter 8. Healing Women

1. "MMIW2S," Coalition to Stop Violence Against Native Women, accessed June 6, 2021, https://www.csvanw.org/mmiw.

2. André B. Rosay, "Violence Against American Indian and Alaska Native Women and Men: 2010 Findings from the National Intimate Partner and Sexual Violence Survey," US Department of Justice, May 2016, accessed June 6, 2021, https://www.ojp.gov/pdffiles1/nij/249736.pdf.

3. Ruth Hopkins, "Sexual Trauma: One Legacy of the Boarding School Era," *Indian Country Today*, last modified September 13, 2018, https://indiancountrytoday.com/archive/sexual-trauma-one-legacy-of-the-boarding-school-era.

4. Coyhis, *The Wellbriety Journey*.

5. "50 Obstacles to Leaving," National Domestic Violence Hotline, accessed June 6, 2021, https://www.thehotline.org/resources/50-obstacles-to-leaving/.

6. "About the Pine Ridge Reservation," Re-Member.

7. Annita Lucchesi and Abigail Echo-Hawk, "Missing and Murdered Indigenous Women & Girls," Urban Indian Health Institute, accessed June 6, 2021, https://www.uihi.org/wp-content/uploads/2018/11/Missing-and-Murdered-Indigenous-Women-and-Girls-Report.pdf.

8. Rosay, "Violence Against American Indian and Alaska Native Women and Men," 50.

9. Ronet Bachman, Heather Zaykowski, Rachel Kallmyer, et al., "Violence Against American Indian and Alaska Native Women and the Criminal Justice Response: What Is Known," August 2008, https://www.ojp.gov/pdffiles1/nij/grants/223691.pdf.

10. "GIC Issues—MMIW Campaign," Global Indigenous Council, accessed June 6, 2021, https://www.globalindigenouscouncil.com/missing-murdered-p1.

11. Christopher Vondracek, "South Dakota Establishes Office for Missing, Murdered Indigenous Persons Cases," *Grand Forks Herald*, April 2, 2021, https://www.grandforksherald.com/news/government-and-politics/6966713-South-Dakota-establishes-office-for-missing-murdered-Indigenous-persons-cases.

12. "Native American Children Reported Missing to NCMEC," National Center for Missing & Exploited Children, 2020, accessed June 6, 2021, https://www.missingkids.org/content/dam/missingkids/pdfs/Native%20American%20Children_2009-2018.pdf.

13. Wyoming Survey & Analysis Center, "Missing and Murdered Indigenous People: Statewide Report Wyoming," (Laramie: University of Wyoming, 2021), https://wysac.uwyo.edu/wysac/reports/View/7713.

14. "Statement of Charles Addington Deputy Bureau Director—Office of Justice Services Bureau of Indian Affairs, United States Department of the Interior, before the House Committee on Natural Resources Subcommittee for Indigenous Peoples of the United States Oversight Hearing 'Reviewing the Trump Administration's Approach to the MMIW Crisis,'" September 11, 2019, https://www.doi.gov/ocl/mmiw-crisis.

15. National Congress of American Indians Policy Research Center, "Policy Insights Brief: Statistics on Violence Against Native Women," February 2013, "https://www.ncai.org/attachments/PolicyPaper_tWAjznFslemhAffZgNGzHUqIWMRPkCDjpFtxeKEUVKjubxfpGYK_Policy%20Insights%20Brief_VAWA_020613.pdf.

16. Kaitlin Grable, "Big Oil Is Fueling the Crisis of Missing and Murdered Indigenous Women," Greenpeace, May 5, 2021, https://www.greenpeace.org/usa/justice-for-missing-and-murdered-indigenous-women-will-move-us-closer-to-climate-justice/.

17. Jenna Kunze, "House Votes to Reauthorize Violence Against Women Act, Commits to Safety for Native Women," Native News Online, March 17, 2021, https://nativenewsonline.net/currents/house-votes-to-reauthorize-violence-against-women-act-commits-to-safety-for-native-women.

18. Carolyn Smith-Morris, "Addressing the Epidemic of Missing & Murdered Indigenous Women and Girls," Cultural Survival, March 6, 2020, https://www.culturalsurvival.org/news/addressing-epidemic-missing-murdered-indigenous-women-and-girls.

19. Indian Law Resource Center, "Violence Against Indigenous Women in the United States, Particularly Alaska Native Women, in the Context of the Covid-19 Pandemic," June 18, 2020, AlaskaNativeWomenResourceCenterILCandNIWRCJointSubmisson.docx (live.com).

20. Suzy Cook and Sierra Clark, "Indigenous Communities Work to Find Justice among Epidemic of Violence, WKAR Public Media, May 4, 2021, https://www.wkar.org/news/2021-05-04/indigenous-communities-work-to-find-justice-among-epidemic-of-violence#stream/0.

21. Jenna Kunze, "House Votes to Reauthorize Violence Against Women Act, Commits to Safety for Native Women," Native News Online, March 17, 2021, https://nativenewsonline.net/currents/house-votes-to-reauthorize-violence-against-women-act-commits-to-safety-for-native-women.

22. Jenna Romaine, "Haaland Announces New Indigenous Missing & Murdered Unit," The Hill, April 20, 2021, https://thehill.com/changing-america/respect/equality/549275-haaland-announces-new-indigenous-missing-murdered-unit/.

23. Lucchesi and Echo-Hawk, "Missing and Murdered Indigenous Women & Girls," 6.

Chapter 9. Rising

1. The Women's March Organizers, *Together We Rise: Behind the Scenes at the Protest Heard Around the World* (Dey Street Books: New York, 2018), 214–15.

2. Tara Paniogue, "L.A. Designer Bethany Yellowtail Creates a Silk Scarf for Women's March on Washington," *Los Angeles Times*, January 21, 2017, https://www.latimes.com/fashion/la-ig-bethany-yellowtail-20170120-story.html.

3. Shayna Plaut, "Learning Resistance and Building Solidarity—Black Lives Matter North of the 49th," *Georgia Straight*, July 22, 2016, https://www.straight.com/news/740886/shayna-plaut-learning-resistance-and-building-solidarity-black-lives-matter-north-49th.

4. Glenn Welker, "Tse-tsehese-staestse (Cheyenne) Literature," last modified June 16, 2016, accessed June 6, 2021, http://www.indigenouspeople.net/cheyenne.htm.

5. Jens Korff, "Bullying & Lateral Violence," Creative Spirits, last modified August 13, 2020, accessed June 6, 2021, https://www.creativespirits.info/aboriginalculture/people/bullying-lateral-violence.

6. Coyhis, *The Wellbriety Journey*.

7. Don L. Coyhis, *Understanding Native American Culture: Insights for Recovery Professionals and Other Wellness Practitioners*, ed. Richard Simonelli, 2nd ed. (Aurora, CO: Coyhis Publishing & Consulting Inc., 2009), loc. 458 of 1740, Kindle.

8. Karen Fish and Jaime Stief, "Symposium: Decolonizing Our Relationships through Lateral Kindness," National Collaborating Centre for Determinants of Health, blog, September 14, 2017, http://nccdh.ca/blog/entry/symposium-decolonizing-our-relationships-through-lateral-kindness.

9. SAMHSA, "Lateral Goodness: Strength-Based Approaches for Addressing Lateral Oppression in AI/AN Communities," October 24, 2014, YouTube video, https://www.youtube.com/watch?v=jbrDHBhQZlc.

10. The Spirit of 1848 Caucus, *APHA 2019 Reportback* (Philadelphia: American Public Health Association, November 2–6, 2019), http://www.spiritof1848.org/2019_spirit%20of%201848%20APHA%20reportback_final_secure_1114.pdf.

11. Nick Estes, "Lakȟóta Giving and Justice," *owasicu owe waste sni*, blog, November 26, 2015, accessed June 6, 2021, https://nickestes.blog/2015/11/26/lakota-giving-and-justice/.

12. Gavin Haines, "Time to Be Kind: Why Kindness Matters," Positive. News, April 1, 2019, https://www.positive.news/lifestyle/time-to-be-kind-why-kindness-matters/.

13. van der Kolk, *The Body Keeps the Score*, 38.

Chapter 10. The Original Caretakers

1. Erica Carbajal, "COVID-19 Death Rates Higher among Native Americans: CDC," *Becker's Hospital Review*, December 14, 2020, https://www.beckershospitalreview.com/public-health/covid-19-death-rates-higher-among-native-americans-cdc.html#:~:text=American%20Indian%20and%20Alaskan%20Native,11.

2. *Crow: The Legend*, directed and written by Eric Darnell, Baobab Studios, aired November 15, 2018, YouTube video, https://www.youtube.com/watch?v=KYFrgc6OiLg&t=6s.

3. Amber Dowling, "Michelle Latimer's Identity Crisis Is Raising Impossible Questions for Canada's Indigenous Filmmakers," *Variety*, December 23, 2020, https://variety.com/2020/film/global/michelle-latimer-indigenous-trickster-inconvenient-indian-1234873888/.

4. *Living Planet Report 2020: Bending the Curve of Biodiversity Loss*, World Wildlife Foundation, ed. R.E.A. Almond, M. Grooten, and T. Petersen (Gland, Switzerland: World Wildlife Fund, 2020), accessed June 6, 2021, https://f.hubspotusercontent20.net/hubfs/4783129/LPR/PDFs/ENGLISH-FULL.pdf.

5. Daniel Dodgen, Darrin Donato, Nancy Kelly, et al., "Ch. 8: Mental Health and Well-Being," in *The Impacts of Climate Change on Human Health in the United States: A Scientific Assessment*, US Global Change Research Program (Washington, DC: 2016), 217–46, http://dx.doi.org/10.7930/J0TX3C9H.

6. Marshall Burke, Felipe González, Patrick Baylis, et al., "Higher Temperatures Increase Suicide Rates in the United States and Mexico," *Nature Climate Change* 8 (July 23, 2018): 723–29, https://doi.org/10.1038/s41558-018-0222-x.

7. Indi Howeth, "Climate Change Is a Threat Multipler," Action for Climate Emergency, November 14, 2020, https://acespace.org/2020/11/14/threat-multiplier/.

8. Rowan Walrath, "Climate Change Isn't Just Frying the Planet—

It's Fraying Our Nerves," *Mother Jones*, February 18, 2019, accessed June 6, 2021, https://www.motherjones.com/environment/2019/02/climate-change-isnt-just-frying-the-planet-its-fraying-our-nerves/.

9. Ashlee Cunsolo Willox, *Climate Change & Inuit Mental Health* (Nova Scotia: Cape Breton University), 2, https://edition.pagesuite-professional.co.uk/html5/reader/production/default.aspx?pubname=&edid=1c4051ec-525a-4ff8-b68d-776d666c5b61.

10. Cunsolo Willox, *Climate Change*, 4.

11. Paolo Cianconi, Sophia Betrò, and Luigi Janiri, "The Impact of Climate Change on Mental Health: A Systematic Descriptive Review." *Frontiers in Psychiatry* 11, no. 74 (2020), https://doi.org/10.3389/fpsyt.2020.00074; Susan Clayton and Bryan T. Karazsia, "Development and Validation of a Measure of Climate Change Anxiety," *Journal of Environmental Psychology* 69, no. 101434 (2020), doi: 10.1016/j.jenvp.2020.101434.

12. "Solastalgia," Climate Psychology Alliance, last modified April 21, 2021, accessed June 6, 2021, https://www.climatepsychologyalliance.org/handbook/484-what-is-solastalgia.

13. Sean B. Carroll, *The Serengeti Rules: The Quest to Discover How Life Works and Why It Matters* (Princeton, NJ: Princeton University Press, 2016).

14. Brodie Farquhar, "Wolf Reintroduction Changes Ecosystem in Yellowstone," Yellowstone National Park Trips, Outside, June 30, 2021, https://www.yellowstonepark.com/things-to-do/wildlife/wolf-reintroduction-changes-ecosystem/.

15. Wayne Walker, Alessandro Baccini, Stephan Schwartzman, et al., "Forest Carbon in Amazonia: The Unrecognized Contribution of Indigenous Territories and Protected Natural Areas," *Carbon Management* 5, no. 5–6 (December 2014): 479–85, https://doi.org/10.1080/17583004.2014.990680.

16. Claudia Sobrevila, *The Role of Indigenous Peoples in Biodiversity Conservation: The Natural but Often Forgotten Partners*, The World Bank, May 2008, https://documents1.worldbank.org/curated/en/995271468177530126/pdf/443000WP0BOX321onservation01PUBLIC1.pdf.

17. Ella Archibald-Binge and Rhett Wyman, "'It's Miraculous': Owners Say Cultural Burning Saved Their Property," *Sydney Morning Herald*, January 6, 2020, https://www.smh.com.au/national/nsw/it-s-miraculous-owners-say-cultural-burning-saved-their-property-20200103-p53okc.html.

18. Benjamin Wachenje, "Defending Tomorrow," Global Witness, July 29, 2020, https://www.globalwitness.org/en/campaigns/environmental-activists/defending-tomorrow/?gclid=Cj0KCQjw1a6E BhC0ARIsAOiTkrHfw9Gc9DSEyMnj3cMMRDA29IVSN1HYPdyTbJ_i_ hp6EKxoOSTGoawaAppJEALw_wcB.

19. Anna V. Smith, "Some Indigenous Communities Have a New Way to Fight Climate Change: Give Personhood Rights to Nature," *Mother Jones*, September 29, 2019, accessed June 6, 2021, https://www.motherjones.com/environment/2019/09/some-indigenous-communities-have-a-new-way-to-fight-climate-change-give-personhood-rights-to-nature/.

20. Jessica Fu, "Amid Severe Drought in Oregon Farming Region, Competing Needs for Water Spark Tense Debate over What Comes First—Farmers, Endangered Fish, or Tribal Food Sovereignty," The Counter, April 2021, accessed June 6, 2021, https://thecounter.org/oregon-farms-water-klamath-river-drought-salmon/amp/?__twitter_impression=true.

21. "Chippewa Establish Rights of *Manoomin* on White Earth Reservation and throughout 1855 Ceded Territory," 1855 Treaty Authority, January 11, 2019, https://static1.squarespace.com/static/5ceea3dff402670001e6ca05/

330

t/610c2292b9d9a51dd0582f72/1628185234841/right-of-manoomin-media-statement.pdf.

22. Charlie McKenna, "Passamaquoddy Tribe Regains Control of Island in Maine after 150 Years," *Boston Globe*, updated May 26, 2021, https://www.bostonglobe.com/2021/05/26/metro/passamaquoddy-tribe-regains-control-island-maine/.

23. Mike Ludwig, "UN Report Says Indigenous Sovereignty Could Save the Planet," Truthout, May 7, 2019, https://truthout.org/articles/un-report-says-indigenous-sovereignty-could-save-the-planet/.

24. "Environmental Justice and Philanthropy: Challenges and Opportunities for Alignment," Building Equity & Alignment for Environmental Justice, https://static1.squarespace.com/static/5d14dab43967cc000179f3d2/t/5efdeb402845322eabcbc51d/1593699136404/LA+One+Pager_Funding+Disparity.pdf.

25. Kat Stafford, "Pledge Drive Urges Funding Racially Diverse Climate Efforts," AP News, February 4, 2021, https://apnews.com/article/racially-diverse-climate-efforts-ff2195a10532f28ed80a08750f7f3e9d.

26. Mack Lamoureux, "Neo-Nazis Are Using Eco-Fascism to Recruit Young People," *Vice*, September 25, 2020, https://www.vice.com/en/article/wxqmey/neo-nazis-eco-fascism-climate-change-recruit-young-people.

27. Brady Dennis, Chris Mooney, and Sarah Kaplan, "The World's Rich Need to Cut Their Carbon Footprint by a Factor of 30 to Slow Climate Change, U.N. Warns," *Washington Post*, December 9, 2020, https://www.washingtonpost.com/climate-environment/2020/12/09/carbon-footprints-climate-change-rich-one-percent/.

28. Jon Queally, "'A Goddamn Terrifying Time to Be Alive': Naomi Klein Explains Why a Global Green New Deal Comes First and Being Hopeful Comes After," *Common Dreams*, September 17, 2019, https://www.commondreams.org/news/2019/09/17/goddamn-terrifying-time-be-alive-naomi-klein-explains-why-global-green-new-deal.

29. David Lawrence, "The Regrowth of Eco-Fascism," *HOPE not hate*, retrieved June 6, 2021, https://www.hopenothate.org.uk/magazine/climate-change-far-right/the-regrowth-of-eco-fascism/.

30. Sam Adler-Bell, "Why White Supremacists Are Hooked on Green Living," *New Republic*, September 24, 2019, https://newrepublic.com/article/154971/rise-ecofascism-history-white-nationalism-environmental-preservation-immigration.

31. Alex Amend, "Blood and Vanishing Topsoil: American Ecofascism Past, Present, and in the Coming Climate Crisis," Political Research Associates, July 9, 2020, https://www.politicalresearch.org/2020/07/09/blood-and-vanishing-topsoil.

32. Peter Dockrill, "We're Headed For a Class-Based 'Climate Apartheid,' Warns Chilling New UN Report," ScienceAlert, June 26, 2019, https://www.sciencealert.com/hundreds-of-millions-at-risk-of-devastating-climate-apartheid-un-expert-warns.

33. "Disasters: UN Report Shows Climate Change Causing 'Dramatic Rise' in Economic Losses," UN News, United Nations, October 10, 2018, https://news.un.org/en/story/2018/10/1022722.

34. Ethan Varian, "While California Fires Rage, the Rich Hire Private Firefighters," *New York Times*, October 26, 2019, https://www.nytimes.com/2019/10/26/style/private-firefighters-california.html.

35. "The Brain-Gut Connection," Johns Hopkins Medicine, accessed June 6, 2021, https://www.hopkinsmedicine.org/health/wellness-and-prevention/the-brain-gut-connection.

More Nonfiction from the Feminist Press

Against Memoir:
Complaints, Confessions & Criticisms
by Michelle Tea

Black Dove: Mamá, Mi'jo, and Me
by Ana Castillo

But Some of Us Are Brave:
Black Women's Studies (Second Edition)
edited by Akasha (Gloria T.) Hull, Patricia Bell Scott,
and Barbara Smith

The Crunk Feminist Collection
edited by Brittney C. Cooper, Susana M. Morris,
and Robin M. Boylorn

Grieving: Dispatches from a Wounded Country
by Cristina Rivera Garza, translated by Sarah Booker

I Had a Miscarriage: A Memoir, a Movement
by Jessica Zucker

Parenting for Liberation:
A Guide for Raising Black Children
by Trina Greene Brown

Radical Reproductive Justice:
Foundations, Theory, Practice, Critique
edited by Loretta J. Ross, Lynn Roberts, Erika Derkas,
Whitney Peoples, and Pamela Bridgewater Toure

Tastes Like War: A Memoir
by Grace M. Cho

You Have the Right to Remain Fat
by Virgie Tovar

The Feminist Press publishes books that ignite movements and social transformation. Celebrating our legacy, we lift up insurgent and marginalized voices from around the world to build a more just future.

See our complete list of books at
feministpress.org

THE FEMINIST PRESS
AT THE CITY UNIVERSITY OF NEW YORK
FEMINISTPRESS.ORG

Sarah Eagle Heart (Waŋblí Šiná Wíŋyaŋ, Eagle Shawl Woman), Oglála Lakota, is an Emmy Award–winning social justice story-teller, entrepreneur, and philanthropic leader. Sarah cofounded Zuyá Entertainment to create multiplatform stories based on her unique worldview infused by her Lakota culture.

Ms. Eagle Heart cofounded Return to the Heart Foundation to support innovative Indigenous women–led projects for climate justice, narrative change, civic engagement, healing, and restorative and regenerative development. Prior to this role she served as CEO of Native Americans in Philanthropy.

Ms. Eagle Heart holds a BS in mass communications and a BS in American Indian studies from Black Hills State University, as well as an MBA from the University of Phoenix. She is also an exclusive public speaker with the American Program Bureau. She is based in Los Angeles, California, and Pine Ridge Indian Reservation, South Dakota.

PHOTO © JAY VALLE

Emma Eagle Heart–White (Waŋblí Wíyaka Wíŋyaŋ, Eagle Feather Woman), Oglála Lakota, is a psychotherapist, life coach, survivor, and advocate. She began her career on the Oneida Nation of Wisconsin in the healing field as a youth advocate for Native American students within the public school system and continued her advocacy on behalf of Native American survivors of domestic abuse and sexual violence. Today she works as a psychotherapist and recently founded Owášte Healing and Wellness LLC, where she continues her passion for healing, advocacy, wellness, life coaching, energy work, and brainspotting therapy. She holds a BS in educational policy and community studies, as well as an interdisciplinary degree in American Indian studies from the University of Wisconsin–Milwaukee. She holds an MA in counseling with a community emphasis from Lakeland University in Plymouth, Wisconsin, and is currently working toward her PsyD doctorate degree in clinical psychology.